Marx's *Capital*

Marx's *Capital*

Philosophy and political economy

Geoffrey Pilling
Senior Lecturer in Economics, Middlesex Polytechnic

Routledge & Kegan Paul
London, Boston and Henley

First published in 1980
by Routledge & Kegan Paul Ltd
39 Store Street,
London WC1E 7DD,
9 Park Street, Boston, Mass. 02108, USA and
Broadway House,
Newtown Road,
Henley-on-Thames,
Oxon RG9 1EN

Set in 10/12 Linotron 202 Sabon by
Input Typesetting Ltd, London
and printed in Great Britain by
Redwood Burn Ltd
Trowbridge & Esher

British Library Cataloguing in Publication Data
Pilling, Geoffrey
   Marx's 'Capital'.
   1. Marx, Karl. Kapital, Das
   I. Title
   335.4   HB501.M37   80 40198
ISBN 0 7100 0516 4

Contents

Acknowledgments

Many people have helped directly or indirectly in what follows. For several years I have enjoyed the pleasure and benefit of joint theoretical and political work with Cliff Slaughter, Tom Kemp and Cyril Smith. It was Tom who first interested me in *Capital* through a series of classes he gave while I was a student in Leeds. Many of the things I have been taught by them are certainly present in the following. But I must stress that none of them saw this work in either draft or final form. So it is necessary to go beyond a usual formal disclaimer and make clear that they are in no sense responsible for any of its weaknesses. I am grateful to Madeleine Wahlberg for reading a draft of Chapter 2 and making helpful comments on its content and style. Part of the material formed the basis of a series of lectures given in Middlesex Polytechnic and I thank those students who sharpened and clarified my ideas in the course of many discussions. Finally my thanks to Frances Dolan for all her help in the preparation of the manuscript.

The author and publishers would like to thank Lawrence & Wishart Ltd for permission to quote from their editions of *Capital*, Parts 1–3, and *Theories of Surplus Value*, Parts 1–3.

List of abbreviations

The following abbreviations have been used throughout the text:

I   *Capital*, I, Lawrence & Wishart, London, 1961
II   *Capital*, II, Lawrence & Wishart, London, 1957
III   *Capital*, III, Lawrence & Wishart, London, 1959
G   The *Grundrisse*, Penguin, Harmondsworth, 1973
LCW   The Collected Works of Lenin (in 50 Volumes) London, Lawrence & Wishart

1 · Introduction

After more than thirty post-war years, during which time most commentators believed that the oustanding questions in economic theory had been resolved, considerable doubt once again pervades the subject. In the opinion of increasing numbers, economics has singularly failed to find any coherent answers to the mounting problems facing capitalist economy throughout the world. Our purpose is not to examine this crisis in conventional economic theory, but we can certainly note the growing scepticism about the ability of Keynesianism to provide the basis for a viable economic policy in the capitalist world. After years during which it was complacently taken as read that 'Keynes had answered Marx' many now see in Keynesian deficit financing the source of the inflationary pressures currently threatening the stability of the western monetary system. Apart from this question of Keynesianism, of equal significance has been the attack launched against several of the principal tenets of neo-classical theory. It has been argued, for instance, that attempts to relate the return to capital to its 'contribution' are based upon circular reasoning, since it is impossible to conceive this return independently of the rate of profit. Other serious blows have also been struck at the marginal productivity theory of distribution in so far as it has been demonstrated that no unique relationship holds between the degree of capital intensity and the distribution of income. One effect of this work (for a selection see Hunt and Schwartz, 1972) has been seriously to undermine one traditional neo-classical justification for the existing pattern of income distribution by reference to technology.

This new crisis in economic theory, stimulating as it has a return to the preoccupations of nineteenth-century political economy, has led to a revived interest in Marxian economics. This new interest has in part been reflected in the emergence of bodies such as the

Conference of Socialist Economists. It is within such bodies that several aspects of Marxist political economy have been debated. But it must be acknowledged at the outset that little, if anything, has been settled in the course of these debates. The arguments have been heated, acrimonious, often abusive, but quite inconclusive. (Fine and Harris, 1976, provide a useful survey of some of these debates.) The fact that these controversies have often ended with a mere reassertion of previously-held positions is no doubt a reflection of political and ideological differences which can only be resolved in practice. But another important aspect of many of these disputes has been the relative neglect of the fundamental questions of Marxist method. Thus discussion has been interminable about the nature of Marx's value theory and its true relationship to the more 'concrete' categories such as prices, wages, rate of profit, etc. Yet in most cases these aspects of Marx's work have been considered apart from *Capital* as a whole. Marx's work cannot be reduced to a series of *results*, to be tested against the 'facts' of capitalist development. What is involved here is nothing less than the struggle between the Marxist method and the method of empiricism. It was this empiricism which Marx had to overcome in his critique of political economy. And it is this same empiricist tradition which has dominated much Marxism in Britain. Until this tradition is faced up to and overcome, then the disputes in Marxian economics will remain unresolved.

As an instance of the impact of empirical methods of thought on these questions of political economy, let us take the example of the post-war boom. It was, of course, during this boom that Keynesianism came to prominence in the field of economic policy. But it must be recognized that this same Keynesianism also left its imprint upon Marxism. Many writers on *Capital* concluded that capitalism had indeed entered a new phase in its history. Special terms were coined to designate this new phase – 'neo-capitalism' and 'permanent arms economy' being amongst the most prominent. And from such notions definite political conclusions were drawn – by some that the major struggles in the world had passed from the metropolitan capitalist centres and had found a new epicentre in the colonial and semi-colonial world. Others concluded that in this new phase the working class no longer constituted a revolutionary force – the responsibility for carrying forward the revolution now fell to the students and other layers increasingly alienated by capitalism (Marcuse's view was prominent in this area).

Now nobody would seek to deny that capitalism did indeed experience a significant period of extended reproduction after 1945. Indeed, far from denying this phenomenon, the task of Marxism is to explain its significance. But it is here that we run up directly against the problem of empiricism in its conflict with the method of Marxism. For if we wish to form an adequate conception of this period we must get to the *essence* of this boom, to its real contradictory nature. And this we cannot do simply by 'reading off' a series of surface phenomena (indices of production, of living standards, etc). In the historical development of capitalism there have been booms and there have been booms. There was the long secular boom from 1850 onwards, and there was the boom which preceded (and in several respects precipitated) the 1929 Wall Street Crash. As Lenin insisted, Marxism demands a 'concrete analysis of a concrete situation'. The period of relative expansion after 1945 cannot be taken as a thing-in-itself, to be judged against some abstract criteria. This has always been the essential feature of those works seeking to 'revise' Marx. A series of empirical data is advanced as evidence that Marx was either wrong or in need of updating. As against this method a real analysis of the post-war expansion has to be posited on to the *whole line* of capitalist development. For Marxism, the twentieth century represents the epoch not of capitalism as such, but of imperialism, the highest stage of capitalist development, the epoch when the productive forces find themselves in a *historically* irreconcilable conflict with the existing property relations. It is against *this* background that the nature of the post-war boom must be evaluated and it is not without significance to note in this connection that many who saw in the post-war boom period an entirely new phase of capitalist development also sought to reject Lenin's notion of imperialism. To deal with any phenomenon concretely means to treat *all* aspects of the phenomenon concerned in their origin and development. Specifically, in connection with the post-war period, it must be stressed that capitalism emerged after 1945 considerably weakened, weakened by a loss of territory in eastern Europe and China and having to face a working class which was quite different from the class defeated in the struggles of the 1930s. It is this *weakness* which must be the starting point for any investigation of post-war economy, a weakness which was relatively hidden by the movement of those indices to which conventional economic theory confines its attention. It was out of *weakness* that capitalism was obliged to abandon the old gold standard and revert to a Keynesianism which in practice involved a controlled expansion of money and credit. One is reminded of what Trotsky said in this connection:

> During the nineteenth century, gold as a universal means of value became the foundation of all monetary systems worthy of the name. Departures from the gold standard tear world economy apart even more successfully than do tariff walls. Inflation, itself an expression of disordered economic ties between nations, intensifies the disorder and helps to turn it from a functional into an organic one. (Trotsky, 1978)

Without at this point going into the question in detail, it is clear that the Bretton Woods monetary arrangements (from which followed the establishment of the International Monetary Fund and other bodies) gave to capitalism a strength which was entirely superficial, but a 'strength' to which many Marxists none the less fell victim. The restoration of post-war Europe rested upon the strength of the dollar. But this strength was not absolute, it was relative – relative, that is, to the strength of world economy as a whole. The convertability of the dollar into gold at a fixed rate (initially 35 dollars to an ounce of gold) could continue only within certain limits. By 1971 – after years of accumulating American payments deficits with the rest of the world – these limits were transgressed. From that time onwards the Bretton Woods arrangements were effectively ended, with capitalist economy now facing its most severe recession since the 1930s and its worst inflationary pressures since the end of the war.

It must be remembered that in studying the vast literature of nineteenth-century political economy, Marx enjoyed one enormous advantage over his contemporaries. He came to the study of political economy having already worked over and mastered the highest achievements of classical German philosophy, and in particular the achievements of Hegel. Marx brought to bear on his reading of economic literature certain definite philosophical conquests, and these must always be kept in mind when considering his treatment of political economy. Here Marx's experience contrasts most sharply with those brought up in the Anglo-Saxon world. The problem has been particularly acute in so far as the work of Marxists has tended to reflect the intellectual division of labour found in academic circles. Thus those who have in the past taken an interest in the economic 'side' of Marx's writings have paid scant, if any, attention to this philosophical heritage. Marx's conclusions in *Capital* were taken as given, and erected into dogma to be defended against opponents. This, of course, was the Marxism which dominated the Second International, a 'Marxism' which concentrated almost exclusively on secondary, episodic, questions and ended up in abject capitulation to neo-Kantianism in the philosophical field and to opportunism in politics.

This indifference to the basic questions of Marxist method still predominates amongst many of those writing on *Capital*. In what is undoubtedly one of the most significant commentaries on *Capital* ever to appear, Roman Rosdolsky in his *The Making of Marx's Capital* is absolutely correct in his observation that,

> Of all the problems in Marx's economic theory the most neglected has been that of his method, both in general and specifically, in its relation to Hegel. Recent works contain for the most part platitudes which to echo Marx's own words betray the authors' own 'crude obsession with the material' and total indifference to Marx's method. (p. xii)

And this same author goes on to say, with equal justice:

> What would one make of a psychologist who was interested only in Freud's results, but rejected the question of the *manner* in which Freud obtained those results as being irrelevant or even 'metaphysical'? One could only shrug one's shoulders. But this is precisely how most present day critics of, and 'experts' on, Marx judge his economic system. Either they totally refuse to discuss his dialectical method because they are opposed to 'metaphysics' . . . or the critique is restricted to a few platitudes better left unsaid. (p. xii)

The significance of Rosdolsky's book cannot be reduced to a series of topics which he takes up — such as the important distinction between 'capital in general' and 'many capitals'. It lies deeper than this: it consists in the fact that Rosdolsky has consciously aimed to re-introduce a proper consideration of Hegel into the study of Marx's *Capital*. And in so doing, his book promises to reverse a long period during which Hegel was consciously or otherwise driven out of examinations of this work. If, as Marx tells us, the dialectic in its rational (materialist) form became a scandal and an abomination for bourgeois professors, the same is true equally of those who dominated the working-class movement from the 1930s onwards. Under Stalin, Marxism was transformed into a crude mechanical caricature of the materialism of Marx and Engels, a caricature used to justify the current political line of a parasitic bureaucracy in the USSR. This theoretical degeneration certainly left its stamp on studies of *Capital*. (It is significant to note that Rosdolsky's book is a product of a tradition which fought against this degeneration. And the same point must be made about those advances in Marxist political economy of the 1920s, associated with Marxists such as Preobrazhensky and Rubin.)

Rosdolsky quite rightly refers to the dialectic as the 'soul' of *Capital*. There is no doubt that his work as a whole was directly inspired by Lenin's own comments on the relation of Marx's *Capital* to Hegel's *Logic*. We shall return to this theme. But it is important to recall that in his analysis of the degeneration of the Second International Lenin was never content merely to trace its roots to the emergence of a new stage of capitalism at the end of the last century (imperialism): he sought always to probe the theoretical and philosophical method employed by Kautsky and others. Lenin's major philosophical works of this period, *Materialism and Empirio-Criticism* (LCW, Vol. 14) and above all the *Philosophical Notebooks* (LCW, Vol. 38), have great importance for any attempt to understand the methodological basis of Marx's *Capital*. In these works, Lenin takes up a struggle against the baleful influence of neo-Kantianism. And in the course of this struggle Lenin was obliged to return to Hegel. It is this 'return' which must be stressed. For Lenin was not content merely to read Hegel through the eyes of Marx and Engels. He went back to Hegel bringing to this study all the richness of his theoretical and practical activity in the Marxist movement. In his philosophical work in this period Lenin had one major aim: to establish the irreconcilable opposition between the philosophy of Marxism (dialectical materialism) on the one hand and the 'latest trends' in bourgeois philosophy which he reveals as in essence involving a return to Kantian dualism. As is now well known this critical re-examination of Hegel culminates in a sharp renunciation of the former 'Marxism' which had first compromised and then capitulated to this new form of Kantianism: 'It is impossible to understand Marx's *Capital* and especially its first chapters without having thoroughly studied and understood the *whole* of Hegel's *Logic*. Consequently half a century later, none of the Marxists understand Marx' (LCW, vol. 38, p. 180). Many are now happy to repeat Lenin's aphorism, but few seem bothered to have thought out its many implications.

It is our contention that Lenin's statement means the following: it is necessary to re-work *Capital* thoroughly, always keeping Hegel in mind. Further, this must be carried out as part of a struggle against the shallow empiricism which has passed for good coin in most studies of Marx's *Capital*. What follows can only be the start of such an attempt. This must not be taken as the usual disclaimer aimed at excusing any weaknesses. For more than sixty years Lenin's advice has for the most part been either ignored or in some cases consciously opposed. A considerable and conscious theoretical effort will now be needed to repair this damage. This should not, however, be read in a pessimistic light. The degeneration of Marxism – of which the distortion of the true nature of Marx's *Capital* was a part – was a product of the defeat of the working class at the hands of Stalinism and its accomplices.[1] Without dealing with the matter in detail, it can be said that we have now entered a quite new period in which capitalism is facing more and more acute problems throughout the world. It is in the context of this new situation that this contribution to the development of Marxist theory is made.

The plan of the work is as follows: first, as a means of highlighting the significance of *Capital*, Marx's critique of polical economy is examined at some length. The aim here is to bring out Marx's attitude to the achievements of political economy taken as a whole. If Marx's own work cannot be broken up into unconnected bits to be 'used' at will, this is equally true of the work of political economy. The philosophical method which underpinned Marx's review of the work of Smith, Ricardo, Mill, etc. is here stressed. This leads us to a consideration of the nature of Marx's concepts which we find in *Capital*. It need hardly be said that nearly all opponents of *Capital* from Böhm-Bawerk onwards have aimed at disproving the key concepts of this work – the nature of value, surplus value, money etc. Here again, however, we should be careful not to get drawn into a defence of these aspects of Marx's work taken in isolation from the rest. Hence we attempt to discuss the nature of Marx's concepts, to show that in elaborating his concepts Marx was operating on a philosophical plane quite different from that accepted by most who read *Capital*. This leads us to a detailed examination of the opening chapters of *Capital*. Marx stressed that it was the *beginning* of any science that constituted its real difficulty. This, together with Lenin's emphasis upon the need to consider Hegel in connection with the *first* chapter of *Capital*, provides the starting point for this aspect of the work. Finally, Marx's notion of fetishism, often looked upon as incidental to his work, but in fact a central category which in many ways lies at the basis of his entire critique of political economy, is examined. It is clear that the emphasis is placed on the opening sections of *Capital*, although these are treated in relation to the work as a whole. This emphasis is quite deliberate. For the aim has been to establish the philosophical method of *Capital*. It is only in this light that the so-called 'concrete' questions which have so exercised the attentions of most writers on *Capital* can be properly considered. In this sense, the following lays no claims to completion. It should be regarded, in this respect, as an attempt to clarify some methodological questions and provide a more adequate basis on which further work can be constructed.

2 · Marx's critique of classical economics[1]

It seems hardly necessary to stress the fact that Marx was among the warmest admirers as well as the keenest students of that trend in economic thinking for which he invented the term 'classical political economy'. It is important to remember that Marx used this term in a way radically different from that of many later writers, in particular Keynes. By classical political economy Marx meant to designate that strand in economic theory originating in France with Boisguillebert (1646–1714) and in Britain with William Petty (1623–87) and reaching its high point with the work of Smith and Ricardo (1772–1823) who 'gave to classical political economy its final shape' (Marx, 1971a, p. 61). It is important to keep this definition in view because the term 'classical economics' has often been used in a much broader sense – for Keynes it was a school embracing all those who, following Ricardo, subscribed to one version or another of Say's Law, who believed, that is to say, in the self-regulating nature of capitalist economy. On such a definition, classical economics culminated with Marshall and Pigou.[2] (For Marx's characterization of classical economy, see Marx, I, footnote, p. 81[3].) Marx was always conscious of the enduring achievements of this school when contrasted with the work of the 'vulgar school', which emerged in the period following Ricardo's death. In Marx's estimation, classical political economy constituted a decisive stage in the investigation of the capitalist mode of production; around 1830 this phase begins to draw to a close, a close intimately bound up, for Marx, with the appearance of a new social and political force increasingly conscious of itself, the working class. Marx did not, of course, mean to imply that in a somewhat mystical manner the modern working class 'killed' political economy. Rather he wished to stress that the method-

9

ological limitations of classical political economy increasingly paralysed it in the face of this new phenomenon.

The ahistorical nature of political economy

The fact that political economy was unable to grasp the significance of the emergence of the working class and the implications of its struggle against capital only underscored, for Marx, the grave methodological and philosophical weakness which he detected in the work of Ricardo. For Marx's considerable respect for the classical economists should not blind us to the fact that he saw in them a series of weaknesses which were to prove fatal. It is, of course, the case that the attack upon Ricardianism after 1830 was increasingly inspired by narrow ideological and political considerations, a point rightly stressed by Meek (1967). And such attacks were sharpened by the fact that a trend within the emerging working-class movement ('Ricardian Socialism') tried consciously to deploy Ricardian theory as a weapon against the capitalist order. But this is by no means the end of the story. For it is also undoubtedly the case that the opponents of Ricardo (Bailey is a good example) were able to seize upon real, unresolved, contradictions in the Ricardian system. It is this aspect of the problem on which we will concentrate.

In considering the deficiencies of Ricardo's work which had opened it up to these attacks, attacks which Ricardo's followers were unable to combat, Marx was to centre his entire critique of political economy on what he considered its decisive weakness – its tendency to view society *ahistorically*, or, more specifically, its inclination to treat capitalist economy as one working directly in accordance with the laws of nature. All Marx's detailed criticisms of political economy's erroneous conceptions of value, money, capital, etc., which fill the pages of *Capital* and even more so of *Theories of Surplus Value*, rest finally upon this, his basic criticism. It is one anticipated, though not as yet exhaustively worked out, in *The Poverty of Philosophy* where we find the following:

> Economists express the relations of bourgeois production, the division of labour, credit, money, etc. as fixed immutable,

eternal categories. . . . Economists explain how production
takes place in the above mentioned relations, but what they
do not explain is *how these relations themselves are produced*,
that is the historical movement that gave them birth . . . these
categories are as little eternal as the relations they express.
They are historical and transitory products. (Marx, 1955,
p. 91; author's italics).

This attack by Marx upon the ahistorical standpoint of the classical
economists must be carefully considered, for it can easily be misunderstood. Many have taken Marx simply to mean that Smith
and Ricardo were either unaware of or not interested in pre-capitalist economic forms of production. This is, however, quite wide
of the mark; Smith was concerned perhaps more than anybody
else to demonstrate the superiority of the capitalist form of production as a means of creating wealth in contrast with feudal
economy. Others, perhaps somewhat less naive, have assumed that
Marx aimed simply to make Ricardo's analysis dynamic, to 'set in
motion' the work of the classical school, as Althusser puts it
(Althusser and Balibar, 1970, p. 60). Neither of these interpret-
ations of Marx's principal objection to the standpoint of classical
economy can be sustained on the basis of a reading of the appro-
priate texts.

Marx, as a materialist, understood that the categories of political
economy were a product of historical development and specifically
of the historical development of the social relations of production.
This point must be emphasized if only because of the attack
launched by Althusser and others against this conception, which
we believe to be at the very centre of Marxism. In his review of
the history of political economy, Marx at all times insists upon the
objectivity of the categories of the science: 'They are socially valid
and therefore objective thought forms', he writes. Marx was here
stressing a vital point – namely, that science always necessarily
develops through definite forms outside the individual consciousness. Men always start with certain definite aims and motives and
the leading figures of political economy were, in this respect, no
exception. But the history of political economy cannot be reduced
to a review of the conscious aims and motives of its leading representatives. Science develops always under determined historical

conditions in that it must always commence its work in and through the categories which have been historically handed down to it, categories which reflect the work of all previous thinkers in the field. Thus, just as Smith's work can only be understood in connection with the legacy of Physiocracy, so Ricardo's work was very much an attempt to deal with the unresolved questions bequeathed to him by Smith.

Marx attacked the political economists precisely because they took the categories of their science *uncritically*. His charge of ahistoricism meant essentially this: the political economists fetishistically accepted the available concepts as fixed and unalterable. Political economy took its categories for granted precisely because it did not know the historical process through which they had been created. It was unable to reproduce this real process in thought and therefore saw in the categories of bourgeois political economy the expression of the essence of bourgeois production. In short, it fell under the illusion that the relations of modern economy not only appeared according to the categories of political economy, but that these relations really were as they appeared.

In this light, it is perhaps possible to begin to see the central importance which Marx's investigations of the history of political economy hold for his work as a whole. In bourgeois social science, the history of any discipline is invariably taken either as 'background' material before the 'substantive' exposition of the subject commences, material which has no organic connection with the principles of the subject, or the development of the subject matter is viewed teleologically – history is reduced to a search for examples from the past designed to show that all previous efforts in the subject were, more or less, crude anticipations of the subject as it exists today. Marx, in his review of the work of Petty, Smith, Ricardo and others, rejected this essentially idealist position. He is not interested in past thinkers merely from the point of view of tracing the origin and growth of his own ideas, nor merely in paying his intellectual debts, as it were. The *Theories of Surplus Value* (intended by Marx, we remember, as a fourth volume of his work) is not a history of economic thought in the conventional sense. It was, Engels tells us,

A detailed critical history of the pith and marrow of Political

Economy, the theory of surplus-value and develops parallel
with it, in polemics against predecessors, most of the points
later investigated separately in their logical connection in the
manuscripts for Books II and III. (Engels, Preface to II).

By 'critique' Engels here means that the categories of political
economy were to be subjected to criticism not by formally comparing them with some object lying outside them but by drawing
out the contradictions in these concepts and showing how, in
practice, these contradictions had been resolved. This was a task
which could be carried out only by somebody conscious of the fact
that these categories were themselves a product and a manifestation
of the actual emergence of the social relations of capitalist
production.

To make more specific Marx's notion of the ahistorical, let us
take an illustration – the law of value. At one point Marx draws
attention to the fact that for thousands of years – ever since the
appearance of commodity production in the ancient world – men
had striven to discover the nature of value. It was only in the
eighteenth century that they were able – in the shape of political
economy – to make significant progress along this road. And this
progress was made possible only because the social conditions in
which political economy operated – the fact that commodity production was becoming predominant – made possible the clarifica-
tion of issues which previously had, of necessity, remained obscure.
Now when Marx criticized the political economists for the ahistorical nature of their work, he meant that they could not grasp
that their own science had emerged and developed only under these
determinate conditions. Political economy laboured under the
serious misapprehension of all bourgeois thought that the categories of its subject (value, capital, money, labour, etc.) were not
only the product of merely individual minds but that the laws
which these minds had (inexplicably) discovered were valid for all
epochs. They conflated the laws specific to a determinate mode of
production with laws they thought to be universally valid; they
confused social with natural law. Political economy was fond of
the parable of Robinson Crusoe. Marx did not object to the indulg-
ence in this type of story as such. He did object, however, to the
fact that the modern (eighteenth-century) individual was projected

back into history. The individual was not conceived as developing historically through definite social relations, but as posited once and for all by nature. History was confused with nature; pre-capitalist economic forms were treated with the same disdain as Christians treated pre-Christian religious forms.

Now in drawing attention to this ahistorical outlook of Ricardo and others, Marx was not making a general criticism about the starting point of these thinkers which, once having been made, could be left behind, as it were. Marx's *Capital* is not political economy plus some different sociological-cum-historical 'framework'. For Marx, the ahistoricism of political economy is a *fatal* weakness which ultimately permeates every aspect of its work and is the ultimate source of its disintegration. But before trying to demonstrate this, let us briefly review the history of political economy to illustrate Marx's conception that its categories were the product of a definite historical development, and, in this sense, objective.

The main stages in the history of political economy

For Marx, Physiocracy was the first genuine school in political economy. It consisted of a group of writers all of whom sought to provide a critique of mercantilism, a system which had imagined that value and its magnitude resulted from exchange. Against this the Physiocrats counterposed the notion that forms of production were physiological forms arising from the necessities of production and independent of will and politics. They thereby turned the attention of economics towards a study of the social conditions of production. We know of course that the decisive weakness of this school lay in the fact that this production was seen only in its immediate, concrete form; for according to Quesnay and his followers labour on the land was alone productive of value, a conception which persisted with Smith, although in the case of the latter it occupies only a subordinate position. This narrowness in the Physiocratic view was, Marx held, a reflection of the then limited stage reached in eighteenth-century French economy which remained predominantly based upon agriculture. Despite this limitation, the work of the Physiocrats none the less constituted a decisive step forward for all the work that was to follow in the investigation of capitalist economy. This was so because the source of the major contradictions in the Physiocratic system stemmed from its efforts to analyse feudalism from a consistently bourgeois standpoint.

When Marx turns to deal with the work of Adam Smith he again stresses that the advances which this work involves have their ultimate source in the economic changes taking place in the latter half of the eighteenth century. The Physiocrats had been able to begin the investigation of surplus value (the difference between the value of labour power and the value created by it) only because it appears most palpably in the sphere of agriculture, the primary branch of production. The total means of subsistence which the labourer consumes is smaller than the total means of subsistence he produces. However, in manufacturing – which was emerging much more rapidly in Britain than in France during this period – the worker does not *directly* produce either his means of subsistence or an excess of them. Under manufacturing the process is mediated, is an indirect one, operating through the various acts of circulation of all commodities within the capitalist system. The development of the value concept, which is the most important single feature of Smith's work – a concept missing in Physiocracy – was an expression of this indirect, mediated form taken by production under capitalism. And this was equally true in the case of surplus value; while this surplus appeared in the form of a surplus of use-values (agricultural products) no *abstract* conception of its nature was either possible or necessary for pre-Smithian economics.

Here, Marx considered, lay the true significance of Smith's work – he was the first to attempt an investigation of the abstractions of value and surplus value. Specifically, the advance marked by *The Wealth of Nations* (1776) was to be found in the fact that it grasped that *labour in general* (and not one of its forms) is value-creating. Marx again draws attention in his commentary on Smith to the material basis for this step forward. The notion of 'labour in general' was itself possible only in a rapidly changing economy in which the traditional bond between an individual and his labour was being shattered. The indifference to the particular type of labour when considering value – Smith's real, if at times inconsistent, point of criticism against the Physiocrats – implied the existence of a highly developed variety of concrete forms of labour, none of which predominated and all of which were being dissolved by the rapid extension of the market.

But as in the case of the French economists, so now in the case of Smith: Marx sees definite limits to these important advances. Marx regarded Smith as a transitional figure and one to whom all later schools, including that of modern (neo-classical) theory, can, with some justification, trace their origin. From the point of view of the *method* of political economy Smith continued and extended the classificatory work of his predecessors, notably that of William Petty. At the same time Smith was the first to attempt an abstract analysis of the capitalist mode of production – a search for the *laws*, that is the *regularities*, of its development. It was this latter side of his work which was to be carried forward by Ricardo some fifty years later. Marx characterizes Smith's work in the following way: on the one hand Smith tried to uncover those laws which would reveal the essential qualities of the economic system which was then emerging in Britain. Herein lay the significance of his idea of the 'hidden hand' summed up in the well-known statement, 'It is not from the benevolence of the butcher, the brewer or the baker that we expect our dinner but from their regard to their own interest' (Smith, 1976, pp. 26–7). Here is Smith's conception of an economic system which worked independently of the aims of any individual. This aspect of Smith's work Marx refers to as its 'esoteric element'. On the other hand, Marx also finds in Smith's writings a considerable 'exoteric element', that is, one concerned not with the *inner* structure of economic relations, but with their immediately outward manifestation, as those relations present themselves in the sphere of *competition*. It was this 'naive duality' (Marx's phrase) which Ricardo identified as the major weakness at the heart of *The Wealth of Nations*. It is a duality most clearly shown in Smith's conception of value. On occasions, Smith sees the value of commodities as determined by the quantity of labour involved in their production, as when he gives the example of beaver and deer:

> In that early and rude state of society which precedes both the accumulation of stock and the appropriation of land, the

proportion between the quantities of labour necessary for acquiring different objects seems to be the only circumstance which can afford any rule for exchanging them for one another. If amongst a nation of hunters, for example, it usually costs twice the labour to kill a beaver which it does to kill a deer, one beaver should naturally exchange for or be worth two deer. It is natural that what is usually the produce of two days or two hours of labour, should be worth double what is usually the produce of one day's or one hour's labour. (Smith, 1976, p. 65)

In other places, however, Smith drops this labour *exchange* theory in favour of a labour *command* notion of value, or, what amounted to the same thing, a theory which sees exchange-value as determined by the level of wages.[4] Thus we find Smith saying, 'The value of any commodity, therefore, to the person who possesses it, and who means not to use or consume it himself, but to exchange it for other commodities, is equal to the quantity of labour which it enables him to command' (p. 65). That is to say, the appearance of wages along with profits and, once private property and land is established, rent, for Smith overthrow the determination of value by labour-time. All three 'factors' had to be taken into account and he adopts what is essentially an 'adding-up' theory of value.

In every state of society the price of every commodity finally resolves itself into some one or other or all of these three parts; and in every improved society all the three enter more or less, as component parts, into the price, of the far greater part of commodities. (p. 68)

Ricardo's achievement

Ricardo's greatest single achievement was that of all his contempories he recognized most clearly this dual conception of value in Smith and aimed, by overcoming it, to make political economy a coherent and unified science. This he did by endeavouring to demonstrate that the determination of value by labour-time could be made consistent with the existence of wages, profits and rent. Indeed, he went further and attempted to show that the determination of value by labour-time was the only sound basis on which the distribution of the social product between wages, profit and rent could properly be explained, a task which he took to be the major one facing political economy. From the very outset of the *Principles* Ricardo notes the different and ultimately incompatible conceptions of value in *The Wealth of Nations*.

> Adam Smith, who so accurately defined the original source of exchangeable value and who was bound in consistency to maintain that all things become more or less valuable in proportion as more or less labour was bestowed on their production, has himself erected another standard measure of value, and speaks of things being more or less valuable in proportion as they will exchange for more or less of this standard measure. Sometimes he speaks of corn, at other times of labour, as a standard measure; not the quantity of labour bestowed on the production of an object, but the quantity which it can command in the market: as if these were two equivalent expressions, and as if, because a man's labour had become doubly efficient and he could therefore produce twice the quantity of a commodity, he would necessarily receive twice the former quantity in exchange for it. (Ricardo, 1951, pp. 13–14)

This same point is made when Ricardo, once more objecting to Smith's inconsistency, writes:

> In the same country double the quantity of labour may be required to produce a given quantity of food and necessaries at one time than may be necessary at another and a distant time; yet the labourer's reward may possibly be very little diminished. If the labourer's wages at the former period were a certain quantity of food and necessaries, he probably could not have been sustained if that quantity had been reduced. Food and necessaries in this case will have risen 100 per cent if estimated by the quantity of labour necessary to their production, while they will scarcely have risen in value if measured by the quantity of labour for which they will exchange. (p. 15)

Ricardo knew that the duality to which he was here drawing

attention had to be eliminated if political economy was to progress as a science. It was through his efforts to grapple with the theoretical problems left by Smith that Ricardo was forced to develop a quite different method in the analysis of economic phenomena. It was this new procedure which constituted for Marx 'Ricardo's great service to the science'. Political economy, Ricardo came to insist, must begin with one fundamental principle – the determination of value by the quantity of labour bestowed upon the production of a commodity. All those economic phenomena (from the realm of competition) which appear to contradict this law must be rendered compatible with it, and the law of value thus made the axis of a scientific political economy. '[Ricardo] demonstrates that this law governs even those bourgeois relations which apparently contradict it most decisively' (Marx, 1971a, p. 60). Here lies the clue to the true significance of the English adage 'It's the exception that proves the rule': the task of science for Ricardo was to show that the law of value was, above all, upheld precisely through those phenomena which seemed, at first sight, to overthrow it.

The general method adopted by Ricardo in his *Principles* is as follows: after stating the law of value in a much less ambiguous manner than Adam Smith, Ricardo then proceeds to consider a number of questions in turn. He examines the extent to which the law of value is in contradiction with the manner in which it appears in competition, as it presents itself to the unscientific observer. Ricardo insists, Marx tells us, that,

> The basis, the starting point for the physiology of the
> bourgeois system – for understanding its internal organic
> coherence and life-process – is the determination of *value by
> labour-time*. Ricardo starts with this and forces science to get
> out of the rut, to render an account of the extent to which the
> other categories – the relations of production and commerce –
> evolved and described by it, correspond to or contradict this
> basis, this starting-point. (Marx, 1971b, p. 166)

The nature of this method can be illustrated by reference to the example of rent. The chapter on rent in the *Principles* (Chapter 2) begins, 'It remains however to be considered, whether the appropriation of land and the consequent creation of rent, will occasion any variation in the relative value of commodities, independently of the quantity of labour necessary to production' (Ricardo, 1951, p. 67). Here Ricardo is about to consider the extent to which, if at all, the existence of the concrete category, rent, undermines or at least forces a modification of the basic starting point for political economy – the law of value.

While paying full tribute to Ricardo's attempt to create a systematic science of political economy in this way, Marx none the less drew attention to the basic weaknesses which still remained with Ricardo, ones which prevented him from carrying through his intended task to completion. It would be very wrong to see these defects in Ricardo's political economy as resting merely on the *conclusions* at which Ricardo arrived: Marx's criticisms went far beyond an objection to Ricardo's conclusions, important though his criticisms were in this respect. Marx objected to the very structure and method of Ricardo's work. We have already noted that in his opening chapter he deals with a series of phenomena to discover whether they can be reconciled with the law of value. Ricardo considers wages and considers that their level is independent of the value of commodities. Here was a significant step forward from Smith, who continually allows a consideration of the wage level to intrude into his analysis. Ricardo says 'Labour of different qualities differently rewarded. This is no cause of variation in the relative value of commodities' (1951, p. 20). This point is elaborated a little later when we find:

> The proportion which might be paid for wages is of the utmost importance in the question of profits; for it must at once be seen, that profits would be high or low, exactly in proportion as wages were low or high; but it could not in the lease affect the relative value (of fish and game) as wages would be high or low at the same time in both occupations. (p. 27)

Having from the start rejected Smith's contention that the emergence of wages undermines (or seriously limits) the law of value, Ricardo then continues (in the third section of the opening chapter) to deal with the impact of the fact that fixed and circulating capital exist in different proportions; the fifth section of this same chapter discusses how far a rise or fall in wages calls for a modification of the initial value analysis, given the existence of capital of varying durability and unequal rate of turnover in different spheres of production. Marx, after reviewing the structure of this chapter, makes what is a crucial observation:

> Thus one can see that in this first chapter not only are *commodities* assumed to exist – *and when considering value as such, nothing further is required* [author's italics] – but also wages, capital, profit, the general rate of profit and even, as we see, the various forms of capital as they arise from the process of circulation, and also the difference between 'natural and market price' . . . In order to carry out this investigation he introduces not only, *en passant*, the relationship of 'market price' and 'real price' (monetary expression of value) *but the whole of capitalist production* [author's italics] and his entire conception of the relationship between wages and profits. (Marx, 1971, p. 168)

Here, it would seem, lies the essence of Marx's attack upon political economy and the key to understanding why he rejected both its fundamental conceptions as well as its method of inquiry. For Marx is stressing that Ricardo started by *assuming* 'as given' the very phenomena – the developed relations of bourgeois economy – which he sought to *explain*. This faulty procedure, which at one point Marx likens to 'giving the science before the science' was precisely a reflection of the ahistoricism of political economy. It should be emphasized here that Marx never attacked Ricardo's work because of its abstract quality; on the contrary it was this abstract quality which so appealed to him. He did, however, find fault with the *forced* and *inadequate* nature of the abstractions which Ricardo employed. It was because he commenced by assuming the relations of bourgeois economy that Ricardo tended to counterpose *directly* the outward appearance taken by these relations on the surface of society with their inner source, which Ricardo had identified as the law of value. Entirely missing from Ricardo's work is any examination of the historical and logical paths by which this (inner) law actually develops to produce the surface relations of bourgeois economy. Or, to put this same point another way, Ricardo fails to trace the manifold and contradictory links (mediations) between this relatively hidden inner determination (law of value) and the immediate phenomena, or phenomenal forms, in which this law finds its expression (prices, profits, interest, rent, etc.). When Marx noted that 'all science would be superfluous if the outward appearance and the essence of things directly coincided' (III, p. 797), he was by implication rejecting the entire method which lay at the foundation of Ricardo's work. We are here insisting that the 'mistakes' in Ricardo's analysis were not isolated questions which Marx corrected or attempted to correct. Ricardo's false understanding of the relationship between value and price for instance (the transformation of values into prices) arose from the fact that the immediate, day-to-day expressions of bourgeois production relations (in this case prices) were allowed to stand in the way of his presentation of the law of value.

The structure of Marx's work

In connection with these last points, it certainly can be considered no accident that the structure of Marx's work is not merely different from Ricardo's, but in essence is its very opposite. Whereas in the case of Ricardo all the historically developed economic relations of 'modern society' are dealt with at the very start of his work, quite the reverse is true in the case of *Capital*. Marx, in this work, shows not in an opening chapter, but over three entire volumes, how all the economic relations of bourgeois economy grow – and this growth is both logical and historical – out of the relations of simple commodity production. And in a fourth volume (*Theories of Surplus Value*) the theoretical reflection of this contradictory process in the work of all the leading political economists is examined. Thus Marx is aiming to demonstrate that the essence of all the contradictions of bougeois economy (which to the reformist or the liberal appear to be a series of isolated 'problems' to be tackled independently of each other) has a common source within the commodity relation itself; but at the same time the *growth* and *development* of this, the fundamental contradiction, has to be demonstrated. Thus while it would certainly be wrong to think that all relations of bourgeois economy (let alone of politics, ideology, etc.) can be explained by direct reference to Marx's opening chapter, it would be equally erroneous to believe that these more complex relations can be considered in isolation from Marx's analysis of the commodity. Lenin sums up the point at issue when he writes:

> In his *Capital*, Marx first analyses the simplest, most ordinary and fundamental, most common and everyday *relation* of bourgeois (commodity) society, a relation encountered billions of times, viz. the exchange of commodities. In this very simple phenomenon (in this 'cell' of bourgeois society) analysis reveals *all* the contradictions (or the germs of *all* the contradictions) of modern society. The subsequent exposition shows us the development (*both* growth *and* movement) of these contradictions, and of the society in the summation of its individual parts, from its beginning to its end. (LCW, vol. 38, pp. 360–1)

Thus in the first volume of *Capital* Marx investigates the genesis of capital, revealing that its origins lie in simple commodity production and exchange, and the further development of simple commodity production in the form of money. Having demonstrated that 'capital' is a historically formed social relation (and not something to be assumed as given, as with Ricardo) Marx goes on to deal with the general nature of the relationship between wage labour and capital. In the second volume he is concerned with the turnover of capital and the way in which this and other factors modify the analysis already made. Having completed these tasks, *only now* is Marx able (in the third volume) to deal with the surface phenomena of bourgeois economy and the reflection of these phenomena in the consciousness of the agents of production as well as in political economy. In this way Marx is able to show that the appearances of bourgeois economy are not 'natural' but a product of definite historically formed social relations and, second, that the consciousness of these relations is also not arbitrary – not merely a 'false consciousness' in this sense – but is itself an objective product of these social relations. This tracing of the contradictory connection between 'social relations' on the one hand and 'social consciousness' on the other was precisely what was needed to demonstrate the validity of historical materialism, the 'testing out' of which Lenin considered to be the real task of *Capital*. But at the same time it was the essence of Marx's 'critique' of political economy in this sense: Marx had to show that the conceptions of political economy were not pure 'illusions', in the sense of the mistakes of individual thinkers, but were a product of and expressed objectively existing social relations in a necessarily contradictory and inverted form. Marx indicates the nature of this method at the start of the third volume:

> In Book I we analysed the phemonena which constitute the *process of capitalist production* as such, as the immediate productive process, with no regard for any of the secondary effects or outside influences. But this immediate process of production does not exhaust the life span of capital. It is supplemented in the actual world by the *process of circulation*, which was the object of study in Book II. In the latter, namely Part III, which treated the process of circulation as a medium for the process of social reproduction, it developed that the process of capitalist production taken as a whole represents a synthesis of the processes of production and circulation. Considering what this third book treats, it cannot confine itself to general reflection relative to this synthesis. On the contrary, it must locate and describe the concrete forms which grow out of the *movements of capital as a whole*. In their actual movement capitals confront each other in such concrete shape, for which the form of capital in the immediate process of production, just as its form in the process of circulation, appear only as special instances. *The various forms of capital, as evolved in this book, thus approach step by step the form which they assume on the surface of society, in the action of different capitals on one another, in competition, and in the ordinary consciousness of the agents of production themselves.* (III, p. 25; author's italics)

What Marx calls the 'faulty architectonics' of Ricardo's work stemmed from the fact that he felt no need to investigate the basic economic categories; he pre-supposed them. It was this faulty structure of the work, Marx felt, which led to a series of interconnected theoretical misconceptions, misconceptions which exposed Ricardianism to the successful attack of its opponents. Comparing Smith and Ricardo, Marx emphasizes both his indebtedness to the advances which the *Principles* mark, but at the same time the inadequacy of its method. The point is summarized like this:

Adam Smith . . . first correctly interprets the value and the relation existing between profit, wages, etc. as component parts of this value, and then proceeds the other way round, regards the prices of wages, profit and rent as antecedent factors and seeks to determine them independently, in order to compose the *price of the commodity* out of them. The meaning of this change of approach is that first he grasps the problem in its *inner relationships*, and then in the *reverse form, as it appears in competition*. These two concepts of his run counter to one another in his work, naively, without his being aware of the contradiction. Ricardo, on the other hand, consciously *abstracts* from the form of competition, from the appearance of competition, in order to comprehend the *laws as such*. On the one hand he must be reproached for not going far enough, for not carrying his abstraction to completion, for instance when he analyses the value of the commodity, he at once allows himself to be influenced by consideration of all kinds of concrete conditions. On the other hand, one must reproach him for regarding the phenomenal form as *immediate and direct proof* or exposition of these general laws, and for failing to *interpret* it. In regard to the first, his abstraction is too incomplete; in regard to the second, it is formal abstraction which in itself is wrong.' (Marx, 1971, p. 106)

This same point is repeated by Marx elsewhere, as follows:

Classical political economy seeks to reduce the various fixed and mutually alien forms of wealth to their inner unity by means of analysis and to strip away the form in which they exist independently alongside one another . . . It often attempts directly, leaving out the immediate links, to carry through the reduction and prove that the various forms are derived from one and the same source. *This is however a necessary consequence of its analytical method, with which criticism and understanding must begin*. Classical economy is not interested in elaborating how the various forms come into being, but seeks to reduce them to their unity by means of analysis, because it starts from them as given premises. But analysis is the prerequisite of genetical presentation and of the understanding of the real, formative process and its different phases. (Marx, 1972, p. 500; author's italics)

The philosophy of empiricism

In criticizing what he saw as the formal nature of Ricardo's abstractions and his neglect of a study of the development of economic forms, Marx is, by implication, pointing to the fact that on the philosophical plane, the outlook of political economy was dominated by empiricism. This empiricism derives from John Locke whose 'philosophy served as the basis for all the ideas of the whole of subsequent political economy' (Marx, 1969, p. 367). This empirical outlook is seen in William Petty, considered by Marx as the founding father of political economy. In his *Political Arithmetic* Petty makes his empiricism clear:

> Instead of using only comparative and superlative words, and intellectual Arguments, I have taken the course . . . to express myself in terms of *Number, Weight*, or Measure; to use only Arguments of Sense, and to consider only such Causes as have visible Foundations in Nature. (Petty, quoted in Roll, 1973, p. 100)

The essence of empiricism is that as a theory of knowledge it holds that sensory experience is the only source of knowledge and affirms that all knowledge is founded on experience and is obtained through experience. One reflection of this philosophical method is that it takes a series of facts as 'given' (by experience), that is, takes them *uncritically*, accepting them as fixed and natural phenomena and using them as the basis on which an analytical structure can be built. According to this conception, a general law – such as the law of value – is taken as given, as a point of departure. Such a general law, argues the empiricist, can be upheld only when it can be established as an immediately given principle under which all the facts being considered can be directly subsumed, without contradiction. The 'general' for the empiricist is mechanically constructed out of a series of 'concrete' experiences and in this way all dialectical relations are set aside, since the universal is merely analysed from the empirically concrete. Engels characterizes this method – this starting with so-called 'principles' or 'laws' which are tested against 'the facts' as *ideological* – as a method which *inverts* the true process by which knowledge develops.

> The general results of the investigation of the world are obtained at the end of this investigation, hence are not *principles*, points of departure, but *results*, conclusions. To construct the latter in one's head is ideology, an ideology which tainted every species of materialism hitherto existing. (Engels, 1947, p. 462)

And Engels immediately points out the roots of this ideology: it rested on a lack of understanding of the origin of thought in definite historical-social conditions. 'While in *nature* the relationship of thinking to being was certainly to some extent clear to materialism in history it was not, nor did materialism realise the dependence of all thought upon the historical material conditions obtaining at the particular time.' (p. 462).

This method of *starting* from principles (instead of abstracting them in the course of theoretical work) was essentially the same as starting from abstract definitions, into which the facts are then 'fitted'. (An example of such a method would be that commonly used to 'prove' that the USSR is 'capitalist'. A fixed definition of capitalism is erected – one involving wage labour and commodity production for instance. Certain 'facts' are then taken from the USSR – where undoubtedly wage labour and commodity production exist – and on this basis the USSR is 'shown' to be capitalist.[5]) Engels replied to this sort of method when commenting specifically on *Capital*; reviewing the treatment by various writers of the transformation of values into prices he says that several mistakes made by one writer

> rest upon the false assumption that Marx wishes to *define* where he only investigates, and that in general one might expect fixed, cut-to-measure, once and for all applicable definitions in Marx's works. It is self-evident that where things

and their interrelations are conceived, not as fixed, but as changing, their mental images, the ideas, are likewise subject to change and transformation; and they are not encapsulated in rigid definitions, but are developed in their historical or logical process of formation. This makes clear, of course, why in the beginning of his first book Marx proceeds from the simple production of commodities as the historical premise, ultimately to arrive from this basis to capital – why he proceeds from the simple commodity instead of a logically and historically secondary form – from an already capitalistically modified commodity. (Engels, Preface to III; author's italics)

Let us review Ricardo's method in the light of this statement by Engels. As we have seen, his starting point was the definition of value by labour-time. According to him, this was a general abstract category which encompassed the characteristics of all those economic phenomena (money, capital, rate of profit, etc.) which he was seeking to analyse. For Ricardo, that is, the relationship between the concept of value and those of money, capital, profit, rent, wages, interest, etc. was that between genus and species. Or, putting the matter another way, money and capital were no more than mere *forms* of value, all having a common source, namely labour. Here lay the *formalism* of Ricardo's abstraction, for which Marx took him to task; he sought to discover the similar and identical in all the phenomena he examined. But this he did in an entirely formal manner – the general concepts (money, capital and so on) were merely an aggregation of the particular (value, measured by labour). For Marx, capital could not be considered as merely 'stored-up' labour as with Ricardo. Capital was, for Marx, a definite social relation in which the labour process took on a determinate historical form, the form of a value-creating and *a fortiori* a *surplus-value*-creating process. Labour, for Marx, was the *technical* basis (and thus an indispensable basis) but not the social basis for capital. Capital could never be understood by seeking within it an element which it shared with lower forms of economic relations (value, money); it could only be understood by a concrete investigation of the path whereby it had grown out of these lower economic relations. This involved a theoretical study of its real birth and evolution. 'Theory' and 'history' could not, therefore, be considered separately; to 'define' capital was to understand the process which had brought this social relation into being. Science then had to reproduce this process theoretically in the form of adequate *notions*. This was the essence of Marx's dialectical method, one which separated him sharply from political economy. Writing of his notion of capital, Marx says:

> To the extent that we are considering it here, as a relation distinct from that of value and money, capital is *capital in general*, that is the incarnation of the qualities which distinguish value as capital from value as pure value or as money. Value, money, circulation, etc., prices, etc. are presupposed, as is labour etc. But we are still concerned neither with a *particular* form of capital, nor with an *individual* capital as distinct from other individual capitals, etc. We are present at the process of its becoming. This dialectical process of its becoming is only the ideal expression of the real movement through which capital comes into being. The later relations are to be regarded as *developments* [author's emphasis] coming out of this germ. But it is necessary to establish the specific form in which it is posited at a *certain* point. Otherwise confusion arises. (G, p. 310)

We shall consider later some further methodological implications of this and similar passages. But let us note at this stage that Marx brings out very clearly his conception of the relationship between value and capital. The value concept was arrived at by Marx not through aggregating the abstract general attributes that experience detects in all its special forms (capital, rent, interest, etc.) as the method of empiricism would demand. Marx arrives at the notion of capital in a quite different manner; namely through a thorough examination of one single, quite concrete, actually existing relation between people – that is, the exchange of one commodity for another. In the analysis of the commodity, the universal determinants of value are abstracted. These determinants are later reproduced at higher levels of development and analysis as abstract general determinations of money and labour-power and capital.

The problem of value and profit[6]

In order to look more closely at the 'confusion' which must arise when this method is not followed and to take forward our investigation of the consequences of empiricism for political economy, we can look at the manner in which Ricardo grappled with the problem of the relationship between value and profit. According to Ricardo the law of the average rate of profit – which established the dependence of the scale of profit on the *quantity of capital as a whole* – and the law of value – which established that only living labour produced value – stood in stark contradiction to each other. Nevertheless both laws determine one and the same phenomenon (profit)! It was this antinomy which Malthus seized upon with such delight and made the basis of his attack on the Ricardian school.

Now here was a real problem. For it had been discovered by Ricardo that there was in fact no direct relationship between the law of value and its immediate appearance. As soon as he tried to grasp the nature of profit *theoretically* (that is to understand it on the basis of the law of value) it led to an apparently absurd conclusion. If the law of value was *universal* – as Ricardo insisted that it was – then profit was in principle *impossible*, a proposition clearly denied by immediate experience. All Ricardo's difficulties arose from the fact that he attempted to resolve what was in fact a real material contradiction by means of a redefinition of his concepts. Political economy wanted to subsume the appearances of bourgeois economy directly under what it took to be its basic law.[7] As Marx observed, when dealing with the disintegration of Ricardo's school, in trying to make the laws which determine value agree directly with those determining the rate of profit, political economy presented itself with a 'much more difficult problem to solve than that of squaring the circle which can be solved algebraically. It is simply an attempt to present that which does not exist as in fact existing' (Marx, 1972, p. 87).

In political economy's endeavour to overcome the paradox of law of value and rate of profit, by attempting to make its concepts more precise, was the belief that the supposed error resulted from an earlier error *in thought*; it could not see, thanks to its formal method, that the paradox arose from the actual contradictory nature of the phenomena under investigation. In connection with this type of method, one based on formal logic, Marx notes:

> Here the contradiction between the general law and further developments in the concrete circumstances is to be resolved not by the discovery of the connecting links but by directly subordinating and immediately adopting the concrete [the average rate of profit] to the abstract [the law of value]. This moreover is to be brought about by a *verbal fiction*, by changing the correct name of things. (These are indeed 'verbal disputes', they are 'verbal', however, because real contradictions, which are not resolved in a real way, are to be resolved by phrases.) (Marx, 1972, pp. 87–8)

This comment by Marx serves to bring out another aspect of the empiricism of political economy, that is its adherence to a purely formal method of thought. If there was a contradiction between the law of value and the law by which the rate of profit was formed, then one or other of the terms had to be redefined to solve the problem. If the notion of contradiction can be said to lie at the heart of dialectical thinking, its elimination is certainly the main concern of positivist thought. As Karl Popper says in his widely known 'What is Dialectic?' 'A statement consisting of the conjunction of two contradictory statements must always be rejected as false on purely logical grounds' (Popper, 1972, p. 316). And elsewhere the same writer says, 'all criticism consists in pointing out some contradiction or discrepancies, and scientific progress consists largely in the elimination of contradictions wherever we find them' (Popper, 1966, p. 39). In other words, the existence of a contradiction is an indication of an as yet unresolved error, an error which must be got rid of if scientific progress is to be made. On this view the unearthing of a contradiction and its elimination involve, in principle, a formal operation performed on the theory, or part of it, in order to bring it into accord with another theory, or part of a theory, that has been accepted as true. If we do not succeed in this, we must get rid of the contradictory theory (or that theory that stands in contradiction to the theory we hold to be true) and seek a new solution.

On this view the contradiction of the Ricardian system would be its real weakness. And this was the view of Ricardo's disciples.

James Mill, who did more to popularize Ricardo's views than anybody else, was guilty of exactly this conception. Mill started with Ricardo's work as a purely abstract system of thought, ignoring the (contradictory) reality which this system expressed. Driven on by the criticism of Ricardo's opponents (the leading one of whom was Malthus) and also sensing that Ricardo's work was in contradiction with reality, Mill tried to eliminate the contradictions of Ricardian political economy. What he tried to achieve, says Marx (1972, p. 84), was 'formal, logical consistency'. Mill was caught in a dilemma – on the one hand he wanted to demonstrate that the bourgeois mode of production was the absolute form of production 'and seeks therefore to prove that its real contradictions are only apparent ones' (1972, p. 85). However, 'On the other hand, [he seeks] to present the Ricardian theory as the absolute theoretical form of this mode of production and to disprove the theoretical contradictions, both the ones pointed out by others and the ones he himself cannot help seeing' (1972, p. 85).

Now Marx's attitude to the undoubtedly real contradictions of the Ricardian system was quite different. In the first place, he grasped the true *source* of these contradictions. It lay not in the error of Ricardo's *thought*, but expressed the contradictory economic and social phenomena which Ricardo in his theory was seeking to express. Speaking of Ricardo, and contrasting him directly with Mill, Marx says, 'with the master what is new and significant develops vigorously amid the "manure" of contradictions out of the contradictory phenomena!' (1972, p. 84). Following from this, Marx also held that the further, more deeply, Ricardo investigated the bourgeois social relations, the more openly the contradictions were inevitably revealed in his theory. For Marx, an opponent of metaphysical and purely formal thought, contradiction was the form taken by all development. Thought, if it was to be truly scientific, must *consciously* aim to express the contradictions in the phenomena it was investigating. Mill tried to *eliminate* the contradictions he and others detected in Ricardo's system. In this sense his work, although it aimed at defending Ricardo and although Mill continued the fight of industrial capital against its outdated landed forms, signified the beginning of the 'disintegration' of political economy. In contrast Marx recognized that the contradictions of Ricardo's system 'expressed with social validity' the maturing contradictions of bourgeois economy. This being the case, it was necessary to grasp how these contradictions were *in practice*, *in reality*, finding their solution. This Marx did and sought to express this solution conceptually – in the theory of production prices, the conception of the organic composition of capital, in the tendency of the rate of profit to fall, etc.

What was involved here was nothing less than the opposed conceptions of formal logic and dialectical thinking. Formal logic could *never* resolve successfully the crisis of Ricardian economics. It required dialectics to 'go beyond' Ricardo, and in this sense materialist dialectics is at the very foundation of Marx's successful critique of political economy. For dialectics, far from abhorring contradiction, says that contradictions inevitably arise in the course of scientific progress; the scientist must resolve such contradictions (that is demonstrate how they appear in a higher, more richly contradictory unity), not attempt to sweep them away by formal logic. Marx saw in the contradictions of Ricardo's *Principles* the great *strength* of that work, not a weakness, an indication of deep-going changes in the reality with which Ricardo was grappling; a reflection of the fact that in the scientific investigation of bourgeois economy a decisive turning point, a 'nodal point' had been reached with Ricardo's work.[8]

It was dialectics that enabled Marx to transcend political economy. Yet it is precisely this dialectic that many writers on *Capital* aim to ignore or reject. One writer, seeking to show that Marxism can be 'enriched' by the incorporation of the results of recent theoretical work associated with the Sraffa school, argues that only on the basis of this work can Marx's work be made logically consistent. Following exactly the same method as Popper, he says:

> Perhaps some will argue that we must reject formal logic and adopt 'dialectics'. Presumably 'dialectical logic' allows one to contradict oneself. In fact, the inevitable result of abandoning formal logic for the purposes of theoretical exposition is to descend into pure nonsense. (Hodgson, 1973, pp. 91–2)

We have shown that purely formal logic proved unable to resolve the problem of the relationship between the law of value and the rate of profit. Let all these critics, such as Hodgson, who reject dialectics in favour of formal logic consider another little problem, far more significant than the much vaunted 'capital controversy', namely the problem of the origin of capital. Marx's analysis of the *origin* of capital — and it is only through a grasp of the origin of capital that we can hope to arrive at an adequate definition of this phenomenon — provides one of the clearest examples of how he consciously seeks to bring out the contradictory, that is dialectical, development of all economic forms. Let our adherents to formal logic ponder the following well-known statement:

> Our friend, Moneybags . . . must buy his commodities at their value, must sell them at their value, and yet at the end of the process must withdraw more value from circulation than he threw into it at the start. His development into a full-grown capitalist must take place, *both within the sphere of circulation and without it*. These are the conditions of the problem. (I, p. 166; author's italics)

And immediately before this: 'It is therefore impossible for capital to be produced by circulation, and it is equally impossible for it to originate apart from circulation. It must have its origin both in circulation and yet not in circulation' (I, pp. 165–6). It was the prejudice of mercantilism that surplus value arose only in circulation, 'upon alienation'. The later development of political economy, starting with the Physiocrats, turned attention towards production. Yet mercantilism did contain an element, a side, of the truth. It was this: a simple commodity owner, considered in relation to his own commodity, can never be a source of self-expanding value, but only of value. It is therefore not possible that a producer, outside the sphere of circulation, can, without coming into contact with other commodity-owners, expand value, annex surplus value, in short convert commodities or money into capital.

Yet surely, the formal logician, following Popper, will retort: to say that surplus value has its origin both in circulation and yet not in circulation is patent nonsense; an indication of some fault in thought which must be corrected if science is to progress. Marx shows that the 'solution' is not made in this way at all — by some redefinition of the terms 'production' and 'circulation' for example. On the contrary, the basis of the solution arose by grasping that the worker sold his labour-power and not his 'labour' (as political economy imagined). Now the use-value of this commodity labour-power possessed the property of being a source of value; it was a commodity whose actual consumption is the materialization of labour, that is to say the creation of value, and whose circulation is therefore production. In other words the conversion of money and commodities into capital arises in the sphere of the circulation of the commodity labour-power, the very circulation of which is the process of production! No doubt such a conclusion will offend if not outrage our formal logician, and for Hodgson it must surely be nothing if not 'pure nonsense'. According to the canons of formal logic, production and circulation are mutually incompatible – surely everybody knows that to be circulated a commodity must first be produced! Yet it is such rigidity of thought which in fact always comes up eventually against the inexplicable.

While we are dealing with the production-circulation problem let us note in passing the treatment given to this question by Cutler *et al*. In the course of rejecting Marx's value theory, the following occurs in a passage purporting to summarize Marx:

> Value analysis can analyze the exploitation in capitalist production because of the concept of the value-creating power of labour and the assumption that commodities despite divergence 'represent' values. This means that for the purpose of analysis of exploitation the differences between production and circulation are obliterated, or rather, that categories of exchange are interiorized within circulation. (Cutler, *et al*, 1977, p. 35)

Of course Marx far from 'obliterating' the difference between production and circulation, grasps these categories in their real unity; shows how these two opposites actually become 'identical' and how their identity–opposition provides the only basis for explaining the nature of capital as 'self-expanding value'.

Formal logic and the 'exceptions' to the law of value

Now with all respect to Hodgson, there is no doubt whatsoever that Ricardo's confinement to a formal logic – that as its basic principle denied contradiction – led to the conclusion that there was, in fact, a series of *exceptions* to the law of value. Under pressure from Malthus and others, Ricardo accepted that changes in the rate of profit (rate of interest) as well as labour-time could affect relative commodity values. This would occur, Ricardo conceded, when the organic composition of capital (this was of course Marx's category, in Ricardo it is the relationship of fixed and circulating capital) was not identical in every industry. For the rate of profit to remain uniform the rise or fall in wages – to which corresponds an inverse movement in profits – must have unequal effects on capital of different organic composition. If wages rise, then profits fall and so does the price of commodities in whose production a relatively large amount of fixed capital is used. Where the opposite is the case, the results will likewise be opposite. That is, the establishment of an equal rate of profit yielded by capital of different organic composition contradicts the law of value. And similarly, Ricardo admitted, with capitals having different rates of turnover and different degrees of durability. Summing up his discussion on the matter of fixed and circulating capital Ricardo says:

> It appears that the division of capital into different proportions of fixed and circulating capital, employed in different trades, introduces a considerable modification into the rule, which is of universal application when labour is almost exclusively employed in production; namely, that commodities never vary in value unless a greater quantity of labour be bestowed on their production, it being shown in this section that without any variation in the quantity of labour, the rise of its value merely will occasion a fall in the exchange of goods, in the production of which fixed capital is employed; the larger the amount of fixed capital, the greater will be its fall. (Ricardo, 1951, pp. 37–8)

In short, the exchange of commodities could not be considered as ultimately independent of wages, that is of distribution. After setting out to show that Smith was mistaken on this matter, Ricardo actually yields the case to him.

On the problem of the *durability* of capital and its impact on the law of value, Ricardo, in a letter of 1818 to James Mill, stated:

> I maintain that it is not because of this division into wages and profit – it is not because capital accumulates that

exchangeable value varies, but it is in all stages of society due to only *two* causes: one the more or less quantity of labour required, the other the greater or lesser durability of capital: – that the former is never superseded by the latter, but is only modified. (Ricardo, 1952, p. 377; author's italics)

Ricardo, as Sraffa (Introduction to Ricardo, 1951) has persuasively argued, was here trying to dispose of one of Adam Smith's objections to the law of value. More germane to the argument here, however, is that Ricardo accedes to the proposition that value has *two* causes: labour-time (a social phenomenon) and the *durability* of capital (a natural-technical phenomenon). We shall return to this matter of the relationship of the 'natural' and the 'social' but this passage from Ricardo seems once more to underscore the fact that he had failed, in the last resort, in his major aim – to establish the entire science of political economy on the foundation of the law of value. As Marx comments:

Because Ricardo, instead of deriving the difference between cost price and value from the determination of value itself, admits that 'values' themselves . . . *are determined by influences that are independent of labour-time* and that the law of value is sporadically invalidated by these influences; this was used by his opponents, such as Malthus, in order to attack his whole theory of value. (Marx, 1971b, p. 101; author's italics)

This last reference to Malthus reminds us that there was one way out of the Ricardian antinomies. This lay in separating entirely the law determining value from that determining the rate of profit. Cost price and value could be identified completely: what in Ricardo was a sporadically occurring exception (which he could not in the first instance adequately explain) could now be elevated to the status of a law. Economics, in the period following Ricardo's death, took precisely this turn. It came to the conclusion that profit originated not only in labour, but in a diversity of what were essentially discrete 'factors'. It was necessary, so the argument now ran, to take into account the role of land, of machines, of supply and demand, etc. Thus was born the Trinity Formula: 'capital-interest; land-rent, labour-wages'. All the contradictions left unresolved by Ricardo could now be disposed of. Rent, profit and wages no longer confronted each other as alienated forms having a common source, an inner unity, but now became in the conception of the 'vulgar' school, heterogeneous and independent of each other. Now they were considered merely different from one another, but in no sense fundamentally antagonistic. The problems which Ricardo's genius had brought to the forefront of science disappeared; but so too had disappeared any *theoretical* approach to economic phenomena, in favour of the most shallow eclecticism. The notion that the durability of capital might play a role in the determination of value (for Ricardo an exceptional case) was now extended to the point where it was eventually alleged by the vulgar school that all social phenomena could be explained entirely in terms of a 'given technology'.

As distinct from Ricardo's opponents, Marx resolved the problems of classical political economy *theoretically*. To do this involved him, above all, in a rejection of the empiricism of political economy, along with its concomitant adherence to formal logic. Marx's dialectical method allowed him to trace the entire chain of connecting links between the law of value and the determination of the rate of profit. This he did in his prices of production theory in which the contradictions of the lower economic forms (the analysis of value) are overcome not in a formal manner (through the redefinition of terms, etc.) but are sublated in a richer, more diverse and concrete theoretical conception.

Dialectics and formal logic

We have stressed that for Marx one of the limits of political economy lay in its implicit confinement to a purely formal logic, a logic which prevented it from grasping the laws of capitalist development. Now this should in no way be taken to mean, as Hodgson implies, that Marxism rejects formal logic completely. In point of fact it draws a sharp distinction between Aristotelean logic and its later degeneration at the hands of the scholastics ('Clericalism killed what was living in Aristotle and perpetuated what was dead', LCW, vol. 38, p. 367). Aristotle's logic, by virtue of its close connection with the scientific developments of his age, and the entire process of knowledge, cannot strictly speaking be called 'formal' logic in the sense in which this word is used in the logic of modern times. Aristotle did not place the logical forms of investigation in any rigid opposition to their concrete content. He tried to elicit the logical forms and connections from the basic characteristics of existence. It is this which explains the depth and richness of his thought. In the hands of the scholastics, logic degenerated into a mere proof-producing instrument, having no connection with the real content of the world, whereas in fact 'even formal logic is primarily a method of arriving at new results, of advancing from the known to the unknown – and dialectics is the same, only much more eminently so' (Engels).

Engels is here in effect drawing attention to the fact that materialist dialectics does not reject formal logic but rather *determines its limits*. The three principles of formal logic (non-contradiction; excluded middle; identity) are not false. They are however limited and all they can do is to prevent fallacies, without, however, rendering or reproducing the movement of ideas which reflect the movement of the material world.

Let us take these three principles of formal logic:

1 The principle of contradiction. Here the principle of a purely formal contradiction is formulated as follows: a proposition cannot be true and false at the same time. In other words, the opposition between two contradictory statements is placed on the same level. For dialectical materialism, contradiction reflects the *development* of reality ('Nature is not, but it *becomes*', Engels, 1960). That is why concepts, if they are to grasp adequately the movement of the material and social world, must be fluid. This was Lenin's point, when, drawing attention to the limits of a purely formal logic, he wrote (LCW, vol. 38, p. 143), 'Ordinary imagination grasps difference and contradiction, but not the transition from one to the other, *this however is the most important.*'

2 The principle of excluded middle. This states that something is either A or not A. For materialist dialectics, the principle of the excluded middle is considered to be valid only on the purely formal level of abstract determinations. In concrete reality – which is intrinsically contradictory because of the interpenetration of opposites in all phenomena – it is impossible to situate anything in the rigid 'either A or non-A' dichotomy. This was Lenin's point

when, commenting with approval on Hegel, he says (LCW, vol. 38, p. 138), 'Every concrete thing, every concrete something, stands in multifarious and often contradictory relations to everything else, ergo it is itself and some other.'

3 The principle of identity. This states that A=A (and negatively, A cannot be simultaneously equal and unequal to A). What is missed here by a purely formal logic is the fact that everything is in continual change and therefore at every moment is both identical with itself and becoming distinct from itself. Of course, *within limits* this principle is perfectly acceptable, 'like all metaphysical categories it suffices for *everyday* use, where small dimensions or brief periods of time are in question; the limits within which it is usable differ in almost every case and are determined by the nature of the object' (Engels, 1960, p. 215). Trotsky, in attacking those who thought that the nature of the USSR could be determined with a series of fixed abstractions, makes essentially the same point about the objective limits of the principle of identity when he writes:

> Our scientific thinking is only part of our general practice including techniques. For concepts there also exists 'tolerance' which is established not by formal logic issuing from the axiom 'A' is equal to 'A', but by the dialectical logic issuing from the axiom that everything is always changing. 'Common sense' is characterized by the fact that it systematically exceeds dialectical 'tolerance'. (1966, p. 65)

The real objection to formal logic which Engels, Lenin and Trotsky here express is that formal logic, being concerned with the classi- fication of thought-forms and with their description as forms inde- pendent of any content, remains essentially subjective; this in opposition to dialectical logic which studies these forms in their connection as thought-forms having a definite content. The unity between the laws of thinking and the laws of being postulated by Marxism implies a close connection among the logical forms, forms which in their unity and interconnection reflect the entire concrete content of the world in its self-movement. (We shall return to the nature of concepts and their place in *Capital* in the next chapter.)

Marx's treatment of labour

Having looked at some aspects of Marx's criticisms of the philosophical foundations of classical economics, we can take this discussion forward in a specific direction: by examining Marx's
treatment of labour. There is no doubt that it was his quite new
treatment of labour as against anything found before in political
economy that gave his work an entirely new and revolutionary
content. 'I was the first to point out and to examine critically this
two-fold nature of labour contained in commodities. As this point
*is the point on which a clear comprehension of Political Economy
turns* we must go into more detail' (I, p. 41; author's italics).
Writing later to Engels he says:

> The best points in my book are 1) *the two-fold character of
> labour*, according to whether it is expressed in use-value or
> exchange value (all comprehension of the facts depends upon
> this). It is emphasized immediately in the first chapter; 2) the
> treatment of surplus value independently of its particular
> forms as profits, interest, ground rent, etc. (Marx and Engels,
> 1956, p. 232)

These points made here by Marx are particularly important in view
of the fact that it is almost a commonplace amongst those sym-
pathetic to, as well as those hostile to, Marx to assume that he
shared a basically similar value theory with that of his classical
forerunners, namely a *labour* theory of value. I believe, however,
this notion – of a 'labour theory of value' in Marx – is at best
confusing and at worst quite wrong. Let us look at this matter by
recalling Ricardo's formulation of the law of value, which Marx
recognized as a big advance on Smith: 'The value of a commodity,
or the quantity of any other commodity for which it will exchange,
depends upon the relative quantity of labour which is necessary for
its production, and not on the greater or lesser compensation which
is paid for that labour' (Ricardo, 1951, p. 11). But to imply that
this was the theory of value, or even the basis for it in *Capital*
would be quite wrong. For on one question the whole of political
economy remained silent: it made no analysis of the nature of this
'labour' that determined the magnitude of value, a point to which
Marx many times drew attention:

As regards value in general, it is the weak point of the classical school of Political Economy, that it nowhere and expressly and with full consciousness distinguishes between labour as it appears in the value of products and the same labour as it appears in the use-value of that product. (I, footnote, p. 80)

For Marx, labour was the basis of all social life, in all epochs, independent of any particular mode of production. In all periods of history man created wealth only through a continual struggle against the forces of nature, of which forces he was of course an integral part. The question, however, remained: to discover the particular *social form* which this universal process (the labour process) assumed in each epoch of history. Replying to those who thought it necessary (or indeed possible) to 'prove' the law of value, Marx wrote:

The nonsense about the necessity of proving the concept of value arises from complete ignorance both of the subject dealt with and of the method of science. Every child knows that a country which ceased to work, I will not say for a year but for a few months, would die. Every child knows too that the mass of products corresponding to different needs require different and qualitatively determined measures of the total labour of society. That this necessity of distributing social labour in definite proportions cannot be done away with by the *particular form* of social production but can only change the *form it assumes,* is self evident. What can change in changing historical circumstances, is the form in which these laws operate. And the form which this proportional division of labour operates, in a state of society where the interconnection of social labour is manifested in the *private exchange* of the individual products of labour, is precisely the *exchange value* of these products. The science consists precisely in working out *how* the law of value operates. So that if one wanted at the very beginning to 'explain' all the phenomena which apparently contradict this law [this was of course aimed at the method of political economy], one would have to give the science *before* the science. (Marx, 1934, pp. 73–4)

What is the meaning of this passage? Marx here points out to his friend Kugelmann that in every society social labour is distributed in definite proportions. No society can alter this basic law. But the law takes different forms in different societies. Under conditions of commodity production this universal law takes the particular form of the 'value' of the products of labour. Simply to say that 'labour is the measure of value' (and to call this a 'labour theory of value') leaves open what is the crucial question: by what social and historical forces are the activities of men expressed in the *values* of the products of their labour? Now if bourgeois economy is viewed naturalistically (in the sense that its laws are universalized, identified immediately with the laws of nature) as in the case of political economy, then it is equally 'natural' to identify labour in its peculiarly capitalist form with labour in general. It was one of Marx's great merits that he investigated the specific characteristics of labour under commodity production, a problem not even considered by political economy.

In order to highlight this point we can refer to a work which in general derives from the Althusserian school and which manages completely to misinterpret this extract from the above letter to Kugelmann. This work argues that Marx seeks 'to explain the *form* of value (value-in-exchange) as a consequence of certain social relations (those of commodity production) but in the context of a general law of value which applies to all forms of production' (Cutler *et al.*, 1977, p. 26). And again: 'In *Capital* the forms of value (value-in-exchange) is the particular type of solution to a universal economic problem, the allocation of social labour in proportions necessary for a certain composition of the product.' The argument is that (a) 'value' is a universal category and (b) exchange-value is the form taken by this universal category under definite conditions (commodity production). But this argument can find no support whatsoever in *Capital*.[9] Marx there demonstrates that the category value arises only when the products of labour take the form of commodities and that exchange value is a manifestation of this category value, its form of appearance, a manifestation which leads eventually to *money*. The category value does *not* exist on Robinson Crusoe's island. Of course the objects which Robinson needs to satisfy his wants each cost him a definite quantity of his labour-time. But that does *not* give these objects a value.

Value only arises when such objects are *exchanged* and then the labour of the producers becomes realized in the *value* of the commodities. We should also add that while 'value' as a social relation expresses relations between commodity production 'Only where wage-labour is its basis does commodity production impose itself upon society as a whole' (I, p. 587). Only then can the law of value emerge from its embryonic form, which it possessed under precapitalist conditions, to become one of the major moving forces in the law of motion of society. Although this particular work will not detain us here, it is noteworthy that one of its chief aims is to deny the *historical* nature of the categories which Marx discovers in *Capital*, categories which are, in any case, all rejected as having no pertinence to the investigation of modern capitalism.

Thus it is above all necessary to be clear about the specific features of labour under capitalist conditions. For, as one writer has correctly noted, 'All Marxists agree that labour is the content of value. But the problem is, what kind of labour is under consideration. It is known to us that the most different forms may be hidden under the word "labour". Precisely what kind of labour makes up the content of value?' (Rubin, 1972, p. 114). And it was precisely an adequate investigation of the specific kind of labour which created value which Marx found missing in political economy. Instead there was a mere 'bald' analysis of labour:

> without exception the economists have missed the simple point that if a commodity has a double character – use-value and exchange-value – then the labour represented in the commodity must also have a double character, *while the mere bald analysis of labour* as in Smith, Ricardo etc is bound to come up everywhere against the inexplicable. *This in fact is the whole secret of the critical conception.* (Marx, letter to Engels, 8 January 1868, in Marx and Engels, 1956, pp. 238–9; author's italics)

It is surprising that this aspect of Marx's work has been so little commented upon, particularly in a period which has seen increasingly strenuous efforts to reconcile Marx's work with that of political economy. In the *Gotha Programme*, it will be recalled, in commenting on the draft programme for the United Workers Party of Germany, Marx took strong exception to a phrase in Article

One of the Draft: 'Labour is the source of all wealth and all culture'. He comments:

> Labour is *not the source* of all wealth. *Nature* is just as much the source of use-values (and it is surely of such that material wealth consists!) as labour, which itself is only the manifestation of a force of nature, human labour power. The above phrase is to be found in all children's primers and is correct in so far as it is *implied* that labour is performed with the appurtenant subjects and instruments. But a socialist programme cannot allow such bourgeois phrases to pass over in silence the conditions that alone give them meaning. (Marx, 1962, p. 18)

To treat labour independently of the social conditions under which it was performed at each historical period, social conditions which had their basis in the ownership of the appurtenant means of production, was to treat this economic category ahistorically. Marx insisted that labour is an entirely social category ('having a purely social reality' I, p. 47) and containing not a single atom of matter. That is why, when Marx deals with the relationship of 'labour' to 'value' he always has in mind *abstract* labour. It was this labour, abstract labour, which 'creates' value, that is to say creates and re-creates a set of social relations which are attached to things. Under capitalism the *private* labour of each individual is transformed into its opposite, *social* labour, only through the transformation of *concrete* labour into abstract labour.

Abstract labour

Now by 'abstract labour' Marx does not mean, as is commonly thought, some mental generalization, some mere product of the mind. If this were so – if abstract labour is conceived of as merely a category arrived at by picking some *common* element found in all labour – then one would be forced inexorably to the conclusion that if abstract labour is a mental image, then so too must be its product, 'value'. Only concrete labour, producing empirically available use-values would have the status of 'real' labour.

Let us, therefore, try to explore in more detail Marx's notion of abstract labour. The products of labour take the form of commodities when these products are made for exchange on the market. As such, they are the products of autonomous private labour, carried out independently of each other. Each person carries out one determinate form of labour as part of a social division of labour. Of course we must remember that if this social division of labour were a *planned* one, the products of individual labour would not take the form of *commodities*. While the production of commodities is impossible without a division of labour, a division of labour is perfectly possible in the absence of commodity production – as in the case cited by Marx of a patriarchal peasant society. Further, under commodity production labour is not *immediately* social; it becomes social labour only through the mediation of exchange relations on the market.

Now in exchanging products men *equalize* them – that is, the market, as an objective process, abstracts from the physical– natural aspects in which one use-value differs from another; and in so doing the market abstracts from that which serves to differentiate this labour. Thus:

> Along with the useful qualities of the products themselves, we put out of sight both the useful character of the various kinds of labour embodied in them and the concrete forms of that labour; there is nothing left but what is common to them all . . . human labour in the abstract (I, p. 38)

and,

> The labour . . . that forms the substance of value is homogeneous labour, expenditure of one uniform labour-power. The total labour-power of society, which is embodied in the sum total of the values of all commodities produced by that society, counts here as one homogeneous mass of human labour-power, composed though it be of innumerable individual units. Each of these units is the same as any other, so far as it has the character of the average labour-power of society, and takes effect as such.(I, p. 39)

From these quotations alone, it should be clear that in the formation of abstract labour we are not dealing with a mental process, but something that takes place in the actual process of exchange itself.

> When we bring the products of our labour into relation with each other as values, it is not because we see in these articles *the material receptacles* of homogeneous human labour. Quite the contrary: whenever by an exchange we equate *as values* our *different products*, by that very act we also equate, as human labour, the different kinds of labour expanded upon them. We are not aware of this, nevertheless we do it. (I)

What is the real significance of this category abstract labour? Let us, in answering this question, return to classical political economy. Ricardo and his predecessors confused the universal character of labour (as the source, along with nature, of wealth in all societies) with its particular characteristic under capitalism, as the creator of value. It necessarily followed that when Smith and Ricardo wrote about primitive societies, the hunter and the fisherman should already own commodities and exchange fish and game in the proportion in which labour-time is embodied in these commodities. As Marx says of Ricardo in this respect, 'He commits the anachronism of making these men apply to the calculations, so far as their implements have to be taken into account, the annuity tables in current use on the London Stock Exchange in the year 1817' (I, p. 76).

This absence of any consideration of the *historical* character of the labour embodied in commodities had its immediate source in the lack of a thorough analysis of the commodity itself. Smith, in this case followed uncritically by Ricardo, had distinguished the 'value in use' and 'value in exchange' of commodities. But the historical implications of this distinction remained unexplored, namely the fact that only in 'modern society' (capitalism) does the production of use-values take the predominant form of the creation of exchange-values. This lack of a proper investigation of the commodity was, for Marx, connected with another weakness on the part of political economy – its tendency to ignore the *value-form* in favour of an almost exclusive concern with the *content* of value.

It is one of the chief failings of classical economy that it has never succeeded by means of its analysis of commodities, and in particular, of their value, in discovering that *form* under which value becomes exchange-value. Even Adam Smith and Ricardo, the best representatives treat the form of value as a thing of no importance, as having no connection with the inherent nature of commodities. The reason for this is not solely because their attention is absorbed in the analysis of the magnitude of value. It lies deeper. The value-form of the product of labour is not only the most abstract, but also the most universal form, taken by the product in bourgeois production. *If then we treat this mode of production as one eternally fixed for every state of society*, we necessarily overlook that which is the differentia specifica of the value-form, and consequently of the commodity form, and its full developments, money-form, capital-form etc. (I, footnote, p. 81; author's italics)

This exclusive concern for the content of value and the neglect of the value-form would be tantamount, said Marx, to the method of a physiologist who held that 'the different forms of life are a matter of complete indifference, that they are all only forms of organic matter' adding 'It is precisely these forms that are alone of importance when the question is the specific character of a mode of social production' (Marx, 1969, p. 295). All the implications of this method cannot be examined, but it is clear that Ricardo's basic errors involved a false identification of the 'social' and the 'natural'; for example, he saw money not as an abstract and universal expression of the value relationship which had developed historically out of commodity production (Marx's conception) but merely as a means of overcoming the deficiencies inherent in barter; nor could Ricardo ever grasp the real character of capital, which he saw only in its immediate shape as stored-up labour rather than as a social form assumed by these means of labour.

Political economy, in the person of Ricardo, saw labour as the measure of the magnitude of value, and was concerned almost entirely with the quantitative aspect of value – that is the particular quantitative exchange relations between commodities. It failed to see that when it treated the difference between various types of labour in a *quantitative* sense, their *qualitative* unity was implied

– that is their reduction to *abstract* labour. Here were involved differences between Marx and Ricardo which cannot be grasped if they are seen merely as disputes about economic theory. Marx rejected the social philosophy underlying political economy, which saw society as an aggregation of individuals, each engaged in his individual labours, each tied together by market forces. Marx once more sees Locke's philosophy as the source of this view, 'because it was the classical expression of bourgeois society's idea of right as against feudal society' (1969, p. 367). Locke conceived labour entirely in its concreteness; for Locke, labour constituted the limit to private property, hence the appeal of the notion of a 'labour theory of value' to the bourgeoisie in the period of its ascendancy. It was this view of labour as a personal subjective activity (Smith's 'toil and trouble'), rather than a nature-imposed necessity taking on definite social forms, which dominated political economy. (It should be pointed out in passing that Locke's position was very advanced for his time. And this was true not only from a philo-sophical viewpoint – here his materialist empiricism was employed as a weapon against scholastic speculation – but also from the standpoint of political economy. At a time when the bourgeois form of property was far from being the sole form, Locke chose it as the sole and authentic one. In so doing he laid a solid foundation for the struggle which continued through Smith to Ricardo against the historically outdated feudal property forms.)

Despite his considerable admiration for Benjamin Franklin, Marx also notes his confusion of labour in its bourgeois form with labour in general. He speaks significantly of Franklin's 'restricted economic standpoint', which took the transformation of the prod-ucts of labour into exchange values for granted (Marx, 1971a, p. 56). In connection with William Petty, Marx says his case 'Is a striking proof that recognition of labour as the source of material wealth by no means precludes misapprehension of the specific social form in which labour constitutes the source of exchange-value' (1971a, p. 54).

Adam Smith also reveals his lack of any *historical* appreciation of labour. He too tended to treat it *subjectively*. He tries to accom-plish the transition from concrete to abstract labour by means of the division of labour. This division of labour, from which arises commodity production, for him has its basis in the famous 'propensity to truck, barter and exchange'. Not only is this position idealist but it also *inverts* the real relationship between commodity production and the social division of labour.

Stressing that at the centre of a scientific political economy must be a concern with labour as a social process Marx says of Ricardo:

> Ricardo's mistake is that he is concerned only with the magnitude of value. Consequently his attention is concentrated on the *relative quantities of labour* which different commodities represent, or which commodities as values embody. But the labour in them must be represented as *social* labour, as alienated, individual labour. (Marx, 1969, p. 131)

And again stressing political economy's limited concern with the measure of value, Marx says:

> Commodities as values constitute one *substance*, they are mere representatives of the same substance, social labour. The *measure of value* (money) presupposes them as value and refers solely to the expression and size of their value. The *measure of value* of commodities always refers to the transformation of value into price and already presumes the value. (Marx, 1972, p. 40)

And in an earlier work, *Wage Labour and Capital*, Marx says: 'What is the common social substance of all commodities? It is *labour*. To produce a commodity a certain amount of labour must be bestowed upon it, worked up in it. And I say not only labour, but *social* labour.'

It should be clearer from the above discussion why Marx gives such importance to the category abstract labour. By abstract labour we mean labour which is cut off, separated, *alienated* from its particular goal. Under capitalism the labour of society is no mere summation of the labour of every individual (as political economy, following Locke's lead, implied). The labour process in capitalist society has an independent existence which stands against the labour of each individual; the labour of each individual has any (capitalist) validity only if it obeys the objective laws of this social labour process. An individual may labour for (say) ten hours, but his labour, viewed socially, may only be counted as five hours, as in Marx's illustration of the hand-loom weaver, given early in the first chapter of *Capital*. And when we use the word 'count' we do not wish to imply that anybody does the 'counting' – it is done in and through the process itself. The acquisition of this independence on the part of the process of labour from the concrete labour of the subjects who take part in it reaches its high point with modern labour, that is *wage-labour*. The worker owns his labour-power. On the basis of the separation of the vast majority from the means of production this labour-power becomes separated from its owner, taking on its own independent existence, becoming a commodity. And not only does it assume an alien form (as a value), but when realized on the market it becomes part of capital, namely *variable capital*.

A 'measure' of value

These comments by Marx about the nature of social labour raise another directly related topic. For in these statements Marx is by implication rejecting what for political economy was one of its main tasks – the search for some 'measure' of value, or what amounted to the same thing, the attempt to arrive at a true *definition* or *concept* of value. (We shall deal later in more detail with this question of *Capital*'s concepts.) We have seen that in a commodity-producing economy the equalization of labour is achieved through the equalization of the products of labour. This is but another way of saying that all varieties of concrete labour are reduced to abstract labour through the market and thus become social labour. But nobody can or does 'measure' these many forms of labour empirically. To imagine that this is so would be to ignore an essential feature of commodity production – its spontaneous, anarchic nature. Considerable misunderstandings will arise (as Rubin, 1972, has rightly pointed out) if the law of value is seen as an 'instrument' which makes possible the comparison and measurement of the various products in the act of exchange. It has been widely (and wrongly) believed by many economists and others that Marx emphasized labour precisely as this 'practical' standard of value. As opponents of Marx, such writers have directed their efforts to showing that labour could not be accorded this privileged status; they have argued along these lines because of the absence of precisely established units with which to measure the various forms of labour which are different from each other with regard to intensity, skill etc.

Such a line of attack utterly misconceives the nature of Marx's value theory. It is both *impossible* and unnecessary to discover a measure of value which will make possible the equalization of labour or the products of labour. It may be a simple point, but none the less profound, to insist that this equalization of labour takes place objectively, spontaneously and indirectly – that is, independently of any participants within the capitalist system. It is in this real, objective process that value is measured. Out of the process of the production and circulation of commodities money (gold) arises. Gold is not some 'external' measure, standing outside the world of commodities. Nor was it 'selected' by conscious planning on the part of economists or politicians. This measure (gold) was historically selected, after long trial and error, in the sense that it was its physical–material properties which enabled gold to select itself as the most suitable money-commodity. The matter can be reformulated thus: it is not money that renders commodities commensurable; on the contrary, it is because all commodities as values are realized human labour, and therefore commensurable, that their values find their measure in one and the same commodity. By a social and historical process this commodity is converted into money. Unless the *objective* nature of these processes is grasped, then the significance of all Marx's categories of political economy is lost. We have already spoken of the social character of the labour which creates value, summed up in Marx's concept of abstract labour. Marx insists that the measure of value is not labour-time, but *socially-necessary* labour-time, that is labour-time required to produce a commodity at a definite stage in the development of the productive forces. And it is only when the producer of a product tries to sell this product on the market that he discovers its real, objective value (if any). During periods of capitalist slump the piles of unsold goods signify that the concrete labour embodied in them was socially unnecessary. Such labour cannot, through the market, be transformed into *abstract* labour and therefore creates no value. But the owner of capital can never discover this beforehand, even though he may be armed with the latest 'market research' techniques and may even have read *Capital*. The essence of capitalist production here is that he can only discover whether the labour incorporated into his products was socially necessary *at the end of the process.*

Our task is not, therefore, to seek some measuring rod for the processes of capitalist production. The very process is its own measure. Value does not measure commodities; commodities discover their own measure of value. The task of Marxism is to discover how this is done, to discover the *laws* and *tendencies* of this process, laws and tendencies which do not appear empirically on the surface of society but appear always in the form of crises:[10]

> in the midst of the accidental and ever-fluctuating exchange relations between the products, the labour-time socially necessary to produce them asserts itself as a regulative law of nature. In the same way, the law of gravity asserts itself when a person's house collapses on top of him. The determination of the magnitude of value by labour-time is therefore a secret hidden under the apparent movements in the relative values of commodities. (I)

In short, instead of the vain search for some formal standard by which to measure the magnitude of value, Marx set out to *abstract* the laws of the development of capitalism ('law of motion'), that is to uncover the (highly contradictory) processes whereby this problem was actually resolved in practice.

Now political economy ran into insurmountable difficulties in the course of its futile search for a measure of value. Smith sometimes saw this abstract standard in 'commandable labour' (wages), sometimes in corn. Others discovered it in labour or in money. Marx's comment underlines his distance from all those who continue to look for such a standard: 'The problem of an "invariable measure of value" was simply a spurious name for the quest for the concept, the nature of value itself, the definition of which could not be another value' (Marx, 1972, p. 134). And Marx points out that Bailey had rendered at least one service during the course of his attack on classical political economy in that 'he revealed the confusion of the "standard of value" (as it is represented in money, a commodity which exists together with other commodities) with the immanent standard and substance of value' (1972, p. 137). Nor was Ricardo exempt from the criticism levelled here by Marx.

Ricardo often gives the impression, and sometimes indeed writes, as if the quantity of labour is the solution to the false, or falsely conceived problem of an 'invariable measure of value' in the same way as corn, money, wages, etc. were previously considered as panaceas of this kind. In Ricardo's work this false impression arises because for him the decisive task is the definition of the magnitude of value. Because of this he does not understand the specific form in which labour is an element of value, and fails in particular to grasp that the labour of the individual must present itself as abstract general labour and in this form, as *social* labour. Therefore he has not understood that the development of money is connected with the nature of value and with the determination of this value by labour-time. (1972, p. 137)

On this matter of the 'measure of value' Marx is in fact making a point of even wider significance which will occupy us later – namely the fact that in this false search for a 'measure' of value was involved an equally wrong procedure which believes that science must *start* with a series of concepts, which can then be tested to see whether they correspond to their empirical manifestation. In his critical comments on Adolph Wagner (Wagner had accused Marx of 'illogicality' in splitting the concept of value into exchange-value and use-value) Marx says, *inter alia*, 'Above all I do not proceed on the basis of "concepts" and thus not from the "value-concept". . . . What I proceed from is the simplest social form in which the product of labour in contemporary society manifests itself; and this is the "commodity" ' (Marx, 1976, p. 214).

It is clear that many Marxists have quite failed to grasp the true implications of this and similar statements which Marx made about his method. It has been widely assumed that Marx, like his predecessors in the classical school, was interested in finding a standard of value, a 'constant' on which the science of political economy could be based. Many such writers often hold that Marx 'chose' labour because it presented fewer difficulties than those associated with other possible standards. Maurice Dobb, for a long period looked upon in some circles as perhaps the leading writer on Marx's *Capital*, takes exactly this position:

In the case of land or capital there were serious practical objections to taking them as a basis: difficulties which would have exceeded any of those which are charged against the labour theory. Classical Political Economy was already focusing attention on the non-homogeneous character of land and was using the differences in the quality of land, along with its scarcity, as the basis of the classical theory of rent. Acres are more dissimilar than man-hours of labour. In the case of capital there was the more crucial objection that it is itself a value, depending upon other values, in particular on the profit to be earned. (Dobb, 1940, p. 18)[11]

Dobb's 'defence' of Marx here is entirely misconceived. It simply is not true that 'acres (of land) are more dissimilar than man-hours of labour' as Dobb will have it. Every use-value is not only the product of different individuals, but the result of individually different kinds of labour. When we consider labour as the creator of use-values (that is, labour as a process common to all societies) it is *impossible* to compare not only labour of different skills but even labour in the same trades, occupations, etc. 'Different use-values are, moreover, products of the activity of different individuals and therefore the result of individually different kinds of labour' (Marx, *Contribution*, p. 29). What is entirely missing in Dobb and others who share his position is any analysis of labour. They implicitly consider labour only from its material, not its social side, notwithstanding their insistence in other places that Marx's political economy is concerned with social phenomena. Such insistence is purely formal if it is not connected with the whole of Marx's work.

Let us, in ending this part of the discussion, recall that Ricardo begins his work with an attempt to define value precisely. He implicitly assumes that the category already exists and attempts to explain the production and exchange of commodities on this basis. Having started with value, Ricardo then sought for some commodity with which it (value) could be measured. Here was a vicious circle. Ricardo failed to see that this 'value' was an expression of social relations which emerged only with commodity production. To start from a concept of value and to try from this to explain the production and exchange of commodities was precisely the *opposite* of a correct scientific procedure. The value relation had to be deduced from the commodity. This is why Marx protested against the spurious charge that he started from an arbitrary conception of value. To have done so would have been to fall into the same trap as the political economists who took the concepts of modern society *uncritically*, 'as they were handed down'.

> Political Economy has generally been content to take just as they were, the terms of commercial and industrial life, and to operate with them, entirely failing to see that by so doing, it confined itself within the narrow circle of ideas expressed by those terms. (Engels, Preface to the English edition of II)

Marx saw his task as providing a *critique* of categories of political economy, of demonstrating that they were expressions, in fetishistic form, of definite social conditions. His critique of political economy was therefore the theoretical form of his revolutionary critique of those same social conditions.

Capital and surplus value

Apart from the distinction between 'concrete' and 'abstract' labour, Marx regarded the second revolutionary element of his work as lying in the treatment of surplus value. This was in no sense a separate element in Marx's work, in so far as his ability to arrive at what he regarded as the first correct understanding of the nature and source of surplus value derived primarily from his analysis and rejection of Ricardo's false understanding of value.

> In order to understand what surplus value was, Marx had to find out what value was. He had to criticise above all the Ricardian theory of value. Hence he analysed labour's value-producing property and was the first to ascertain *what* labour it was that produced value and why and how it did so. He found that value was nothing but congealed labour of *this* kind.' (Engels, Preface to II)

Of course, the existence of that portion of value which, since Marx, we know as surplus value had been recognized by political economy; it was further understood that this surplus consisted of the product of labour for which its appropriators had not given an equivalent. The political economists had, however, largely confined their investigations to discovering the proportions in which the product of labour was divided between the classes (this was above all the case with Ricardo); the socialist critics of capitalism on the other hand, had found that this division was unjust and sought utopian means to overcome this injustice. 'They all,' said Engels, 'remained prisoners of the economic categories as they had come down to them' (Preface to II).

Both the political economists and the 'Ricardian socialists' alike took the existence of surplus value for granted. But for Marx the problem was to explain the existence of this surplus value and its relation to capital. For Marx this capital was not merely a thing (as it remains for all academic economists) but the dominant social relation of modern society attached to things.

> Capital is not a thing, but rather a definite social production relation, belonging to a definite historical formation of society, which is manifested in a thing and lends this thing a specific social character. Capital is not the material and produced means of production . . . it is the means of production monopolised by a certain section of society, confronting labour-power as products and working conditions rendered independent of this very labour-power, which are personified through this antithesis in capital. (III, pp. 814–15)

Thus when John Eatwell writes, 'In classical and Marxian theory surplus is defined simply as social product less that share of product which must be paid to the labourers' (Eatwell, 1974, p. 286), he really only reveals his lack of understanding of Marx's concept of surplus value. Joan Robinson's position is almost exactly that of Eatwell in this respect. Rejecting Marx's 'primitive labour theory of value', she admits that Marx none the less grasped the fundamental feature of capitalism, namely,

> that the possibility of exploitation depends on the existence of a margin between total net output and the subsistence minimum of the workers: If a worker can produce no more in a day than he is obliged to eat in a day he is no potential object of exploitation. This idea is simple and can be

expressed in simple language without any apparatus of specialised terminology. (Robinson, 1966, p. 17)

What both Eatwell and Robinson do here is certainly 'simple': they confuse surplus value with surplus labour. Surplus labour is not, however, unique to capitalism – it is as old as human civilization. If all we need to know about capitalism is that it produces surplus labour we certainly have no need of an 'apparatus of specialised terminology'! But a proper analysis of capital demands an investigation of the 'specific economic form in which unpaid surplus labour is pumped out of the direct producers'. For this alone 'determines the relationship of rulers to ruled', and also distinguishes the various historical epochs one from another. (III, p. 791)

As Rosdolsky (1977, Chapter 33) has pointed out, this confusion by Joan Robinson of surplus labour and surplus value goes hand in hand not only with a rejection of Marx's value theory but also a confusion about capital as a thing.[12] Robinson writes, rebuking Marx for his 'logic chopping theorising':

> Next Marx uses his analytical apparatus to emphasise the view that only labour is productive. In itself, this is nothing but a verbal point. Land and capital produce no value, for value is the product of labour-time. But fertile land and efficient machines enhance the productivity of labour in terms of real output. . . . Whether we choose to say that capital is productive, or that capital is necessary to make labour productive, is not a matter of much importance. What is important is to say that owning capital is not a productive activity. (Robinson, 1966, pp. 17–19)

And drawing attention to the increasingly complete separation of ownership from control, she goes on:

> it seems simple to say that owning property is not productive, without entering into logic-chopping disputes as to whether land and capital are productive, and without erecting a special analytical apparatus in order to make the point. Indeed a language which compels us to say that capital (as opposed to ownership of capital) is not productive rather obscures the issue. It is more cogent to say that capital, and the application of science to industry, are immensely productive, and that the

institutions of private property, developing into monopoly, are deleterious because they prevent us from having as much capital, and the kind of capital that we need.

Here are innumerable confusions. First, capital is equated with 'efficient machinery' and the 'application of science to industry'. Capital is simply, for Joan Robinson as for all political economists, 'stored up labour'. On this view, as Marx long ago indicated, the first capital was the first stone picked up by the first savage.[13] Second – and this is a reflection of the first error – capital and land are lumped together. A social relation is joined up with the basic prerequisite for the production of wealth in all societies. Third, the point about the productivity of capital is completely misunderstood. We have already tried to explain the sense in which Marx saw labour as the 'creator' of value. *Abstract* labour creates value: that is a definite social form of labour produces and reproduces definite social relations of production. But this does not mean that the 'objective factors of production' are to be denied any form of 'productivity'. On the contrary, to the extent that these factors raise the level of production they are certainly productive, *but productive of use-values* (a category which Joan Robinson continually confuses with value). Marx is explicit on this point:

> The use-values, coat, linen, etc. i.e. the bodies of commodities, are combinations of two elements – matter and labour. If we take away the useful labour expended upon them, a material substratum is always left, which is furnished by Nature without the help of man. The latter can work only as Nature does, that is by changing the form of matter. Nay more, in the work of changing the form he is constantly helped by natural forces. We see, then, that labour is not the only source of material wealth, of use-values produced by labour. (I, p. 43; see also Marx, 1972, p. 264)

Capital is, however, productive in a quite different sense. It is productive as the dominant social relation of modern society. For Marx capital was productive because it was able to 'enforce surplus labour' on a scale far surpassing any previous social relation. It is not, therefore, a question of obliterating the distinction between capital and labour. As Rosdolsky has said in exposing Joan Robinson's confusion, labour is the horse producing surplus value, capital is the whip across its back. Hence for Marx productive labour is labour which when exchanging against capital produces surplus value. Here 'productive' has an entirely social meaning – concerned with man's relationship to man – and is not to be confused with the material relation of man to nature.

Let us turn for a moment to a work already mentioned (Cutler *et al.*, 1977) which manages completely to misinterpret Marx's position on the relationship of labour to value. Like so many others, this work labours under the illusion that Marx sought and had a need for some measure of value. In the case of this particular book, it sees this need in terms of the need to uphold the notion of surplus value. 'For the production of the concept of surplus value wages and the product of labour must be expressed as and composed *as values*, they must be measurable in a term common to both (labour-time) and shown to represent discrepant quantities of that term' (Cutler *et al.*, 1977, p. 31). And a little later:

> Surplus value arises in the difference between the value of labour power and the value of the product created by the labour actually expended. The analysis of the two quantities cannot work unless value-terms in labour-time are supposed and form the basis of calculation. In order for it to be shown that the two sums are not equal (value of wages-value created by labour) it is necessary that comparable terms be present on both sides (wages and the product can be expressed as quanta of the same measure). *When the assumption that labour-time is the 'substance of value' is abandoned then the two sides of the equation become incommensurable.* . . . Remove the assumption of the value-creating power of labour and the pertinence of equivalent exchange and the result is that the analysis cannot be done. There is no reason to ascribe profit to 'unpaid' labour.

So if we abandon the notion that labour-time is the substance of value, dire results follow for Marx's analysis of exploitation. The only problem is that Marx has absolutely no need to 'abandon' any such notion – for the simple reason that he never held it in the first place.

Cutler *et al.* are guilty of an old elementary mistake, they manage to confuse completely the *substance* and *measure* of value. Marx, we repeat, nowhere says that labour-time is the substance of value. The substance of value is abstract labour; the 'measure' of this value is time. Value is a social relation, connected to things (products of labour); the labour which 'creates' it is therefore labour of a definite social type, created only in and through certain social relations. Now this social labour is measured through those social relations, that is through a purely *objective process* which takes place independently of the consciousness of the producers. All labour, considered in its concreteness, differs qualitatively. The labour of one blacksmith must differ qualitatively from that of another, just as the blacksmith's labour as a particular form of labour differs from all other particular types of labour. Now precisely because labour, considered as a use-value creating process, does and must differ qualitatively it is irreducible; all such labour is not social and not measurable. Concrete labour only becomes social, that is it only acquires value, through its transformation (reduction) into abstract labour. This abstract labour is alone capable of 'quantification' that is, reducible to time. But this measurement is an objective process. Measure is the objective category in which quality (concrete labour) and quantity (abstract labour) are resolved in a higher unity.

Cutler *et al.*, like so many others, have singularly failed to understand this. This is clear when in their discussions of measurement (which they see as an essentially subjective category) they say of Ricardo 'he bases the exchange of equivalents on equal magnitudes of the same objective substance, labour-time' (Cutler *et al.*, 1977, p. 24). Again this is simply wrong. Nowhere does Ricardo hold that labour-time is the measure of value. For him it was always the *quantity* of labour. And if anything of the discussion has been understood it will be seen that this was quite different from Marx's notion. One consequence was that Ricardo embarked on a search for some abstract measure of value, an indication that labour as a basic human activity was continually confused with labour in its specific form as a value-creating process. And this confusion persists with Cutler *et al.*

The class struggle

The failure on the part of political economy to separate out the natural from the social, resulted in its entirely superficial view of the place of the class struggle in the analysis of bourgeois society. This is an important question if only because many have seen the significance of the recent revival in political economy as lying in the fact that the class struggle has been reintroduced into the analysis of capitalism. It is certainly true that the neo-classical (vulgar) school tried to eliminate any consideration of class antagonisms from its system – this it did with its asocial 'factors of production' and its claim that the distribution of income was a function of technology. And it is equally true that this marked the sharpest contrast with the Ricardian tradition where a consideration of the interrelations of classes was brought to the forefront of the analysis. Marx certainly saw this emphasis on class relations as one of the greatest strengths of Ricardo's work. (The American writer, Carey, denounced Ricardo for precisely this same emphasis.) Furthermore, Marx, in explicitly rejecting the notion that he was the first to discover the class struggle in history (this was the achievement of earlier French historians), gave priority to English political economy for having been the first to investigate the 'anatomy' of this struggle. But does this mean that Marx and Ricardo shared a similar theoretical position in their attitude to this class struggle? This is by no means the case.

Let us first make a general point, not about political economy, but about historical materialism. Marx and Engels never held the view that the basic contradiction of the bourgeois mode of production was to be found in the antagonism between wage labour and capital. Nor, extending this point, did they see the class struggle as the basic contradiction in history. The materialist conception of history, on the contrary, saw the fundamental contradiction in history as one between the development of the productive forces on the one hand and the existing social relations of production on the other. A glance at the *Preface to the Critique of Political Economy* proves this to be so. In this short Preface, where the essential points of historical materialism are outlined, there is no mention of classes, or of class struggle. Marx does, however, speak about the 'basis' of society, a basis which lies in the social relations of production, relations which 'correspond' to the stage reached in the development of the productive forces. Only at a given level of the growth of the productive forces do the relations of production take the form of classes, which in turn disappear at a higher level. Class antagonisms are not, therefore, to be taken as things-in-themselves; they are rooted in the deeper, more basic contradictions between the productive forces and the production relations. These antagonisms are a driving force in class society *solely* because they are the expression, the result, of this deeper contradiction, which in the case of capitalism consists of the contradiction between the increasingly socialized nature of production and its ever-narrowing private appropriation.

It should be clear that this was not Ricardo's view of the class struggle. He starts his work by assuming, as given, the existence of the three basic classes – workers, capitalists (tenant farmers) and landowners. They appear in the opening chapter of the book, and he proceeds to reveal their antagonism as a function of their economic interests. (As we know – and this stood to his credit – Ricardo became increasingly unsure whether the development of machinery would actually benefit the working class.) Despite this achievement Marx attacks Ricardo for 'naively taking this antagonism for a social law of nature' (Preface to Marx, 1971a). What Ricardo took as 'given' Marx had to explain. Only at the very *end* of Volume III (in the famous unfinished chapter) does Marx start to deal with the class relations of the bourgeois system as they appear on the surface of society. It is precisely in this class struggle that the outward forms of society are continually 'smashed up' as Marx at one point says (Marx and Engels, 1956, p. 250). Thus the structure of Marx's work is once again seen to be the very opposite of Ricardo's and this opposition is in no way fortuitous. For Marx set out not merely to prove that the interests of the two basic classes of bourgeois society were antagonistic (this had been recognized by the leading bourgeois thinkers as well as in the practice of the working class), but to uncover the historical roots of this antagonism. For only in this way could it be scientifically demonstrated that capital not only produces this antagonism, but provides also the material basis for overcoming it. In short, Marx set out to prove that the working class is not merely an *exploited* class, but a *revolutionary* class, a revolutionary class because it is the most important and decisive element in the productive forces of modern society. These productive forces are driven into increasingly sharp historical conflict with the social relations of bourgeois society. Here lies the ultimate source both of capital's crisis and of the social revolution alike. Marx's task (and the task of Marxism) was to make the working class aware of this spontaneous process. Hence Trotsky's aphorism 'Marxism is the conscious reflection of an unconscious process.'

This naive conception of the class struggle found in political economy was in turn bound up directly with its treatment of economic crisis. Because they invariably confused material and social phenomena, the political economists did not so much deny the possibility of economic crises as attribute such crises to *nature*, rather than to society. Once more it is Ricardo who brings out this point most clearly. The cornerstone of his view of economic crises lies of course in his theory of rent. He starts by defining the rate of profit as uniquely determined by the rate of surplus value to variable capital ($p^1 = {}^s/_v$). He then proceeds to confine his discussion of changes in the profit rate to one centred on changes in the value of labour power. Accepting the 'principle of population', as advanced by Malthus (which by pronouncing the supply of labour infinitely elastic assumes wages constant at subsistence level), Ricardo was then able to limit his analysis to one concerning the productivity of labour in agriculture. He believed – on the basis of the 'law' of diminishing returns – that the productivity of labour in this sector would decline over time. This, in turn, would force up wages and hence bring about a reduction in profits. Thus his famous dictum 'The interest of the landlord is always opposed to that of every other class in the community'.

The fact that Ricardo was forced to rely upon the Malthusian law of population – with its corollary, the notion of differential rent – marked another betrayal of his central aim to found political economy on the law of value. For the decline in the rate of profit was not deduced – and given Ricardo's empiricist method could not be deduced – from the law of value. It also landed Ricardo in another difficulty. According to him, as population rises – and given constant wages – rent increases and profits fall. He thus makes landed property the source of the decline in profit; yet, with the development of the industrial revolution, landed property was being increasingly subordinated to industrial capital.

Without examining all aspects of Ricardo's work on the nature of capitalist crisis, it is clear that for him such crises rest finally upon *nature*. For he held that, in the last instance, the rate of profit is determined by the fertility of the soil. Given the protection of agriculture by the tariff system, there must be a secular decline in the rate of profit as increasingly infertile soil is brought into cultivation to feed a growing population. And the corollary to this conclusion was that this decline in the profit rate could be arrested if sufficient fertile land were available:

> Profits of stock fall only because land equally well adapted to produce food cannot be procured; and the degree of the fall of profits, and the rise of rents, depends wholly on the increased expense of production. If therefore, in the progress of countries in wealth and population new portions of fertile land could be added to such countries, with every increase in capital, profits would never fall, nor rents rise. (Ricardo, 1951, p. 18)

Marx certainly praised Ricardo in his efforts to understand the movement of the rate of profit. Not only did he probe this question much more deeply than Smith (who saw profit falling as a result of competition, which was no explanation at all) but Ricardo did grasp the significance of the rate of profit as the motor of capital accumulation: 'What worries Ricardo is the fact that the rate of profit, the stimulating principle of capitalist production, the fundamental premise and driving force of accumulation, should be endangered by the development of production itself' (III, p. 254). But, adds Marx, Ricardo was concerned here, as in so many other matters, only with the quantitative aspect of the problem and was at best only vaguely aware of the real forces lying behind this tendency. He saw the problem, says Marx, 'in a purely economic way – that is from the bourgeois point of view, within the limitations of capitalist understanding, from the standpoint of capitalist production itself' (III, p. 254).

And it was precisely because Ricardo assumed the capitalist economy to be natural that he was unable to examine the social roots of its breakdown, expressed amongst other things through the law of the tendency of the rate of profit to fall. In this connection Marx observes: 'Those economists, therefore, who, like Ricardo, regard the capitalist mode of production as absolute, feel at this point that it creates a barrier to itself, and for this reason, attribute the barrier to Nature (in the theory of rent) not to production' (III, p. 254).

As we have attempted to show, this fusing of the natural and the social was not confined to the treatment of the falling rate of profit. It permeated every single aspect of political economy. When Marx speaks of Ricardo's 'purely economic' way of viewing things he means essentially this: the fact that political economy transformed the properties of commodities, money, capital, etc. which arose from their *social existence* into properties belonging naturally to them as *things*. Here was the fetishism of political economy, a fetishism which was directly related to empiricism in that it attributed to the objects in their immediately perceptible form properties that in fact did not belong to these objects and had nothing in common with their perceptible appearance. This is why Marx speaks of that 'fetishism peculiar to bourgeois Political Economy, the fetishism which metamorphoses the social, economic character impressed on things in the process of social production into a natural character stemming from the material nature of those things' (II, p. 225).

It was this fetishism, this 'purely economic' way of treating phenomena which Marx rejected *in toto*. Of course, Marx rejected many of the particular conclusions of the classical economists. But much more important as we have attempted to show, was his rejection of the faulty method which he considered led inescapably to these wrong conclusions and theoretical inconsistencies. In short, Marx's critique of political economy was of a philosophical nature, rather than one concerned with the details of economic theory alone. It is therefore to some further aspects of these philosophical questions that we now turn our attention.

3 · The Concepts of *Capital*

In its most profound sense, *Capital* is a work which elucidates the history of capitalism and it does this by means of 'an analysis of the concepts which *sum up* this history' as Lenin at one point puts it. The nature of the concepts Marx develops in his work and the role played by them are therefore of decisive importance in understanding the nature of this work. It is no accident that nearly all the attacks launched against *Capital* have been directed against the fundamental concepts of the work – the law of value, the notion of surplus value, etc.[1] It has been asserted that these categories do not correspond to the observed development of capitalism; either this or they are merely theoretical constructs, a legacy of Marx's unfortunate flirtation with Hegelianism.

In examining the nature of Marx's concepts, let us recall one decisive point which emerged from his critique of classical economics. In this critique Marx (here following the lead of Hegel) recognizes that every science necessarily evolves through its own categories and that it is only through the development of such categories that thought is able to gain a more rigorous understanding of the objects and processes it is studying. Marx's concern was never confined to pointing out the errors of Ricardo and others – he was above all concerned to show the limitations of a method that had produced a series of concepts which, while explaining bourgeois economic relations 'with social validity', proved incapable of probing to the 'law of motion' of capitalist society. In his critique of the categories of bourgeois economy Marx was directly influenced by Hegel. It was Hegel who drew an important distinction between the mere formation of *images* of things and the drawing of *notions*. It will be important to keep this distinction in mind for what follows. Hegel says on this point: 'The mind makes general images of objects long before it makes *notions* of them;

67

and it is only through these mental images and by recourse to them, that the thinking mind rises to know and comprehend *thinkingly*' (Hegel, 1975, p. 3). And Hegel proceeds to characterize philosophical thought as 'a peculiar mode of thinking – a mode in which thinking becomes knowledge, and knowledge through notions' (1975, p. 4). Elaborating on this distinction between 'image' and 'concept' Hegel further says: 'It may be roughly said that philosophy puts thoughts, categories, or in a more precise language adequate *notions*, in place of generalized images we ordinarily call ideas. Mental impressions such as these may be regarded as the metaphors of thoughts and notions' (1975, p. 6).

It was in tracing this path along which 'thinking becomes knowledge' that Hegel insisted on the objectivity of the basic categories of thought. Real scientific thought was impossible if it confined itself to the immediate impressions given in sensation. It was necessary to posit these sensations on to a body of existing knowledge, a body of knowledge built up historically by previous thinkers in the particular field concerned. There is no doubt that Marx and Engels fully agreed with Hegel on this point. The categories of thought were not the product of minds considered in their individuality; the development of knowledge, like the development of history generally, was the product of 'many wills'. It is important in this respect to note that Marx did not confine his studies in the history of political economy to one or two individuals. It is, of course, true that he gave particular prominence to Ricardo; but he also studied thoroughly Ricardo's opponents, even though he considered their work often contained much 'vulgar' material (Malthus would be a case in point). And this is no accident: Marx studied all the aspects of the development of political economy, for it was only in this process – in the 'clash of many wills' – that the science had in reality developed. Ricardo's own development provides a striking example of the objective character of the categories of political economy. His early works are almost wholly concerned with monetary questions, the question of fixed currency and the bullion price. Despite the fact that Ricardo had studied Smith's *Wealth of Nations* before these early writings, there is no evidence that he was at that stage in any way concerned with the more abstract questions (law of value, rate of profit, etc.) which were to dominate his latter work, notably the *Principles*. He was forced to consider the problem of the law of value by practical necessity – in his case by the problem of the Corn Laws and the analysis of class relations which this involved. And this in turn obliged him to attempt to resolve the theoretical inconsistencies in Smith's work. He was forced to 'connect up' with the basic concepts of political economy, as these had been developed up to that point.

The objectivity of concepts

In considering this point about the objectivity of conceptual knowledge let us consider Marx's well-known statement in the *18th Brumaire*:

> Men make their own history, but they do not make it just as they please; they do not make it under circumstances chosen by themselves, but under circumstances directly encountered, given and transmitted from the past. The tradition of all the dead generations weighs like a nightmare on the brain of the living.

The important point for us here is that what is true of man's economic, political, etc. history is true equally of his *intellectual* history. Every new development in knowledge, in all spheres of investigation, necessarily grows out of the old forms in which that knowledge has historically emerged. And the form taken by human thought is always a series of interrelated concepts, concepts which do not reflect the whim of individual thinkers, but reflect man's practice in the particular sphere of science concerned. It is for this reason alone that all attempts to separate Marx's thought off *completely* from his predecessors can only lead to sterility, as with efforts by some members of the Althusser school to paint Marx as an *a-Ricardian*.[2] The diversity in pre-Ricardian and Ricardian economic thought reflected the contradictory, diverse, nature of the reality under investigation. Marx had to *work over* this body of literature, recognizing that as a reflection of man's social practice it marked an important stage forward in the efforts to understand the nature of the bourgeois mode of production. Thus, Marxism, the theory of modern socialism, cannot be metaphysically separated from the highest achievements of bourgeois thought, on the grounds that it has a different 'object'. 'Like every new theory, modern socialism had, at first to connect itself with the intellectual stock-in-trade ready to its hand, however deeply its roots lay in (material) economic facts!' (Engels, 1947).

We know that Marx did not dismiss the concepts developed by classical economy as merely 'bourgeois'. Ricardo's work came nearest to reflecting the true interests of industrial capital (in its conflict with the landed interest) precisely because it came closest to a truly objective grasp of bourgeois economy. And this 'paradox' is explained precisely by the fact that at the time he was writing, the industrial bourgeois still had undisputed leadership in the struggle for the development of the productive forces. Their immediate class interests *did*, at this period, coincide with the elaboration of an objective, 'disinterested' view of social and class relations. Only when their leadership in the historical development of these productive forces was challenged – as it was with the appearance of the working class – did this position alter. Because this was the case, Marx had to subject the categories of political economy to the most detailed scrutiny – as part of the task of uncovering the material and social forces which had given birth to these categories. This was the very essence of the 'critique' of political economy. In short he had to show the *necessity* of the categories of political economy as a reflection of man's developing and unfolding social practice. For Marx, new concepts arise in science because, penetrating ever more deeply into the world of phenomena, man reveals new aspects of these phenomena which simply cannot be fitted into the existing categories of thought. New concepts are demanded if these new aspects are to be adequately expressed and established. And they in turn become necessary only when the material and social conditions for the new concepts exist or are coming into being. Engels' example from the history of chemistry is worth repeating in this connection:

> We know that late in the past century, the phlogistic theory
> still prevailed. It assumed that combustion consisted essentially
> in this: that a certain hypothetical substance, an absolute
> combustible named phlogiston, separated from the burning
> body. This theory sufficed to explain most chemical
> phenomena then known, although it had to be considerably

strained in some cases. But in 1774 Priestley produced a certain kind of air 'which he found to be so pure, so free from phlogiston, that common air seemed adulterated in comparison with it'. He called it 'dephlogisticated air'. Shortly after him Scheele obtained the same kind of air in Sweden and demonstrated its existence in the atmosphere. He also found that this kind of air disappeared whenever some body was burned in it or in ordinary air and therefore he called it 'fire-air'. From these facts he drew the conclusion that the combination arising from the union of phlogiston with one of the components of the atmosphere (that is to say from combustion) 'was nothing but fire or heat which escaped through glass'. (Preface by Engels to II)

As Engels remarks, Priestley and Scheele 'had produced oxygen without knowing what they had laid their hands on' (Preface to II). They remained prisoners of the conventional categories of chemistry. It fell to Lavoisier (to whom Priestley had communicated his findings) to analyse the entire phlogistic chemistry in the light of this discovery. It was Lavoisier who came to the conclusion that this new kind of air was a new chemical element and that combustion was not the result of this mysterious phlogiston leaving a burning body, but of this new element combining with that body. Priestley and Scheele, although they had produced oxygen prior to Lavoisier, because they remained trapped in the old concepts, were unable to grasp what they had done. Thus although Lavoisier 'did not produce oxygen simultaneously and independently of the other two, as he claimed later on, he nevertheless is the real *discoverer* of oxygen vis-à-vis the others, who had only *produced* it without knowing what they had produced' (Preface to II, p. 15).

Form and content of knowledge

For Marx a study of the concepts of political economy as they had arisen in the pre-1830 period was decisively important for he held that without conceptual thinking, no *conscious* thinking was possible. Unlike the political economists he could not take the *forms* developed by the subject as ready and given. These forms had to be investigated, because it was only through them that the *content* of bourgeois relations developed and revealed itself. Here is one important aspect of Marx's rejection of the empirical method of political economy. Empiricism, as a theory of knowledge, rests upon the false proposition that perception and sensation constitute the *only* material and source of knowledge. Marx as a materialist, of course, never denied that the material world, existing prior to and independently of consciousness, is the only source of sensation. But he knew that such a statement, if left at that point, could not provide the basis for a consistent materialism, but at best a mechanical form of materialism, which always left open a loop-hole for idealism. It is true that empiricism lay at the foundation of seventeenth- and eighteenth-century materialism in England and France. But at the same time this very empiricist point of view provided the basis for both the subjective idealism of Berkeley and the agnosticism of Hume. How is it possible, starting with the proposition that sensation is the sole source and material of knowledge, to end up either denying the objectivity of the external world (subjective idealism) or denying the possibility of an exhaustive knowledge of that external world (scepticism)? To take the latter case, the argument runs as follows: to men are given directly perceptions and sensations; they provide the only legitimate source of knowledge. But in these perceptions are to be found no internal necessary connections. How do we know that one thing is the *cause* of another? We see only one thing followed by another; if this is constantly repeated we come to *expect* the second whenever the first occurs. This is merely a psychological expectation, not a causal connection. These were essentially the conclusions drawn by Hume from the empiricist theory of knowledge. It followed that any statements about the objectivity of the categories of philosophy or science (causality, interaction, law, etc.) are purely metaphysical, reflecting nothing in the sensed material of knowledge. On this view, logical categories are only schemes which we use (purely out of convention and habit) for the organization of sense-data. But such schemes remain, necessarily, wholly subjective. They are subjective first in relation to the external world, the existence of which, according to scepticism, can never be established; second in relation to the very sense data themselves, since they are determined by the very constitution of the subject – that is by the aggregate of the individual's former psychical experiences.

Marx's objection to empiricism rests upon this: that its attention is directed exclusively to the *source* of knowledge, but not the *form* of that knowledge. For empiricism the form assumed by our knowledge tends always to be ignored as something having no inherent, necessary, connection with the content, the source of our knowledge. To return again to a previous example in the light of this: Ricardo saw in labour the source and measure of value, capital, etc. But he failed to consider the form assumed by this labour. Here was an expression not so much of the weakness of his economic theory as of his philosophical stance, empiricism. Here we can see why Marx considered it vital to examine economic forms and why political economy ignored this matter. (It must be said that this neglect is unfortunately to be found in much Marxist writing on *Capital*.)

To examine this matter further, let us consider Kant's position, a position which appears to be at the root of many misunderstandings about *Capital*. In an effort to vindicate scientific reason in the light of Hume's rejection of causation and of knowledge of the external world, Kant argued that the mind is an instrument which, by its very construction, always apprehends isolated, individual facts in rational form. Kant realized that without categories, rational thought was impossible; but for him these categories have their basis in our *thoughts*, thought which is necessarily sundered from the material world. Sensation and the logical moments of knowledge do not on this view have a common basis – there is and can be no transition between the two. (Or as the Althusserian would put it, 'Our constructions and our arguments are in theoretical terms and they can only be evaluated in theoretical terms – in terms, that is to say, of their rigour and theoretical coherence. They cannot be refuted by any empiricist recourse to the supposed "facts" of history' (Hindess and Hirst, 1975, p. 3).) Concepts, according to Kantianism, do not grow up and develop out of the sensed world but are already given before it, in the *a priori* categories of reasoning. These categories are supposed to grasp the multifarious material given in sensation, but themselves remain *fixed* and *dead*. 'Sensation' and 'reason' were counterposed to each other in a thoroughly mechanical manner, with no connection between them. And the same was true of the content of knowledge and its forms. On this last point Rubin is surely absolutely correct when he states:

> One cannot forget that on the question of the relation between content and form, Marx took the standpoint of Hegel and not of Kant. Kant treated form as something external in relation to the content, and as something which adheres to the content from the outside. From the standpoint of Hegel's philosophy, the content is not in itself something to which form adheres from the outside. Rather, through its development, the content itself gives birth to the form which is already latent in the content. Form necessarily grows from the content itself. (Rubin, 1972, p. 117)

We shall return to this question of economic form specifically in connection with the value-form. But let us note here that it was Hegel, on the basis of his criticism of Kantianism, who attempted to resolve the problem (of the connection between the 'sensed' and the 'logical', the 'content' and the 'form') by showing that thought is a dialectical process of movement, from thought of a lower grade to that of a higher grade. According to Hegel, concepts developed by thought ceased to be dead, *a priori* products of the individual mind, but forms endowed with life, the life of the movement of thought itself. This is Lenin's point when he says, 'What Hegel demands is a logic the forms of which would be forms with content, inseparably connected with that content' (LCW, vol. 38, p. 92) and Lenin notes Hegel's attack on logic considered entirely from the subjective standpoint:

> Logic is the science not of external forms of thought, but of the laws of development 'of all material, natural and spiritual things', i.e. of the development of the entire concrete content of the world and of its cognition i.e. the sum-total, the conclusion of the *history* of knowledge of the world. (LCW, vol. 38, p. 92)

In this respect there can be no doubt whatsoever that Marx adopted Hegel's position (against Kant). In stressing the historical and objective nature of concepts, Hegel prepared the way for introducing the role of *practice* into human thought, even though his conception of this practice remained too narrow. Marx followed Hegel's lead in insisting that the movement from the 'sensed' to the 'logical' was a process in which social man penetrated ever more deeply through the appearance of phenomena, deeper and deeper into their essence. It was this *social practice* that lies at the very heart and foundation of the development of man's conceptual thinking. The form taken by man's knowledge, summarized in the concepts of science, represents an index, a résumé, of his education and in particular the education of his senses. Speaking of the growth of human thought, Engels says that

> the results in which its experiences are summarized are
> concepts, that the art of working with concepts is not inborn
> and also is not given with ordinary everday consciousness but
> requires real thought and that this thought has a long
> empirical history, not more or less than empirical natural
> science.

Empiricism and the empirical

Now this reference by Engels to the 'long empirical history' involved in the elaboration of scientific concepts should warn us against confusing the 'empirical' with 'empiricism', a confusion which, for instance, runs through the whole of Althusser's work. Before saying something about Althusser, let us note a statement by Lenin. 'In order to understand it is necessary empirically to begin understanding, study, to rise, from empiricism to the universal. In order to learn to swim it is necessary to get into the water' (LCW, vol. 38, p. 205). Lenin is drawing attention to the fact that for Marxism the empirical is a necessary, unavoidable, stage in the development of conceptual thinking. Marx supported Hegel's view of knowledge as a process from the sensed to the logical (conceptual), but Marx never forgot that Hegel was an idealist. The *Phenomenology* is concerned with the path along which, according to Hegel, consciousness moves, raising itself from the level of sensation to that of 'pure thought'. But Hegel's idealism meant that he rejected the material basis of sensation: he was therefore obliged to represent the ascent of consciousness as one in which thought was gradually emancipated or 'purified' from sensuous reality. Marx's view here departed sharply from that of Hegel. For Marx the logical growth of knowledge takes place on the foundation of a continual working on the ever richer material of sensation; in the course of this the mind abstracts richer and therefore increasingly adequate concepts. Here there is no confusion whatsoever between 'empiricism' and the 'empirical'. The construction of *Capital* would have been impossible had Marx not spent hour upon hour sifting through a mass of empirical material, against which the real criticism of the categories of political economy was to take place. Lenin expressed this point, saying of Marx: 'he took one of the economic formations of society – the system of commodity production – *and on the basis of a vast mass of data (which he studied for not less than twenty-five years)* gave a most detailed analysis of the laws governing this formation and its development' (LCW, vol. 1).

The insistence by Hegel that thought must rise from the immediate, the sensed, to the apparent, to the *universal* provided the germ for Marx's revolutionary conception of *practice* as the decisive component in the development of human knowledge.[3] Human thought does not occupy some hermetically sealed compartment, standing outside the real object under investigation. Knowledge must and can only start from perception; it is from these perceptions that abstractions are made which in turn must be subjected to continual testing in practice, that is testing against the historically evolved concepts of the science. It is only in this light that we can overcome the erroneous conception that Marxism is a fixed body of knowledge, rather than a *theory* of knowledge, a theory of how knowledge develops through man's practice. Both Hegel and Marx objected to the Kantian position in that Kant, in effect, wanted knowledge outside the process of knowledge; their fundamental reproach to Kant is this, that he wished to learn to swim before getting into the water. (To take a previous example, it is clear that all those who interpret Marx's value theory as the search for an 'invariant measure of value' are guilty of foisting a Kantian position on to Marx, a position which he entirely rejected.)

In the light of the distinction between the 'empirical' and 'empiricism' let us pause to consider the case of Althusser. One aspect of Althusser's work is that he is guilty of transforming Marx's many statements on the inadequacy of empiricism to mean that the empirical must be rejected entirely as purely ideological. Reading Marx through the distorting lens of structuralism, Althusser wants to pretend that Marxism is anti-empiricist in the sense that there is a reality lying beyond and entirely separated from the immediate appearances of the world. On this view – one quite at variance with Marx – the essence of phenomena inhabits a realm divorced completely from the manner in which these, the phenomena, were actually historically formed, from the path along which they actually appeared. And this sphere – the essence of phenomena – is to be discovered through 'theoretical practice' – that is, in a process of thought separated entirely from historical practice. And because he separates out the 'essence' from the path by which that essence actually takes on the form of its appearance, he must separate out logic form history. Thus we find in *Reading Capital*:

> Knowledge working on its object . . . does not work on the real object but on the peculiar raw material which constitutes in the strict sense of the term, *its 'object'* (of knowledge) and which, even in the most rudimentary forms of knowledge is distinct from the *real object*. For that raw material is ever-already, in the strong sense Marx gives it in *Capital, raw material*, i.e. matter already elaborated and transformed, precisely by the imposition of the complex (sensuous-technical-ideological structure) which constitutes it as an *object of knowledge*, however crude, which constitutes it as the object it will transform, whose forms it will change in the course of its development process in order to produce knowledge and which are constantly *transformed* but will always apply to its *object*, in the sense of the *object of knowledge*. (Althusser and Balibar 1970, p. 43).

Stripped of the pomposity which characterizes the Althusserian style, what does this passage mean if not that there is supposedly a rigid distinction to be drawn between reality and the way in which we come to perceive that reality? And from this must inexorably follow an attack upon Marx's insistence on the *historical* nature of all the categories evolved in the study of society. (We note in passing that Althusser tries to foist this view mainly on to Engels, rather than Marx. It was in fact a position held by them both.)

This metaphysical separation of 'dialectics' and 'history' runs throughout Althusser's work. Another example of it will have to suffice. Attacking those who have conceived *Capital* as a *historical* work, Althusser says:

> They did not see [that is presumably until Althusser fell from the skies] that history features in *Capital* as an object of theory, not as a real object, as an 'abstract' (conceptual) object and not as a real-concrete object; and that the chapters in which Marx applies the first stages of a historical treatment either to the struggles to shorten the working day or to primitive capitalist accumulation refer to the theory of history as their principle, to the construction of the concept of history and of its 'developed form', of which the economic theory of the capitalist mode of production constitutes one determinate 'region'. (Althusser and Balibar, 1970, p. 117)

Shorn of its verbiage, what does this amount to if not the old ideological prejudice that theory precedes practice? Practice is to be degraded to the level where it merely *illustrates* theory. The abstract is to be sundered entirely from the concrete, this abstract to be arrived at by a process metaphysically standing apart from the process of reality. Only when science has developed can it then be applied to history. Hence the concern of this school to find adequate concepts which alone will allow us to understand the movement of reality. Once more Althusser, if he will pardon the expression 'inverts' the real path by which knowledge grows. Marx's categories in *Capital* arose through a long process in which all the perceived developments and changes within capitalism were posited on to all the previous attempts – inside and outside the working-class movement – to grasp the real nature and significance of this new mode of production. Only in this process was political economy 'tested out' and its inadequacies exposed. For instance, Marx's ability to grasp the real nature of surplus value would have been impossible without the discovery of the category 'labour-power'. Only with this discovery was Marx able to resolve a number of the theoretical problems which had beset political economy. But, and it is a vital 'but', such a 'discovery' by Marx was possible only because the category labour-power was actually being brought into being by the development of capital, brought into being in the shape of the modern working class, a class selling this commodity, labour-power, as the basis for its existence.

In short, the Althusser position is one totally incompatible with that of Marx. The way man perceives reality is *not* purely ideological, not something *entirely* separated from reality, but always the starting point for knowledge, for the elaboration of concepts. Althusser's position, far from being 'rigorous' in fact leads to a position where the individual can believe or do anything in practice, because for him theory constitutes an autonomous sphere. Althusser and his followers have in effect merely been engaged in the very old and entirely petty dispute as to whether truth is located in the immediately sensed or in the essence of things. Hegel (followed by Marx) put an end to this squabble by insisting that it was not a question of 'or' but of 'and'.[4] Truth was a process which involved both the immediate and the mediated – truth was not a body of dogma (to be discovered by the practitioners of Theoretical Practice) but a process, a process which moved always from appearance to essence. Speaking specifically of Marx's analysis of the commodity, Lenin shows how much richer is his position as against the arid structuralism of Althusser. 'A double analysis, deductive and inductive – logical and historical (forms of value). *Testing by facts or by practice respectively*, [author's emphasis] is to be found here in *each* step of the analysis' (LCW, Vol. 38, p. 320).[5]

Empiricism and the commodity

Returning to our main theme, both Hegel and Marx wished to stress as against empiricism that rational knowledge is a deeper, richer form of knowledge of the material and spiritual world when compared with that furnished by mere direct apprehension of it in sensations and representations. Now these considerations, although seemingly remote from the concerns of Marxist political economy as it has developed over the last fifty years, have, in fact, an immediate bearing on an attempt to understand *Capital*. Let us take a statement by Marx about the analysis of the commodity:

> The reality of the value of commodities thus represents
> Mistress Quickly, of whom Falstaff said, 'A man knows not

where to have her.' This reality of the value of commodities contrasts with the gross material reality of these same commodities (the reality of which is perceived by our bodily senses) in that not an atom of matter enters into the reality of value. We may twist and turn a commodity this way and that – as a thing of value it still remains unappreciable by our bodily senses. (I, p. 47)

What is the meaning of this passage? This: that man can see and touch the material envelope of different commodities. He can weigh them, measure them, test their hardness, etc. But such sensuous knowledge cannot itself in any way disclose the universal connection between commodity producers, cannot possibly discover the social relations which are attached to these sensuously perceptible things, cannot discover within the commodity the 'germ' of money, cannot possibly comprehend capital in the whole process of its birth, development and decay. In this task – the task which Marx set himself in *Capital* – abstraction is required if the true nature of these economic relations is to be understood. 'In the analysis of economic forms . . . neither microscopes nor chemical agents are of use. The force of abstraction must replace both' (I, p. 8). The nature of the commodity is not to be disclosed through a knowledge of its chemical etc. properties. Lenin's comment here is right to the point, when he notes Hegel's repudiation of those philosophies which reject conceptual knowledge because such concepts are without the spatial and temporal material of the sensuous. Lenin says: 'Hegel is essentially *right: value* is a category which disposes with the material of sensuousness but it is truer than the law of supply and demand' (LCW, Vol. 38, p. 172).

We have argued that in so far as Marx stressed the objectivity of thought-concepts he stood on the same ground as Hegel as against empiricism or Kantianism. According to Hegel, the categories of thought are generated dialectically one after the other and it is through the dialectical movement of these concepts that the Absolute Idea unfolds and its content is transformed into nature, through which process it becomes embodied in material entities. It would be easy to dismiss such a conception as merely idealist. This has been the stance of many who thought that they were thereby defending the positions of materialism. What such a position misses out is that in its idealist form Hegel's conception contains a profound truth, a truth which was fully assimilated by Marx. The truth was this: although Hegel treats the categories of thought as the creation of a world spirit (God), his service to philosophy lay in the fact that in the dialectical transformation of the categories he sensed the movement of the world: 'He brilliantly *divined* the dialectics of things (phenomena, the world, *nature*) in the dialectics of concepts' (LCW, vol. 38, p. 196). This was certainly the 'rational kernel' which Marx extracted from Hegel and it was Lenin's main concern in his reading of Hegel. All those who tend to dismiss Hegel as merely an idealist, approach philosophy more from the standpoint of vulgar materialism than from a dialectical materialism which was formed on the basis of the conquests of the *whole* of philosophy, including the contribution made to human thought by the Plato-Hegel tradition in philosophy (the 'intelligent idealist' trend). When Lenin undertook his study of Hegel he did so precisely to combat that trend inside the working-class movement which started from positions close to those of mechanical materialism. Despite formally arguing against Kantianism, they ended up capitulating to it. Lenin had Plekhanov and others in mind when he says 'Marxists criticized (at the beginning of the twentieth century) the Kantians and the Humists more in the manner of Feuerbach (and Büchner) than of Hegel' (LCW, vol. 38, p. 179).

In this respect Hegel stands infinitely closer to dialectical materialism than the whole of modern positivism, which is ultimately forced to the conclusion that in the face of our (supposed) inability to establish causality and necessity in nature the *mind* must carry out this task, according to the principles of formal logic. By a concept, in stark contrast to this subjectivist view, Marx meant an abstraction which approached the essence of a series of phenomena; a concept was not to be derived mechanically – by 'adding up' all the features common to a series of phenomena. Hegel also vigorously attacked this latter view, and here lies the significance of his distinction between a concept and 'general image'. By a general image Hegel meant an abstract common element found in every single representative of a class. (For instance, one found an element common to all observed capitalisms – say the existence of commodity production. An image of capitalism is constructed which abstracts this element, commodity production. It is of course again 'easy' using this method to 'prove', for example, that the USSR is 'capitalist'.) This method of constructing concepts (as merely general images) was one adopted by Kant. 'The concept is . . . a general image or representation of that which is common to many objects, consequently a general idea provided that it can be included in several objects' (Kant, *Logik*, quoted in Ilyenkov, 1977, p. 184).

Abstract identity

Hegel rejected this Kantian view of the concept on the grounds that it was confined to what he called *abstract identity* or *abstract universality*. Some aspect common to a range of objects is isolated (abstracted) as that which is 'general' to them, to be set against a 'particular' which, on this view, can exist on its own. The *necessity* of the aspects chosen can never be demonstrated and, given that this necessity cannot be established, these 'aspects' out of which the general is constructed must remain ultimately *arbitrary*. In short, regularity in appearance is not sufficient to establish necessity. This Hegel points out when he notes the inadequacy of the *consensus gentium* as a proof for the existence of God. The fact that everybody agrees with the existence of God, is no necessary proof for God's existence. Unless the nature of this individual consciousness is thoroughly explained and its inner necessity established, the proof is inadequate:

> Among the so-called proofs of the existence of God, there used to stand the *consensus gentium*, to which appeal is made as early as Cicero. The *consensus gentium* is a weighty authority, and the transition is easy and natural, from the circumstance that a certain fact is found in the consciousness of every one to the conclusion that it is a necessary element in the very nature of consciousness. In this category of general agreement there was latent the deep-rooted perception, which does not escape even the least cultivated mind, that the consciousness of the individual is at the same time particular and accidental. Yet unless we examine the nature of this

consciousness itself, stripping it of its particular and accidental elements and, by the toilsome operation of reflection disclosing the universal in its entirety and purity, it is only a *unanimous* agreement upon a given point that can authorize a decent presumption that that point is part of the very nature of consciousness. (Hegel, 1975, pp. 105–6)

Likewise, but from the opposite standpoint, Hegel praises Rousseau. In the *Social Contract* Rousseau held that the laws of the state must spring from the universal will (*volonté générale*) but need not on that account be the will of all (*volonté de tous*). This, says Hegel, is a striking expression of 'the distinction . . . between what is merely in common, and what is truly universal' (1975, p. 228).

Hegel objected to the Kantian method of arriving at concepts because it made it impossible to trace the connection between the individual and the particular. All objects not included in a class were set against those standing outside this class. Identity (conceived as a dull sameness) and opposition were placed into two rigidly opposed criteria of thought. The direction Hegel took in trying to overcome the limitations imposed by such rigidity of thinking led to far richer results, and it was a method which guided Marx throughout *Capital*.

For Hegel a concept was primarily a synonym for the real *grasping* of the essence of phenomena and was in no way limited simply to the expression of something general, of some *abstract* identity discernible by the senses in the objects concerned. A concept (if it was to be adequate) had to disclose the real nature of a thing and this it must do not merely by revealing what it held in common with other objects, but also its *special* nature, in short its *peculiarity*. The concept was a unity of universality and particularity. Hegel insisted that it was necessary to distinguish between a universality which preserved all the richness of the particulars within it and an abstract 'dumb' generality which was confined to the sameness of all objects of a given kind. Further, Hegel insisted, this truly universal concept was to be discovered by investigating the actual laws of the origin, development and disappearance of *single things*. (Even before we take the discussion further, it should be clear that here lay the importance of Marx's logical-historical investigation of the cell-form of bourgeois economy, the commodity.) Thought that was limited to registering or correlating empirically perceived common attributes was essentially sterile – it could never come anywhere near to grasping the *law of development* of phenomena. One crucial point followed from this which has direct and immediate importance for *Capital*. It was this: the real laws of phenomena do not and cannot appear directly on the surface of the phenomena under investigation in the form of simple identicalness. If concepts could be grasped merely by finding a common element within the phenomena concerned then this would be equivalent to saying that appearance and essence coincided, that there was no need for science.

This insistence that the general is no mere mechanical summation of the individual phenomena concerned is reflected in Marx's comment on Feuerbach:

> [he] resolves the essence into the *human* essence. But the human essence is not an abstraction inherent in each single individual. In its reality it is the *ensemble* [author's emphasis] of the social relations. Feuerbach, who does not enter upon a criticism of this real essence, is consequently compelled: (1) To abstract from the historical process and to fix the religious sentiment as something by itself and to presuppose an abstract *isolated* human individual. (2) Essence, therefore, can be comprehended only as an internal, dumb generality which *naturally* unites the many individuals.

What is the significance of Marx's criticism of Feuerbach when considered in the light of the nature of concepts? Really this: that one can never get to the essence of any class (in this case to the essence of man) through finding a series of general attributes possessed by each member of the class taken separately. The essence of man can only be arrived at *historically*. (Feuerbach was, says Engels, a materialist in connection with nature but left materialism behind when he came to consider the social and historical sphere.) And it was only possible to demonstrate that this essence was not something 'fixed' and immutable, a dead generality, but developed and changed as part of the 'whole ensemble' of man's social and historical relations. The essence of anything was in this sense not *internal* but could be grasped only in and through its relations with other things. To grasp the real essence of man it was above all necessary to examine the formation and growth of human society as a whole – and of its separate individuals – as this process has taken place and is taking place. As a separate individual a person is only a member of a class (in this case man) in so far as he actualizes some aspect or side of a culture which has been formed historically prior to and independently of him. To the extent that the human individual embodies this historically developed culture, to that extent he expresses the true, always changing and deepening, universal in man. So this universal is no mechanically repeated 'uniformity' at dead repose in each and every member of society. It is, on the contrary, reality, repeatedly and directly broken up within itself into particular (separate) spheres which complement each other and are in essence mutually connected in their transition, thereby constituting a real living 'ensemble'.

Now in criticizing Feuerbach's inadequate conception of man, Marx drew attention to the lack on the part of 'contemplative materialism' of a real appreciation of the nature of human practice. Feuerbach did not, says Marx (Thesis I), 'conceive human activity itself as *objective* activity'. In probing to the real nature of man, Marx saw the peculiar feature of human life as arising from his *labour*, from his continual transformation of nature (both external and his own nature).

> Labour is the source of wealth, the political economists assert.
> And it really is the source – next to nature – which supplies it
> with the material that it converts into wealth. But it is
> infinitely more than this. It is the prime basic condition for all
> human existence, and this to such an extent that, in a sense,
> we have to say that labour created man himself. (Engels,
> 1960, p. 170)

It was for this reason – because of the role played by labour in the development of man – that Marx regarded with such sympathy Benjamin Franklin's definition of man as a tool-making animal (I, p. 179).

Where does the Kantian understanding of concepts stand in relation to Franklin's notion of man as a tool-making animal? Of course Franklin's definition would have to be rejected. For it is clearly the case that only a relatively small minority of men actually *make* tools. Such a definition would, therefore, have to be rejected as too narrow and restrictive. A 'wider' concept could be constructed by isolating any one of a number of commonly held features found amongst all men (consciousness, speech, etc.) and making these the basis for our understanding of man. And of course this is the usual method found in the social sciences. But it is a method having nothing in common with Marxism. Marx rejected such conceptions because they remained abstract and 'objectivist', for they were never able to grasp the process through which the phenomenon concerned (in this instance man) actually came into being and did in *practice* distinguish itself from other phenomena (the lower animals, for example). In connection with Feuerbach, Marx says:

> Men can be distinguished from animals by consciousness, by religion *or anything else you like* [author's italics]. They themselves begin to distinguish themselves from animals as soon as they begin to *produce* their means of subsistence, a step which is conditioned by their physical organization. By producing their means of subsistence men are actually producing their actual material life. (Marx and Engels, 1970, p. 42)

To recast this point. As in every attempt to form an accurate notion of any phenomena, Marx and Engels had here to answer two related questions in establishing the essence of man. They had first to establish the *continuity* between man and the rest of the world (here Darwin's work played the vital role) and at the same time they had to establish the difference, within this continuity, between man and the rest of the organic world. Like all living matter, man reacts with his environment, a reaction arising from man's unity with organic nature and nature as a whole. But his reaction with nature is *purposive*, unlike that of the animal which remains purely *instinctive*. Man sets out to achieve definite goals and aims; these goals and aims do not arise, we must stress, from 'free will' but are determined by the whole of man's past practice. And man's ability to carry out his necessary struggle against nature at a level qualitatively higher than other animals arises essentially from the development of tools. Here lies man's true *uniqueness* and it explains Marx's respect for Franklin's basically materialist conception. In arriving at a conception of man which grasped, in the same concept, the unity of man with the animal world and at the same time his distinction from that world, Marx and Engels laid the basis for overcoming a one-sided (and therefore ultimately false) view of this problem. On the one hand, if one separates man metaphysically from the rest of nature one is forced ultimately to an idealist view of non-material forces as the ones which distinguish man. (Such views have, for example, taken the form of vitalism in biology.) On the other hand, equally one-sided would be the view that attempted to *reduce* the laws of social development to the level of biology. In other words, one cannot either separate *absolutely* the various forms of matter (the mistake in the first case); nor can one collapse the higher forms into the lower (as in the second case). In this last instance: social processes have certain specific features ('peculiarities') that are *not* inherent in biological phenomena as such, and no matter what biological forms of matter we may study we cannot deduce from them the laws of social phenomena, just as those biological processes cannot in turn be exhausted by the chemical and physical processes which they presuppose.

This latter viewpoint – the one that ignores the *qualitative* differences between material forms – (or rather tries to reduce more complex forms to simple ones) is a reflection of mechanism, the standpoint which dominated seventeenth- and eighteenth-century materialism. The seventeenth-century natural scientists picked out velocity, mass and volume as the simplest and most general aspects of all physical phenomena. (This was precisely the method of conceptualization confined to 'abstract identity'.) These aspects were in turn considered in a purely quantitative manner. The transformation of these aspects into unique, essential qualities of nature led these scientists to a denial of qualitative distinctions in nature, to a purely quantitative view of the world.[6]

Capital and the productive forces

These philosophical observations are of direct significance for a consideration of *Capital*. Let us start from Marx's avowed aim 'to lay bare the law of motion of modern society'. In order to carry out this task successfully, Marx had to demonstrate how the *universal* features common to all economic formations were expressed in a determinate form within 'modern society'. Only in this way could Marx disclose the peculiarities of capital, peculiarities which indicated that it was not some eternal timeless mode of production, as its apologists maintained. Capital, by expressing the universal laws of every mode of production in its own specific form, aided enormously the development of the productive forces; but at the same time, this specific social form is the very source of capitalism's definite (objective) historical limits. Capitalism played a definite and great (progressive) role in the development of man's productive forces. And Marx, unlike Utopian Socialism, fully grasped this role, so brilliantly depicted in the *Manifesto*. But he was able to understand this contradictory role played by capital and thereby overcome a purely moralistic opposition to capitalism *only* because he related capitalism *to the whole line of social development*. The point here is this: the concept of capital was not formed on the basis of seeking some abstract qualities which capital shared with all other modes of production (a view which reaches its most absurd in modern economics' notion of a quite timeless and asocial 'economic problem'). Nor was the concept of the nature of capital achieved by seeking those features which separated it absolutely from all previous economic forms.

Marx proceeded quite otherwise. As an illustration, let us take the labour process. Marx does not start with an examination of the labour process as it manifests itself in its specifically capitalist form. On the contrary, he begins when considering the process of labour with those universal (general) features common to all societies. He tells us:

> The fact that the production of use-values, or goods, is carried out under the control of a capitalist and on his behalf does not alter the general character of that production. We shall, therefore, in the first place, have to consider the labour process independently of the particular form is assumes under given social conditions. (I, p. 177)

Having dealt with the universal aspects of the labour-process (work) Marx *only then* deals with it in its specifically capitalist form:

It must be borne in mind, that we are now dealing with the production of commodities, and that up to this point, we have only considered one aspect of the process. Just as commodities are, at the same time, use-values, so the process of producing them must be a labour-process, and at the same time, a process of creating value. (I, p. 186)

To put this last point from a different angle. The labour-process (the general) is the pre-condition for all human life, the process in which man effects an exchange of matter between himself and Nature, 'the everlasting Nature-imposed condition of human exist-ence, and therefore common to every such phase' (I, p. 184). But this process cannot exist in this general form. Man never confronts Nature outside of definite social relations.

In production, men not only act on nature but also on one another. They produce only by co-operating in a certain way and mutually exchanging their activities. In order to produce, they enter into definite connections and relations with one another and only within these social connections and relations does their action on nature take place.

Stressing that man must always be conceived concretely, Marx and Engels tell us that they always set out

from real, active men, and on the basis of their real life-process we demonstrate the development of the ideological reflexes and echoes of this life-process. ... This method of approach is not devoid of premises. It starts out from the real premises and does not abandon them for a moment. Its premises are men, not in any fantastic isolation or abstract definition, but in their actual, empirically perceptible process of development under definite conditions. (Marx and Engels, 1970)

So this general process (of labour) exists only in connection with a definite, specific social form. And because of this – and here is the crucial point for the argument – the general is here, never produced *completely* in some, 'unadulterated' form. This is not the 'fault' of thought; on the contrary it is an expression of the rich and contradictory nature of all development. All the concrete phenomena under investigation can never be contained completely in any abstract general conception. All Marx's laws – the law of value, law of the falling rate of profit – are always approximations, in the sense of tendencies and not laws, in the sense that they coincide with immediate reality. And this must always be the case – precisely because these laws have been abstracted from reality. The contradiction between 'value' and 'price' for instance reflects no weakness of the law of value – it expresses the actual movement of capital and its accumulation. This approximate nature of all *Capital*'s concepts is true of every (adequate) concept in science and in history:

> Did feudalism ever correspond to its concept? Founded in the kingdom of the West Franks, further developed in Normandy by the Norwegian conquerors, its formation continued by the French Norsemen in England and Southern Italy, it came nearest to its concept – in the ephemeral kingdom of Jerusalem, which in the *Assize of Jerusalem* [The collection of laws of the kingdom of Jerusalem in the eleventh to thirteenth centuries] left behind it the most classical expression of the feudal order. Was this order a fiction because it achieved only a short-lived existence, classically expressed throughout, and only in Palestine, and even that mostly on paper only?
> (Marx and Engels, 1956, p. 565)

Use-value and value

This same methodological principle concerning the nature of the general and its relation to the particular can be seen right at the outset of *Capital* when Marx investigates the commodity. In the analysis of the commodity, we find him starting not with 'value' but 'use-value'. He begins, that is, with the *substance* of wealth, and therefore with a universal category, common to all societies. Only after making clear that commodities are 'in the first place' use-values does Marx deal with the peculiar feature of modern society, namely that use-values are the bearers of a definite social relation, the value relation. 'Use-values . . . constitute the substance of all wealth, whatever may be the social form of that wealth. In the form of society we are about to consider they are, in addition, the material depositories of exchange-value' (I, p. 36). The importance of Marx's statement here is that he is stressing and starting from the *objective* nature of the labour process in which use-values are created. Man's struggle against nature is in no way an arbitrary process – it takes place only in accordance with the laws of nature (matter). And because the labour process is eternal – and with it, therefore, the process of creating use-value ('an eternal nature-imposed necessity', (I, pp. 42–3)) – it cannot be dispensed with in any epoch. It is *universal*. This any child knows. But the implications are crucial. It would be a mistake to deal with the labour process as though it were some natural, technical process, separate from social relations. In the labour process men create their *physical* existence and this must not be lost sight of. But they create more than this – in the labour process is produced and reproduced their social existence. This mode of production, Marx reminds us: 'Must not be considered simply as being the production of the physical existence of the individuals. Rather it is a definite form of activity of these individuals, a definite form of expressing their life, a definite *mode of life* on their part' (Marx and Engels, 1970, p. 42).

But if it is a mistake to see production as a merely non-social (technical) matter it is equally erroneous to conceive of production as *purely* social, that is as one having no natural basis. Clearly involved here is the philosophical problem of the relationship of the 'social' to the 'natural'. While all aspects of this question cannot concern us here, this much can be said: all those who want to draw a rigid distinction between the 'natural' and the 'social' (essentially after the fashion of Kantianism) and who deny the dialectical character of natural phenomena must incline towards this latter mistake. To take one instance of such a mistake in relation to *Capital*: it would be wrong to treat the composition of capital in purely *value* (that is social) terms. When dealing with the organic composition of capital (the relationship of constant to variable capital) Marx insists that the social composition of capital is a *mirror* of the technical composition. This confusion of the social and the technical sides of the organic composition of capital is clear in Sweezy's work; it is a mistake which leads directly to errors in connection with Marx's falling rate of profit, as Yaffe

(1973 and 1975) and others have correctly pointed out. It is in fact quite impossible to understand the basic laws of accumulation and turnover of capital if this two-sided character of capital (as a social phenomenon, but one affixed to things) is not recognized. Similarly it would be a fundamental mistake to believe that use-value plays no role in Marx's investigation of capital, as Hilferding (1973) in his reply to Böhm-Bawerk wrongly thought. (We will return to this point, but see Rosdolsky's discussion of this matter – Rosdolsky, 1977 Ch. 3.)

Capital in general

It should be clear from this last example that the problem of the nature of concepts is in effect the same problem as that concerning the relationship between the individual and the general. We have already had occasion to draw attention to the role of the concept of capital in general – again Rosdolsky's work has here been of considerable importance. Let us review what we said earlier about this concept. Marx could not start from the existence of each individual unit of capital, taken in isolation in an external form, as seen on the surface of economic life. It is this surface of economic life which the 'vulgar' economists regard as the essence of things and the only valid source of knowledge about bourgeois economy. But, beneath this surface and through all the contradictions of competition, there remains the fact that all individual capitals constitute the capital of the whole of society. The existence of the individual capitals in their movement reflects social laws; because of the inherent anarchy of capitalist economy these social laws can only assert and reveal themselves behind the backs of individual capitalists and in opposition to their consciousness in a round-about, mediated manner and only on the basis of continual deviations from an average. For this reason any adequate theory in political economy cannot study economic processes from what would be the entirely superficial standpoint of the market – this would be in fact to study economic processes from the point of view of the *consciousness* of the individual capitalist.

Capital in general was not merely the summation of all individual capitals as they appeared in competition. This political economy understood, but only partially. For its efforts to abstract from the immediate way in which capital appeared (competition) were both formal and incomplete. It had tried to reduce all the economic relations to a common element (labour). It constructed its general notions by taking this common element in all economic forms. Marx's approach is quite different. In seeking the essential nature of capital ('capital in general') he traces the origin and development of capital out of its lower forms (commodities, money). And in doing this Marx reveals the real connection between capital and these lower forms while at the same time pointing to its peculiarities, peculiarities which separated it from these lower forms. Marx shows, to give a specific instance of the results of this approach, that while capital cannot exist independently of money, equally it cannot be reduced to this lower form. There have been many mistakes in the history of political economy arising from efforts to separate out completely the economic forms which, in their process of development, actually constitute a unity. The notion that the contradictions of capital could be overcome through the abolition of money provides one such example. But equally serious mistakes have occurred when higher economic forms have been mechanically reduced to their lower forms – when, for example, capital has been confused with one of its forms such as money capital. Marx's dialectical method alone enabled him to avoid these mistakes. His conclusion: capital is value, but value of a peculiar type, namely self-expanding value; it is a social relation attached to things which appropriates surplus value created in a definite process of production, and it thereby continually reproduces both capital and the relation of capital itself. The origin of this surplus value (which was taken as given by classical economics) was revealed by Marx without any reference whatsoever to individual capitals or the relations between them. Indeed, this point must be even more strongly put. To have dealt with the immediate form of economic relations (as they emerged in the sphere of competition) would have rendered *impossible* an uncovering of the process by and through which surplus value is extracted from the working class. In the form it takes as profit, surplus value seems to be produced in equal amounts by all sections of capital and as such capital appears to be the source of wealth, independent of labour. It was therefore essential that Marx should disclose the nature of this 'capital in general' *before* he dealt with its specific, immediate forms and why capital in general is dealt with before its forms – profit, interest, rent; these latter forms are explicable in terms of particular forms of capital. It is no accident that along with the notion of abstract and concrete labour, Marx considered this latter point to be one of the two best in his entire work. In short, it would have been impossible to get to the essence of what Marx calls the 'finished forms of capital' (G, p. 209) without this abstraction 'capital in general', or what Marx calls 'capital as such, capital in the process of becoming' (G, p. 729).

The example of imperialism

The notion of capital in general is a dialectical abstraction and one which enabled Marx to get to capital in the process of its arising – enabled him to reveal what it held in common with lower forms and at the same time what qualitatively new features it incorporated. This same dialectical method was at the very centre of Lenin's struggle to understand the historical significance of the imperialist stage of capitalism in his fight against Kautskyism. To illustrate this point we can take Lenin's definition of imperialism and compare it with that given by Kautsky.

Lenin's definition:

> Imperialism is Capitalism at that stage of development at which the dominance of monopolies and finance capital is established; in which the export of capital has acquired pronounced importance; in which the division of the world among the international trusts has begun, in which the division of all territories of the globe amongst the biggest capitalist powers has been completed.

Kautsky's definition:

> Imperialism is a product of highly developed industrial capitalism. It consists in the striving of every industrial capitalist nation to bring under its control or to annex all large areas of *agrarian* territory, irrespective of what nations inhabit.

Kautsky's definition of imperialism is entirely abstract and quite worthless. It is abstract because it can in no way disclose the connection between the *highest* phase of capitalist development and the *lower* forms from which it emerged. It is a formal definition arrived at by abstracting a feature common to all imperialist powers – the tendency to annexation. But this is a *political* not an *economic* phenomenon. Kautsky's definition went hand-in-hand with the notion that imperialism had no necessary, historical, relationship to capitalism in its competitive phase. For him imperialism was merely a reactionary *policy* carried out by a predatory wing of the bourgeoisie. For Lenin it was inadequate (and ultimately reactionary) to designate imperialism as merely 'violent'; the roots of this violence had to be discovered – only then would it be possible to point to the means by which this violence could be overcome. Lenin's definition of imperialism was correct because it explained the peculiarities of the latest phase of capitalism; these peculiarities had grown out of nineteenth-century competitive capitalism producing a situation where monopoly became decisive and where financial capital became the predominant form of capital. Lenin's conception of capitalism was arrived at not by picking out a single feature common to each capitalist power (Kautsky's false procedure) but by tracing the actual concrete development of capitalism. All the facets of capitalism in their interconnection had to be studied, and studied in their self-movement. And once more Lenin's conception of imperialism has to be seen as a tendency. It is quite worthless to think that Lenin can be 'refuted' by, for example, showing that monopoly in late nineteenth-century Britain did not reach the predominant position it 'should' have done according to Lenin's theory. This 'exception' can only be understood *dialectically* – by tracing its connection to the growth of world economy and Britain's specific, historical relationship to that world economy. The growth of monopoly (and of protectionism) was arrested in Britain because she was the first industrial capitalist nation who established a specific division of labour with world economy (importing food and raw materials, exporting finished manufactured goods). Similarly Lenin's point about the crucial role played by the export of capital as an important feature of imperialism cannot be considered in isolation from all the other features of capitalism noted by Lenin. Only in their combination, in their ensemble, do we get a 'definition' of imperialism which gets near to the driving forces of this new, higher stage of capitalist development. Whereas Kautsky's method (which derived from neo-Kantianism) allowed the reformists and centrists to concentrate on the purely secondary, episodic features of imperialism, Lenin's method alone leads to the conclusion that imperialism as the highest stage of capitalism opened up the epoch of wars and proletarian revolution. Here is but one instance of the immediate and practical implications of differences which at first sight might appear to be of a purely methodological character.

A recent writer on 'capital in general'

To understand the role of abstraction in the approach to any so-called 'concrete' question in *Capital* let us consider a recent writer (Hodgson, 1973) on Marx's concept of 'capital in general'. We have already met this writer as an explicit opponent of dialectics and an upholder of formal logic. It should, therefore, come as no surprise to discover that he rejects this notion of 'capital in general' which as we have seen is a concept arrived at only by dialectical abstraction. Yet it is the nature of this abstraction that is of interest to us at this point. Let us first see what Hodgson says on this matter and then we will examine his statement. Dealing with the 'basic flaw' in Marx's solution to the transformation problem, he says, 'It must be remembered that the capitalists are *primarily concerned* [author's italics] to increase their profits in *money terms*. This is essentially the meaning of Marx's well-known diagram M–C–M′ ' (1973, p. 51). Having 'explained' this for us, he then proceeds: 'Money capital M is invested in constant and variable capital, production takes place, commodities C are produced, and finally they are sold to reap an enlarged money revenue, M′. It was Marx's aim to explain the source of the profit, the difference between M and M′ ' (p. 51).

The capitalists, Hodgson now tells us,

> will calculate their rate of profit on capital invested in terms of prices, not values . . . this is the rate of profit that the capitalists themselves 'perceive' and upon which they base

their investment decisions. The goad to accumulate takes the form of prices as the capitalists are not *aware of*, or *disposed towards* a calculation in terms of values. (p. 51, author's italics)

Finally Hodgson comes to 'capital in general': Marx's 'error' in connection with the value-price relationship, we are told, 'Stems from his arbitrary assumption that we may treat the social capital as a whole, regarding the capitalist economy as one giant firm. Hence he avoids the main problem: to determine the general rate of profit that pertains to *separate* firms' (p. 52). By the number of basic errors compressed into so short a space one can only be 'disposed' to the view that Hodgson has understood nothing about *Capital*. Let us try to untangle some of these errors.

1 Hodgson is utterly wrong in his interpretation of the M–C–M' circuit. He believes that it indicates that capitalists are 'primarily concerned' as he puts it to increase their profits in money terms. In fact when Marx analyses this circuit he is not at all concerned with the *subjective motives* of the capitalists. Nor is he interested in either *profits* or *production*. It is in the fourth chapter of *Capital* that Marx starts his discussion of the 'General formula for Capital'. As we shall see in a moment this chapter is entirely and explicitly concerned with capital in general and Marx's discussion abstracts at this stage specifically from any consideration of the material composition of capital. Nor is Marx, at this point, concerned with exchange. He deals with the general economic form taken by capital in circulation:

> If we abstract from the material substance of the circulation of commodities, that is from the exchange of the various use-values, and consider only the economic forms produced by this process of circulation, we find its final result to be money: this final product of the circulation of commodities, is the first form in which capital appears. (I, p. 146)

Marx is here deliberately putting aside the question of the particular forms of capital as well as a consideration of individual capitals until later. He is dealing with *capital in general*. Throughout this chapter (Chapter 4) there is no mention of *production*, nor is Marx concerned with *profit* as Hodgson asserts, but only with *surplus value*. In fact Marx's discussion is about merchant's capital, for the very good reason that the first form assumed by capital is that of money and as such it constitutes the germ which is sublated in all the higher, more developed forms:

> As a matter of history, capital as opposed to landed property invariably takes the form at first of money; it appears as moneyed wealth, as the capital of the merchant and the usurer. But we have no need to refer to the origin of capital in order to discover that the first form of appearance of capital is money. We can see it daily under our eyes. All new capital, to commence with, comes on the stage, that is on the market, whether of commodities, labour, or money, even in our days, in the shape of money that by a definite process has to be transformed into capital. (I, p. 146)

Thus the circuit M–C–M' is not concerned with any one particular form of capital but with the *essence* of all forms of capital, in short with capital in general. This is made clear by Marx at the end of this chapter in a passage, which makes it clear that Hodgson has got everything wrong:

> Buying in order to sell, or more accurately, buying in order to sell dearer, M–C–M', appears certainly to be a form peculiar to one kind of capital alone, namely merchants' capital. But industrial capital too is money, that is changed into commodities, and by the sale of these commodities, is reconverted into more money. The events that take place outside the sphere of circulation, in the interval between the buying and selling, do not affect the form of this movement. Lastly in the case of interest-bearing capital, the circulation M–C–M' appears abridged. We have its result without the intermediate stage, in the form M–M', 'en style lapidaire' so to say, money that is worth more money, value that is greater than itself. (I, p. 155)

2 Yet these errors, serious though they are, do not arise merely from a misreading of certain passages in *Capital*. When Hodgson tells us that the capitalist is 'not disposed' to or 'aware' of value-magnitude, he only reveals that he rejects the basic point of materialism, and with it the corner-stone of Marxism. For he starts

from the consciousness of the capitalist! It is *entirely* irrelevant whether the capitalist is aware or unaware of the law of value. However the capitalist computes his rate of profit, the formation and movement of the rate of profit is explicable only in terms of the law of value. It is this law of value and its developed forms which determine the movement of capitalist economy, laws to which the owner of capital is entirely subordinated, He may, as an owner, not recognize the law of value, but it certainly recognizes him! The capitalist may 'conceive' his capital in money form and 'calculate' his rate of profit in money terms – these are entirely secondary questions. But Marxists certainly do not confuse capital with one of its forms, money. Capital is a process which appears in the antithetical forms of money and commodities, it is therefore vital to grasp the nature of this antithesis. To take capital in only one of its forms (money) is precisely to reduce it to a 'thing' to make of it a fetish.

In the circulation M–C–M', both the money and the commodity represent only different modes of existence of value itself, the money its general mode, and the commodity its particular, or so to say, disguised mode. It is constantly changing from one form to the other without thereby becoming lost, and thus assumes an *automatically active character*. If we now take in turn each of the two different forms which self-expanding value takes in the course of its life, we then arrive at these two propositions: Capital is money; Capital is commodities. In truth, however, value is here the active factor in a process, in which while constantly assuming the form in turn of money and commodities, it at the same time changes its magnitude, differentiates itself by throwing off surplus-value from itself; the original value, in other words, expands spontaneously. (I, pp. 153-4, author's italics)

It is of course in a crisis that the true nature of capital forcibly asserts itself. In times of prosperity the capitalist continually throws his money into circulation (M–C); money in such periods is declared to be a 'vain imagination'. But in a crisis things turn into their opposite – now everybody moves out of commodities, demands money (C–M). As Marx puts it, 'As the hart pants after fresh water, so pants his soul after money, the only wealth' (I, p. 136). It is in the crisis that the contradictory nature of the circuit M–C–M' is revealed. The relative unity of the process (in prosperity) turns into an absolute contradiction. 'In a crisis, the antithesis between commodities and their value-form, money, becomes heightened into an absolute contradiction' (I).

It is important in this respect to stress that for Marx capital is not merely expanding value, but *self*-expanding value. The constant drive to expand value ('Accumulate, accumulate! That is Moses and the prophets!) arises not from something 'external' to capital, such as the 'disposition' or motives of the capitalist. It arises from something intrinsic to the very nature of capital itself. From the point of view of the owner of capital he is driven along by *competition*. But this is only the appearance of things, albeit a *necessary* one. For in capital are revealed in outward form the immanent laws of capital ('competition makes the immanent laws of capitalist production to be felt by each individual capitalist, as external and coercive laws', as Marx at one point says). It is for this reason that throughout his work Marx sees the capitalist as the personification of capital. He is a capitalist, and remains so, only in so far as his behaviour is subordinated to the objective, independently existing laws of capital. And this subordination never arises from conscious *plan* or *desire* – it is a force which imposes itself upon the capitalist through laws which operate necessarily behind his back. Of course the capitalist always starts out with 'aims', but these aims are determined entirely by the objective nature of capital. The capitalist 'starts' with a sum of money, M. Naturally, as a 'practical' man he never examines this starting point. He never examines the historical and social conditions which alone enable him to turn this money into capital. But notwithstanding this, he remains a prisoner of these conditions. He remains a capitalist only to the extent that his aims are in accordance with the needs of definite social relations:

> As the conscious representative of this movement, the possessor of money becomes a capitalist. His person, or rather his pocket, is the point from which the money starts and to which it returns. The expansion of value, which is the objective basis or main spring of the circulation M–C–M, becomes his subjective aim, and it is only in so far as the

appropriation of even more and more wealth in the abstract becomes the sole motive of his operations, that he functions as a capitalist, that is, as capital personified and endowed with consciousness and a will. (I, p. 152)

The reality of abstractions

A common objection to Marx's notion of 'capital in general' is that it does not deal with the concrete reality of capitalism. It is an abstraction which cannot deal with concrete matters like the rate of profit for a particular firm. (This is Hodgson's position). Again, the problem to be resolved here is not so much one concerning economics, but philosophy. It is a fallacy to think that because abstractions (such as that of capital in general) are formed through the penetration of the appearance of things, deeper into the essence of the phenomena concerned, this renders such abstractions unreal. On the contrary, they have a powerful *objective* existence precisely because, as abstractions, they embrace the wealth of all the phenomena concerned. Attacking all those who wanted to raise what was immediately given in perception to the status of the sole source of knowledge, Hegel says,

> Abstract thinking, therefore, is not to be regarded as a mere setting aside of the sensuous material, the reality of which is not thereby impaired; rather it is the sublating and reduction of that material as mere *phenomenal appearance* to the *essential* which is manifested only in the Notion. (Hegel, 1969, p. 588)

And Lenin's comment on this passage is significant in considering the method exemplified by Hodgson.

> *Essentially*, Hegel is completely right as opposed to Kant. Thought proceeding from the concrete to the abstract (provided it is correct (NB)) (and Kant, like all philosophers speaks of correct thought) – does not get away *from* the truth but comes closer to it. The abstraction of *matter*, of a *law* of nature, the abstraction of *value* etc., in short all scientific (correct, serious, not absurd) abstractions reflect nature more

deeply, truly, and *completely*. From living perception to abstract thought, and *from this to practice*, – such is the dialectical path of the cognition of *truth*, of the cognition of objective reality. (LCW, vol. 38, p. 171)

It was because abstraction, if accurate, does not get away from the pulse of development but comes closer to it that Marx said, specifically of 'capital in general':

> as distinct from the particular real capitals, is itself a real existence . . . capital in this general form, although belonging to individual capitalists, in its *elemental form* of capital, forms the capital which accumulates in the banks or is distributed through them . . . while the general is therefore on the one hand only a mental mark of distinction it is at the same time a particular real form alongside the form of the particular and individual. (G, pp. 449–50)

We are, of course, once again considering the relationship between the 'individual' 'particular' and the 'general'. The notion of capital in general is not arrived at via a mechanical summation of each unit of capital; it is no mere abstraction based upon some dead uniformity found in each individual capital. The total social capital consists of the contradictory ensemble of all individual capitals in their dynamic interrelations. Dealing with the movement of this social capital, Marx says,

> However the circuits of the individual capitals intertwine, presuppose and necessitate one another, and form, precisely in this interlacing, the movement of the total social capital. Just as in the simple circulation of commodities the total metamorphosis of a commodity appeared as a link in the series of metamorphoses of the world of commodities, so now the metamorphosis of the individual capital appears as a link in the series of metamorphoses of the social capital.

And what is true of individual capitals is true of particular forms of capital (fixed, circulating, etc.). The total social capital is not an arithmetical addition of these forms:

> Capital as a whole, then, exists simultaneously, spatially side by side, in its different phases. But every part passes

constantly and successively from one phase, from one functional form, into the next and thus functions in all of them in turn. Its forms are hence fluid and their simultaneousness is brought about by their succession. Every form follows another and precedes it, so that the return of one capital part to a certain form is necessitated by the return of the other part to some other form. Every part describes continuously its own cycle, but it is always another part of capital which exists in this form, and these special cycles form only simultaneous and successive elements of the aggregate process. (II, p. 104)

And in its development this total social capital (capital in general) asserts itself against the individual owner of capital.

If social capital experiences a revolution in value, it may happen that the capital of the individual succumbs to it and fails, because it cannot adapt itself to the conditions of this movement of values. The more acute and frequent such revolutions in value become, the more does the automatic movement of the now independent value operate with the elemental force of a natural process, against the foresight and calculation of the individual capitalist, the more does the course of normal production become subservient to abnormal speculation, and the greater is the danger that threatens the existence of the individual capitals. (II, p. 106)

Thus the concept of capital in general is an essential abstraction for understanding the movement and general tendencies of the capitalist mode of production. And it is important to stress once more that we are dealing with a tendency, a movement, not with capital in a state of dead repose (it can never, of course, exist in such a state). In its actual contradictory development capitalism more and more brings out the power of social capital against the individual unit of capital. This is brought out clearly in the case of the banking and credit system. For through credit and banking all the actual and potential capital of society is placed at the disposal of industry and commerce. And here lies the driving force to a higher form of society (socialism) within the capitalist mode of production. For banking and credit does away with the private character of capital and thus contains in itself, but only in itself, the abolition of capital itself . . . banking and credit thus become the most potent means of driving capitalist production beyond its own limits, and one of the most effective vehicles of crisis and swindles. (III, p. 593)

It is, however, in share capital that the real character of aggregate social capital is most openly revealed. For in this form capital has worked itself up to its final form, in which it is posited, not only *in itself*, in its substance, but is posited also in its form as social power and product' (G, p. 530). The contrast here between capital 'in itself' and its 'posited existence' is as Rodolsky points out (Rosdolsky, 1978, p. 49) drawn from Hegel's logic. This understanding that capital in general must itself be seen as a particular form of capital, having a definite social power, is derived from Hegel's insistence that the general was a category which was itself at the same time necessarily an individual and a particular. Discussing Aristotle's notion of the soul as determined in three ways (as 'nutrient', 'sensitive', and 'intelligent' which correspond with plants, animals and humans) Hegel writes:

> Aristotle says of them, with perfect truth, that we need look for no one soul in which all three are found and in which a definite form is conformable with any one of them. This is a profound observation, by means of which truly speculative thought (dialectics) marks itself out from thought which is merely logical and formal. (Hegel, 1968, p. 185)

Hegel goes on from this to give the example of the relationship of the triangle to other definite figures, such as the square and parallelogram. Only these 'definite figures', says Hegel, are 'truly anything':

> For what is common to them, the universal figure, is an empty thing of thought, a mere abstraction. On the other hand, the triangle is the first and truly universal figure which appears in the square, etc. as the figure which can be led back to the simplest determination. Therefore, on the one hand, the triangle stands alongside the square, pentagon etc. as a

particular figure, but – and this is Aristotle's main contention – it is the truly universal figure. (p. 185)

The value concept

Let us look at this question of abstraction and the production of concepts in relation to a specific question: the law of value. We shall deal with this law in more detail later, so here we will content ourselves with a brief résumé of Marx's findings. The discovery of the essential nature of this concept belongs to Marx. He points out that the property of value can be abstracted only by examining the relationships entered into by commodities during the course of their exchange. In this process of exchange, commodities are rendered equal despite their different qualitative character. Or more precisely: the very fact that they do have *different* qualitative characteristics alone makes it possible to establish an equality between them. (There is no basis or future in exchanging boots for boots!) Marx shows that a 'third' factor alone makes it possible to establish a relationship of equality between two quite distinct commodities, and this third factor is their *value*. 'Therefore the common substance that manifests itself in the exchange-value of commodities, whenever they are exchanged is their value' (I, p. 46). And Marx proceeds to make clear that the emergence of this category, value, and therefore man's ability to conceptualize it, is related directly to human practical activity. It was on the basis of commodity exchange alone that the category value was formed, but it required a highly developed stage in the growth of such exchange before it was possible to discover this category. 'Although an abstraction, this is an historical abstraction which could only be evolved on the basis of a particular economic development of society' (Marx and Engels, 1956, p. 48). The point Marx is here making can be stated as follows: while the conditions reflected in the simple or accidental form of value alone prevailed it was impossible to abstract the concept of value. For while exchange remained limited and sporadic it could still be concluded that the exchange of commodities was regulated solely by the luck or cunning of the people concerned. It was not possible to establish the necessity, the law, of these exchanges. And the same is true with the developed, or expanded value form. Only with the emergence of the universal form of value was it possible to abstract the *concept* of value. Only when scientists were able to infer on the basis of their investigations that all commodities can be exchanged for each other in certain proportions was it possible to begin to conclude that there must be something *in common* between them, a common substance, namely 'value'. But, and this point must be emphasized in the light of considerable confusion about Marx's concepts, we have only arrived at the point of identifying a common property amongst commodities (value). This in no way necessarily means that the essential nature of this property has been discovered. The abstraction of a new property in a series of phenomena does not yet mean that we are necessarily able to grasp the essential nature of this property, even though the process of forming scientific concepts must always include this stage. At this stage of the formation of the concept of value we can define value only as an 'abstract object', as a general feature of commodities that are exchanged for one another. In this connection Engels writes: 'Marx summarizes the actual content common to things and relations and reduces it to its general logical expression. His abstraction therefore only reflects, in rational form, the content already existing in the things' (Marx and Engels, 1956, p. 357).

To arrive at an adequate *concept* of value it was necessary to discover the *origin* and *source* of this common property. And this was only revealed on the basis of further investigation, particularly of the category labour. Marx showed that value is nothing else but the embodiment of human labour in the abstract, the quantity of which is measured by socially necessary working time. It became possible to get to the essence of value, to define this concept adequately only in the conditions of capitalist production, where the equality and equivalence of all forms of labour was revealed, when the predominant social relationship between people became their relationship as commodity owners, when the producers were finally separated from the means of production and labour power itself became a commodity.

In other words all concepts, far from being generated in thought, are a reflection of man's practice. It is this practice which is the indispensable basis on which all theoretical categories arise. That this is so can be seen if we consider the role which Aristotle played in the attempt to discover the nature of value. '[Aristotle] the great thinker who was the first to analyze so many forms, whether of thought, society or Nature, and amongst them also the form of value' (I, p. 59). After pointing out that Aristotle's genius allowed him to grasp that the money-form was only a further development of the simple form of value (in this respect at least it can be said that Aristotle was ahead of nineteenth-century political economy), Marx goes on to note that Aristotle in addition saw that it was also the case that if two commodities were exchanged it necessarily followed that they were qualitatively equal to each other. Marx here quotes Aristotle: 'Exchange cannot take place without equality, and equality without commersurability' (I, p. 59). At this point, says Marx, Aristotle stopped. He found it impossible to conceive of any commensurability between such qualitiatively different commodities. Now Marx proceeds to make what is a crucial remark which directly bears upon the matters we have been considering. 'Aristotle therefore, himself, tells us, what barred his way to further analysis, *it was the absence of any concept of value* (I, p. 59; author's italics). Aristotle lacked a *concept* of value. His profound insight that when commodities exchange they do so on the basis of some commensurability and further his understanding that money, the universal value form grows out of the particular (the commodity) were by themselves an inadequate basis for the formation of a concept of value. Marx tells us the specific conditions which prevented even the genius of Aristotle from arriving at the value concept. They lay in the social relations of production and particularly in the conditions of labour in the ancient world. Marx says in a passage which reveals the barrenness of the approach taken by Althusser and others:

> There was however an important fact which prevented
> Aristotle from seeing that to attribute value to commodities is
> merely a mode of expressing all labour as equal human
> labour, and consequently as labour of equal quality. Greek
> society was founded upon slavery, and had therefore, for its
> natural basis, the inequality of men and their labour powers.
> The secret of the expression of value, namely, that all kinds of
> labour are equal and equivalent, because and so far as they
> are human labour in general, cannot be deciphered, until the

notion of human equality has already acquired the fixity of a popular prejudice. This, however, is possible only in a society in which the great mass of the products of labour takes the form of commodities, in which consequently, the dominant relation between man and man is that of owner of commodities. The brilliancy of Aristotle's genius is shown by this alone, that he discovered, in the expression of the value of commodities, a relation of equality. The peculiar conditions of society in which he lived, alone prevented him from discovering what 'in truth' was at the bottom of this equality. (I, p. 60)

This passage serves once again to indicate why it was only with the eighteenth century that real strides forward were made in deciphering the value-relationship. Only when the notion of human equality (and the equality of human labour-power) had, because of definite economic conditions become established as a prejudice in men's minds, could the secret of value be discovered. Here also lies the clue to seeing not only why the eighteenth century should bring such advances towards the solution to problems which had engaged man from the ancient world onwards, but at the same time why these advances were of a limited nature. It was precisely because the commodity form of wealth was becoming all pervasive and universal that it was treated as a 'prejudice' to use Marx's word. The existence of generalized commodity production (which constituted the basis for all its advances) was taken axiomatically by political economy, a fact requiring no investigation. It could not grasp the point that the ability to go beyond Aristotle was rooted entirely in these objective conditions. As Lenin notes in connection with the syllogism: 'The practical activity of man had to lead his consciousness to the repetition of the various logical figures thousands of millions of times *in order that* these figures could obtain the significance of *axioms*' (LCW, vol. 38, p. 190).

So the emergence and development of the value concept, like all concepts, was bound intimately with man's social practice. Let us, however, consider more closely how the concept of value actually took shape in the minds of the eighteenth-century political economists. Because here is a very good example of the actual process by which concepts are formed. It was William Petty who, in the modern world, made the most significant steps towards an adequate conceptualization of value. And this is how Petty posed the matter: 'If a man can bring to London an ounce of silver out of the Earth in Peru, *in the same time* that he can produce a bushel of Corn, then one is the natural price of the other.' (William Petty, *A Treatise on Taxes and Contributions*, 1667, quoted in Marx, 1969, p. 356). In other words, in practice (in spite of any logical precepts and axioms which it may have professed) political economy did not arrive at the value category by seeking something abstractly identical in each and every commodity (which general usage long previously had united in the term 'value'). On the contrary, it began with one particular relationship (the case of silver and corn or in Smith's case beaver and deer). This was the simplest economic relationship – simplest because historically the first. It then tried to move from this particular relationship to a more general one – money, capital, profit, etc. And this was undoubtedly the correct, scientific method. Marx levelled no criticism against political economy in this particular direction. The political economists groped their way empirically and spontaneously towards a general conception of value. But having once arrived at the concept, they attempted to verify the conception according to the canons of formal logic, relying on Locke, as we have already noted.

This point can be reformulated in the following way, in attempting to arrive at a concept of value, political economy did, in its best representatives, proceed scientifically from the simple and abstract to the more concrete. But it saw this movement as purely *mechanical*. The general, according to this conception, had to reproduce *exactly* and *wholly* every particular. Each particular, in mechanical addition, was to explain the whole. Society was merely an aggregation of each individual, a position which does in fact express the essence of bourgeois individualism. Here is revealed one of the weaknesses of purely mechanical thought as against the truly dialectical. This is why we have stressed that dialectics sees the relationship between the particular (in this case the exchange of two individual commodities) and the universal as a *law of tendency* in which the universal can only approximately and one-sidedly embrace the wealth of all the individuals.

Hegel expressed this same thought when he attacked the empirical method for its over-concern with *analysis* and its lack of an adequate regard for *synthesis*. In insisting that the whole is not to be regarded as a mere summation of its separate parts Hegel says, specifically in connection with empiricism:

> In the impression of the senses we have a concrete of many elements, the several attributes we are expected to peel off one by one, like the coats of an onion. . . . . Empiricism therefore labours under a delusion if it supposes that while analyzing its objects, it leaves them as they were: it really transforms the concrete into an abstract. As a consequence of this change the living thing is killed: *life can exist only in the concrete and one.* Not that we can do without this division, if it be our intention to comprehend. . . . The error lies in forgetting that this is only one half of the process and the main point is the reunion of what has been parted. (author's italics)

Thought had to proceed to the concrete through a dialectical *combination* of abstraction, or, as Marx puts it, 'The method of advancing from the abstract to the concrete is only the way of thinking by which the concrete is grasped and reproduced in our own mind as concrete' (G, p. 101).

But some care is needed if this passage – often quoted by writers on Marx's method – is to be understood correctly. For it might be thought that science can start from some arbitrary definitions which it then proceeds to 'concretize'. However, we know that the abstractions from which Marx started (and indeed from which every thinker starts) were not arbitrary but the result (to use Engels' phrase from another context) 'of a long and wearisome development of philosophy and science'. We draw attention to this point once more if only to combat that view which would separate Marx *absolutely* from the previous body of political economy, to make him an *aRicardian*. (This is the characterization of Marx made by a follower of Althusser – see de Brunhoff, 1974. According to this view Marx was an *aRicardian* because he had an entirely different object in his studies – he was an historical materialist, not a political economist.) But such a view of history is essentially sterile: history is chopped up into rigidly discrete periods, with all question of transition and development excluded. Speaking of Spinoza, Hegel says, 'one must get rid of the erroneous idea of regarding the system as out and out *false*, as if the *true* system by contrast were only *opposed* to the false. . . . On the contrary, the true system as the higher, must contain the subordinate system within itself' (Hegel, 1969, p. 580). In other words, the 'refutation' of a philosophical system does not mean discarding it, but actually taking it forward; not replacing it by another, one-sided system, but incorporating it into something richer. It is therefore quite wrong to treat Marx's relationship to classical economics as though he were merely interested in a different object – Marx only got to this 'object' through tackling the political economists *on their own terrain.* In this sense English political economy was a necessary stage in the elaboration of dialectical and historical materialism, an indispensable 'component' of Marxism as Lenin puts it. Thus it is in no way a question of Marx starting from a series of different abstractions from those of Ricardo. This would have provided no basis for his dialectical negation of political economy.

> the refutation must not come from outside, that is, it must not proceed from assumptions lying outside the system in question and inconsistent with it. The system need only refuse to recognize those assumptions. . . . *The genuine refutation must penetrate the opponent's stronghold and meet him on his ground; no advantage is gained by attacking him somewhere else and defeating him where he is not.* (author's italics; ibid., p. 581)

Marx stood on the shoulders of his predecessors in political economy. The work of the seventeenth-century political economists, and particularly the work of Petty, was indispensable for Marx's later development. These economists tended

> to begin with the living whole, with population, nation, state, several states, etc. but they always concluded by discussing through analysis a small number of determinant, abstract, general relations such as division of labour, money, value, etc. As soon as these individual moments have been firmly established and abstracted (here was the emphasis upon *analysis,* and so striking in the case of Petty) there begin the economic systems, which ascend from single relations, such as labour, division of labour, need, exchange value, to the level

of the state, exchange between nations and the world market. The latter is obviously the scientifically correct method. (G, p. 101)

But while the latter path (the movement from the abstract to the concrete) reflected the only valid method it would have been impossible without the first path (the movement from the concrete to the abstract). Thus, although Hegel attacked empiricism for its one-sided emphasis upon analysis, analysis is none the less an indispensable element in human thought. It was only after a mass of material had been sifted and analysed that the science could move forward. The point is this: although *thought* moves from the abstract to the concrete 'this is by no means the process through which the concrete itself comes into being' (G, p. 101). The abstractions from which political economy began presupposed a concrete and definite form of society 'Hence in the theoretical method, too, the subject, society, must always be kept in mind as the presupposition' (G, p. 102). It is important to keep this point always in mind, otherwise we can fall into the idealist illusion that concepts merely grow out of concepts, forgetting that all concepts presuppose and are rooted in a definite form of human practice. Just as the capitalist thinks that money breeds money and is uninterested in the material basis for this process so the professional ideologist tends always to see his knowledge as the beginning and the end of his life activity. This is the most basic prejudice of all idealisms. Marx's revolution (and here we are specifically concerned with his revolution in political economy, although the same is true of his work in philosophy and history) came after a long, contradictory, series of efforts by many great minds to grasp the nature of the new social relations involved in the emergence of capitalism. Marx was able to synthesize all these efforts into a new conception and from the standpoint of this new conception grasp the relationship of these earlier efforts to his own work. Hegel expressed this idea about the growth of knowledge and the elaboration of new concepts when he wrote:

> The beginning of the new spirit is the outcome of a
> widespread revolution in manifold forms of spiritual culture;
> it is the reward which comes after a chequered and decisive
> course of development, and after much struggle and effort. It

is a whole, which after running its course and laying bare all its content, returns again to itself; it is the resultant abstract notion of the whole. But the actual realization of this abstract whole is only formed when those previous shapes and forms, which are now reduced to ideal moments of the whole, are developed anew again, but developed and shaped within this new medium and with the meaning they have thereby acquired. (Hegel, 1971, p. 76)

The concept of capital

We have looked at the general nature of Marx's concepts, stressing always the material-practical basis of these concepts. We shall next say something in more detail about the manner in which Marx actually develops his major concept for the investigation of modern society, namely the concept of capital itself. This will involve us in a review of the content and method of the early chapters of *Capital*. Let us, therefore, say something of a preliminary nature about this key concept. For Marx the understanding of this category was a vital condition for any proper investigation of modern society. 'Capital is the all-dominating economic form of bourgeois society – it must form the starting-point as well as the finishing-point' (G, p. 107). This point is repeated with even more emphasis in the same work when Marx says,

> The exact development of the concept of capital [is] necessary since it is the fundamental concept of modern economics, just as capital itself whose abstractly reflected image [is] its concept [is] the foundation of bourgeois society. The sharp formulation of the basic presuppositions of the relation must bring out the contradictions of bourgeois production as well as the boundary where it drives beyond itself. (p. 331)

Now in what respect was capital 'fundamental' to and 'all-dominating' within bourgeois society? In this sense; it was the category which contained *implicitly* all the lower, less concrete categories, categories which were its presuppositions, its historical and theoretical bases. To grasp the nature of capital, therefore, was the necessary pre-condition for understanding the lower economic relations (value, money) out of which capital had historically and logically grown and developed. To 'define' capital adequately meant to grasp conceptually the origin and emergence of this basic relation of modern economy. Only if this were done would it prove possible to understand the necessary connections between all these economic categories, that is to understand the path of *transition* from one category to another. As the *Manifesto* in particular so brilliantly demonstrates, the historical mission of capital was to bring all pre-capitalist economic forms under its sway. To the extent that these earlier relations continue to survive, they do so always in a truncated and distorted manner.

Given that capital now dominated all pre-capitalist social relations, this meant that these earlier relations could not be grasped except in their organic and living relations to capital in modern society. At one point, Marx says it would seem to be correct to investigate the economic categories in the order in which they had *historically* evolved, just as by analogy, it might appear correct to deal with the anatomy of the ape before that of man. As far as political economy goes, this would seem to suggest that one ought to deal first with rent (landed property) then interest (mercantile capital) and only finally profit. But such a method, says Marx, would be 'impossible and wrong'. The economic categories must not be considered in the same sequence in which they were historically decisive:

> Their sequence is determined, rather, by the relation to one another in modern bourgeois society, which is precisely the *opposite* of that which seems to be their natural order or which corresponds to historical development. The point is not the historic position of the economic relations in the succession of different forms of society. . . . *Rather their order within modern bourgeois society.* (pp. 107–8; author's italics)

So *capital* was the central category and this is why landed property (assumed as zero in Volume I) is left out of account until the concept of capital has been 'sharply formulated'. But here we face a seeming paradox. For in the investigation of modern society, Marx starts not with capital but with the *commodity*. Only later (from Chapter 4 onwards) does he begin to deal with capital. This paradox is explained by reference to the distinction, drawn by

Marx, between the *mode of presentation* of his theoretical work and the *path of inquiry* which had enabled him to present his material in abstract form. We know that Marx continuously grappled with the 'mode of presentation', in particular with those sections of Chapter 1 dealing with the value form. As Marx himself tells us:

> Of course the method of presentation must differ in form from that of inquiry. The latter has to appropriate the material in detail, to analyse its different forms of development, to trace out their inner connection. Only after this work is done, can the actual movement be adequately described. If this is done successfully, if the life of the subject matter is ideally reflected as in a mirror, then it may appear, as if we had before us a mere *a priori* construction. (I, p. 19)

This warning must be taken seriously. In *Capital* (and especially its opening chapters which will now be our immediate concern) we are not dealing with a 'mere *a priori* construction'; this is only the appearance of the thing. Marx had to *derive* the concept of capital and this process of derivation involved much patient work over a long number of years. The *fruits* of this uncompleted work can be seen in *Capital*. But – and this has been one of our main points – one cannot take the fruit without a study of the conditions under which it was grown and developed. Thus those who see the categories of the opening chapters of *Capital* as the product of an illegitimate juggling with a few Hegelian phrases are far wide of the mark. Marx's categories are 'a product of the *working up* of observation and conception into concepts' (G, p. 101; author's italics).

This 'working up' of observation and conceptions into the concepts which alone could grasp the contradictory driving forces of bourgeois society, which could grasp the fundamental, inner connection of this mode of production constitutes the enduring, revolutionary essence of Marx's whole work. 'Once the interconnection is grasped, all theoretical belief in the permanent necessity of existing conditions collapses before their practical collapse' (Marx to Kugelmann, July 1868, in Marx and Engels, 1956, p. 252). The manner in which Marx revealed these driving contradictions will be our next concern.

4 · The significance of the opening chapters

We have tried to show throughout our examination of *Capital* that Marx regarded political economy as above all an *historical* science. The aim of *Capital* was to investigate the law of motion of a determinate mode of production, namely capitalism. Political economy was an expression of a society where the products of man's labour were exchanged on the market and above all the reflection of a situation where these conditions became generalized. Political economy is a product of capitalism and it will disappear along with the disappearance of commodity production. Marx, therefore, had one quite specific aim in *Capital*: it was to lay bare the law of motion of modern society. Marx's theory of historical materialism summarized the nature of the conditions which had been at the basis of the transition between the various modes of production. This theory, the materialist conception of history, is tested out in *Capital* against modern society. Thus *Capital* is not *identical* with historical materialism as some have thought. It is Marx's effort to reveal the *specific form* taken by the contradictions which provide the driving force for the transition to socialism, that is for the overthrow of capitalist society. The theoretical limitations of political economy were rooted in this: the struggle of classes within capitalism was as yet not an extensive or intensive enough phenomenon with a power sufficient to pose the question of the overthrow of capitalism. Marx's critique of political economy set out to provide a conscious, scientific reflection of this emergence of the working class in its struggle to overthrow capitalism and effect the transition to socialism. It set out deliberately to reflect, in a scientific manner, the process whereby the working class – the most decisive component in the productive forces of modern society – came into increasingly severe conflict with the very limitations of bourgeois economy. This is really what Lenin meant when he spoke of *Capital* being a 'testing out' of the materialist conception of history. It is this aim of Marx — to express in scientific form the historical-material interests of a new social force as yet unconscious of itself — that gives to Marx's work its powerfully polemical character. It is this highly polemical character which has led many of Marx's opponents to see his work as wholly tendentious, as a work incompatible with the canons of science. In connection with this type of attack — commonplace amongst the 'legal Marxists' of the last century — Lenin retorted:[1]

> The 'system of Marx' has a 'polemical character' not because it is 'tendentious' but because it accurately portrays the theory of all the contradictions that exist in life. Therefore, incidentally, all attempts to assimilate the 'system of Marx' without assimilating its 'polemical character' remain and will remain unsuccessful: the 'polemical character' of the system is only the accurate reflection of the 'polemical character' of capitalism itself.

This polemical nature of *Capital* certainly marks it off from anything found in the previous work of political economy. Marx, as we have already sufficiently stressed, valued highly the work of Ricardo. But Ricardo's writing was dispassionate in the extreme. This is clear enough from the tone of his polemic with Malthus. Malthus for Marx was the 'shameless sycophant' who prostituted science on behalf of the landed interest. One might have thought that Ricardo — whose work reflected the emergence of industrial capital — would have been involved in bitter exchanges with his adversary. This was far from the case. According to a contemporary observer, 'Ricardo's discussion with Malthus and others was carried out in the same peaceful fashion as a chess game or a debate on mathematical problems.' This is explicable in the following terms: while the Ricardo–Malthus polemic was undoubtedly concerned with very real problems (corn laws, banking legislation, etc.) which certainly affected the material interests of the landowner and the bourgeoisie none the less what was at issue, in the final analysis, was a conflict between two factions of a property-owning class. Despite their differences both factions had an overall interest in the preservation and perpetuation of the existing social order. Marx, on the other hand, came forward as the representative of a classs whose historical interests lay in the most decisive and far-reaching social progress; not in the replacement of one class by another but in the abolition of classes. Because the proletarian revolution posed issues which far transcended – in their depth and scope – those of all previous social revolutions, the theoretical struggle involved in the preparation of such a revolution inevitably had a sharper, more polemical character, not previously found.

If Marx always depicts the capitalist as capital endowed with will and consciousness, we can equally depict the book *Capital* as Marx's lifelong struggle to express the historical interests of the working class, to give to these interests a conscious revolutionary expression and aim. This 'purposeful', 'subjective' side of Marx's work should be stressed; nor should we ignore the enormous privations and wants Marx lived through in the writing of *Capital*, a work for which, as he himself said, he sacrificed – 'my health, my happiness in life and my family'. For this subjective side of Marx's work is not a mere 'aspect' but expresses its very *essence*. This must be clearly said in the face of all those efforts to reduce Marxism to some branch of the social sciences – sociology, economics or whatever and to transform it thereby into an 'academic Marxism' which is as acceptable to existing society as was 'legal Marxism' some eighty years ago. In this connection it is necessary to draw the sharpest distinction between Marxism and this 'social science'. The essential point about all social science is that it starts from an uncritical acceptance of the 'facts' of bourgeois society, facts which it then attempts to correlate in order to discover some regularity within them. Involved here is the traditional notion of an objectivity in which the theoretical and practical work of the observer stands separated from these 'facts'. Marxism rejects this view of objectivity as entirely spurious. It is only possible to know what something is if we grasp the process by which, through *our practice*, we have come to know it. For Marx, a struggle to grasp the inner-driving forces of capital and the study of the process by which the working class actually achieves consciousness of these inner forces were not separate problems.

Let us put the matter this way: Marx did not set out merely to explain the necessity of the social relations of capital. This would be an entirely one-sided view of Marx's work, a view which can, under certain circumstances, transform Marxism into its opposite

– into an instrument for 'justifying' these very social relations. The social relations of capitalism exist in a state of *relative*, not absolute, equilibrium, an equilibrium which must be overcome through the struggle of opposed forces which arise on the basis of these social reations. In this way, Marx grasped always that the investigator, if his work was to be truly scientific, must place at the very centre of his endeavours a conscious struggle to understand his own relationship to the forces being analysed; this in turn was, for Marx, inseparable from a study of his own struggle, in theory and in practice, to grasp these facts. Thus in the *Communist Manifesto* we read:

> Finally, in times when the class struggle nears the decisive hour, the process of dissolution going on within the ruling class, in fact within the whole range of the old society, assumes such a violent, glaring character that a small section of the ruling class cuts itself adrift, and joins the revolutionary class, the class that holds the future in its hands. Just as therefore at an earlier period, a section of the nobility went over to the bourgeoisie; so now a portion of the bourgeoisie goes over to the proletariat, and in particular, a portion of the bourgeois ideologists, who have raised themselves to the level of comprehending theoretically the historical movement as a whole.

Here Marx and Engels were in fact writing *of themselves*. On the basis of all their practical and theoretical work they alone at that stage 'comprehended theoretically the historical movement as a whole'. They alone had been able to grasp the historical-revolutionary significance of the appearance of the working class, a class 'in itself' which had consciously to be transformed into a class 'for itself'. The actual struggle to do this – and knowing that every aspect of one's theoretical work was subordinated to this task – was for Marx and Engels the real essence of objectivity. Theory could only be developed as an expression and instrument of a definite social force in history. Marx did not 'criticize' capitalist social relations merely by revealing the unresolved contradictions in the work of political economy. He sought to show that the very development of capitalism actually created an instrument – the modern working class – which was obliged *in life*, in practice, to 'criticize' capitalism, to 'criticize' political economy, a criticism the high point of which was the overthrow of the existing social relations. Here is the very heart of Marx's 'critique' of political economy. Not only must the whole of *Capital* be seen from this point of view, but at the same time it provides the key to understanding how Marx develops his investigation over the three volumes.

The development of Marx's investigation

Let us give a general résumé of the structure of *Capital*. In Volume I is found a development of the basic theoretical concepts which reflect the relations of this specific mode of production. Marx, as we know, begins with the simplest, most fundamental, relation of capitalist society – the exchange of commodities. He at once reveals, in the investigation of a simple commodity, the contradictory nature of this cell-form as a unity of value and use-value. He then shows the contradictory nature of the labour incorporated in the commodity – concrete labour and abstract labour. Marx next reveals that the internal contradiction in the commodity finds the form of its self-movement in the external contradiction which appears as the relationship of the relative and the equivalent form of value, polar opposites indissolubly united with each other. The further development of this antagonistic relationship, which reflects the historical growth of commodity production, goes through three stages – a simple, an expanded and finally a universal form of value. In the last of these stages, the product of labour assumes a double form of the commodity itself and its monetary equivalent. The development of money, in its various functions, being the result of an extension of commodity production and at the same time the condition for the growth of these very same relations, constitutes a development of the initial contradiction. Marx now examines the conditions under which money is transformed into capital, the internal contradiction of the general form of the movement of capital (M-C-M') and the resolution of this contradiction in the buying and selling of labour-power. The appearance of this latter category, labour-power, signifies the extension of commodity relations to a scale where they are predominant, where the law of surplus value is raised to a position where it becomes the most basic law of motion of modern society. Now the most essential productive force – labour-power itself – is turned into a commodity. Production of commodities for sale becomes capitalist. The conversion of money into capital in this way denotes the development of the law of value into a new qualitative law – the law of surplus value. It is this law which constitutes the driving force of the entire capitalist system – the source of its *self-movement*. Marx then shows how the capitalist organization of production involves the concentration in great workshops of hitherto scattered means of production and their conversion, in this process, from productive forces of separate persons into increasingly *socialized* forces. This transformation occurs, of course, under conditions of increasingly narrow individual appropriation. Marx examines how the drive for a continual increase in the rate of surplus value (demanded by the very nature of capital itself as 'self-expanding value') runs up against the twin barriers of the limited length of the working day and the growing resistance of the working class. This in turn is the fundamental source of the intensified contradiction between the social character of production and its individual appropriation. . . . This leads to the transition from simple capitalist co-operation into manufacturing and thence into production by machinery. Marx reveals that the progressive increase in the rate of exploitation demands an uninterrupted expansion of production, that reproduction leads to concentration and centralization of capital and consequently to the ruination of small-scale capital. From another point of view, this very same process of the continual reproduction of capital tends to create an industrial reserve army of labour and with it a trend towards the intensification of class contradictions. In his struggle to penetrate to the essence of capital and its deepening but ever-changing contradictions, Marx shows that these contradictory relations of capital provide the foundation for the emergence and development of a series of interconnected phenomena. To this are devoted the second and third volumes of *Capital*. In the course of the second and third volumes the process of capitalist circulation is examined – commodities produced in capitalist enterprises must be sold and only on this condition will capital be able to realize the surplus value contained potentially in the commodities and produced by wage-labour. In the final volume, the process of capitalist production, conceived of as a whole, as a dialectical unity of production and circulation, is examined. Marx deals here with the division of surplus value into the forms of profit of enterprise, interest, profits of commerce and ground rent. Marx reveals how the law of surplus value is developed in its external forms and how the law of value grows into the law of production prices. He explains how in the expansion of production the organic composition of capital tends to grow and how, under the influence of this tendency, the rate of profit tends to decline, despite the fact that the need to raise this rate continually forces capital to develop the productive forces, although in its own, increasingly contradictory way.

In the course of this development Marx traces the dialectical movement to the realm of everyday appearances through which bourgeois society functions and in which the forces for its revolutionary overthrow are forged. At the end of this, the third, volume, the most fundamental and characteristic illusions of capitalist society (illusions which are accepted uncritically by 'vulgar economy') are revealed in their origin, development and crisis. These illusions are thus shown by Marx to be *necessary* illusions, forms of appearance which express, always in an inverted form, the social relations of capitalist production. Finally Marx arrives at the unfinished chapter 'Classes'; it is in the struggle of classes that these illusions will be broken up as part of the struggle to overthrow the social conditions which generate, sustain and feed these illusions. Here Marx demonstrates concretely that the ideological sphere is no mere layer on top of the cake, nor is it some rationalization of an easily graspable 'class interest'. Although Marx's work does not aim to deal with a complete analysis of capitalism (such a detailed analysis would involve a full treatment of the history of ideological forms, as well as state forms etc.) it does outline the most general forms of social consciousness and reveal the manner in which they are engendered by a definite social being – namely the development of capital. Here is the 'soul' of *Capital*. The emergence and development of the object and its reflection in the consciousness of man (the developing consciousness of the working class) arise *from the same process*. The development of the social relation of capital itself provides the basis for the grasping in consciousness of the laws of this very development. Here object and subject are united through man's practice.

Thus, taking *Capital* as a whole, Marx has given us a picture of the movement of the contradictions of capital in its emergence, development and decay. This is the only way to knowledge of the law of motion of a process and of the manifold concrete forms of its appearance at different moments and under different conditions. As against this dialectical conception, all mechanistic approaches prove not only unable to lay bare the movement of opposites in their emergence and development, but such an approach really stands in the way of such a task. This is so, because from the point of view of mechanics, every process commences from a stable equilibrium, where there are either no contradictions; or they are reconciled and balanced and thereby cannot be the source of further development. On this view, contradiction appears only at a known stage of the movement of a process, as a result of the action of *external* forces, whether these be (in the case of capitalist development) the 'motives' of the capitalist, 'competition' or whatever. In either case, the source of development is kept entirely in the background.

The place of the opening chapters

A correct understanding of the opening chapter of *Capital* was, for Lenin, a vital pre-condition for understanding the work as a whole. And, as we have already noted, if such an understanding was to be achieved it was necessary in Lenin's view to study the *dialectic* of this first chapter. What is the status of this opening chapter in which Marx subjects the commodity form of labour to a detailed investigation? In the Preface to *Capital* Marx himself warns us not to underestimate the importance of the analysis of this, the 'cell-form' of capital, while at the same time also warning that the real problem for any science lies always in its beginning. Thus:

> Every beginning is difficult, holds in all sciences. To understand the first chapter, especially the section that contains the analysis of commodities, will therefore present the greatest difficulty. That which more especially concerns the analysis of the substance of value and the magnitude of value, I have as much as it was possible popularized. The value-

form, whose fully developed shape is the money-form, is very elementary and simple. Nevertheless, the human mind has for more than 2,000 years sought in vain to get to the bottom of it, whilst on the other hand, to the successful analysis of more composite forms there has been at least an approximation. Why? Because the body as an organic whole, is more easy to study than are the cells of that body. . . . To the superficial observer, the analysis of these forms seems to turn upon minutiae. It does in fact deal with minutiae, but they are of the same order as those dealt with in microscopic anatomy. (Preface to I, pp. 7–8)

What should we make of this passage? I think this: The commodity is the cell-form of bourgeois society because it is the basic relationship of that society, basic in a double sense. First the *economic* relation, while of course not the only relation in society, is certainly the simplest and one found historically prior to all others. Our method, Engels tells us, 'starts from the simplest fundamental relations we can find historically, in actual fact, that is economic relations'. Here is a point which has direct bearing upon and implications for the theory of historical materialism. For Engels is, in effect, saying here that economic relations (relations between men in the course of producing their material existence) are the ones found again and again as moments in more complex relations (political, religious, ideological, etc.). The simplest relations are moments which stand at the basis of and are involved in the richer more concrete determinations, but of course these economic relations do not exhaust the higher relations, any more than biology can be understood simply from the point of view of chemistry.

But the commodity form is a fundamental category in a second sense. Historically capital grew out of simple commodity production. 'Small scale production,' Lenin explained, 'engenders capitalism and the bourgeoisie continuously, daily, hourly, spontaneously and on a mass scale' (LCW, Vol. 34, p. 24). Exchange value has, at particular points in time, constituted a dominant and essential economic category: in antiquity and in the economy of the Middle Ages. Under modern capitalism it is in one respect 'antediluvian' in that it has been transcended, sublated into higher and richer economic forms. Yet it none the less remains the basic and fundamental economic relation: but for the exchange of commodities there could be no world market, no commercial, industrial or finance capital. In this respect the study of the commodity-form can be likened to the study of the simplest form of the movement of capital, one that lies at the base of all the higher, more developed forms. The connection between Marx's procedure and the history of science is worth noting. Engels says, in connection with the study of the most elementary forms of motion, 'The investigation of the nature of motion had, as a matter of course, to start from the lowest, simplest forms of this motion and to learn to grasp these before it could achieve anything in the way of explanation of the higher and more complicated forms' (1960, p. 69); and, adds Engels,

> All motion is bound up with some change of place, whether it be change of place of heavenly bodies, terrestrial masses, molecules, atoms or other particles. The higher the form of motion, the smaller this change of place. It in no way exhausts the nature of the motion concerned, *but it is inseparable from the motion. It therefore has to be investigated before anything else.* (p. 70; author's italics)

In this sense, an investigation of the commodity, an analysis of its inherent contradictions, a study of how those contradictions grow and reveal themselves on the surface of society remains an indispensable basis for the study of capitalist development. But, having said this, we should not at the same time be unmindful of a certain danger here. It is this: while a real study and grasp of the early chapters of *Capital* is vital, it would be wrong to think that these chapters can in any way *exhaust* all the complexities in the development of capital, any more than the mechanical form of motion exhausts the higher forms of motion. In response to Lachatre's plan to bring out a French edition of *Capital* in serial form, Marx, while recognizing that this would make it more accessible to the working class ('a consideration which to me outweighs everything else') also warned of the dangers involved in such a proposal. The danger lay in the fact that

> The method of analysis which I have employed, and which had not previously been applied to economic subjects, makes

the reading of the first chapters rather arduous, and it is to be feared that the French public, always impatient to come to a conclusion, eager to know the connection between general principles and the immediate questions that have aroused their passions, may be disheartened because they will be unable to move on at once. (I, p. 21)

This question of the relationship between 'general principles' and 'immediate questions' is further complicated by the fact that Marx's projected plan of work for *Capital* was left incomplete at his death. In 1857 his plan envisaged the following structure for the work:

1 The book on capital
2 The book on landed property
3 The book on wage labour
4 The book on the state
5 The book on foreign trade
6 The book on the world market and crises

Even on the level of *economic* relations (leaving aside political, ideological, etc. factors) Marx's work was therefore incomplete: of the above six projected parts, only the first three were completed (and even here the majority only in draft form which Engels subsequently edited for publication). It is important to keep this incompleteness in mind and for the following reason: it is clearly impossible to get fully to the driving forces of the crises of capital without taking the analysis to the level which Marx was evidently hoping to deal with (Books 4–6).

Let us give a concrete instance of the sort of implications which this involves. It would clearly be naive to attempt an explanation of the structure and crisis of the present world monetary system by mere reference to what Marx says on the question of money in *Capital* (and even more naive to restrict oneself to what he says in the early chapters of Volume I). While, of course, this specific question will not be our concern here, it is apparent that an examination of the role and structure of the International Monetary Fund, established following the 1944 Bretton Woods negotiations, cannot be carried out merely by looking into the pages of *Capital*. For the particular crisis of the world money system, with which Bretton Woods tried to grapple, is a product of the entire development and decline of capital in the present century. A proper study of the world money system from a Marxist standpoint would in point of fact require amongst other things a detailed consideration of imperialism, its development since Lenin, together with a study of the relations between nation states (and particularly the relationship between Europe and America) along with an analysis of the role of the state in the economy ('Keynesianism', etc.). And even this would not be exhaustive. But all these factors and others would have to be analysed in the light of Marx's work in *Capital*.

Engels on Marx's method

Engels gives a characterization of the early chapters of the *Critique* which applies equally well to *Capital*. Reviewing the *Critique* and drawing attention to its dialectical method, Engels writes:

> Even after the determination of the method, the critique of economics could still be arranged in two ways —historically or logically. Since in the course of history, as in its literary reflection, the evolution proceeds by and large from the simplest to the more complex relations, the historical development of political economy constituted a natural clue, which the critique could take as a point of departure, and then the economic categories would appear on the whole in the same order as the logical exposition. This form seems to have the advantage of greater lucidity, for it traces the *actual* development, but in fact it would thus become, at most, more popular. History moves often in leaps and bounds and in a zigzag line, and as this would have to be followed throughout, it would mean not only that a considerable amount of material of slight importance would have to be included, but also that the train of thought would frequently have to be interrupted; it would, moreover, be impossible to write the history of economy without that of bourgeois society, and the task would thus become immense, because of the absence of all preliminary studies. The logical method of approach was therefore the only suitable one. This, however, is indeed nothing but the historical method, only stripped of the

historical form and diverting chance occurrences. The point where this history begins must also be the starting point of the train of thought, and its further progress will be simply the reflection, in abstract and theoretically consistent form, of the historical course. Though the reflection is corrected, it is corrected in accordance with laws provided by the actual historical course, since each factor can be examined at the stage of development where it reaches full maturity, its classical form. (Marx, 1971a, p. 225)

Here Engels is again stressing the unity of 'logic' and the actual historical development. *Capital* is a reflection of the actual course taken by the emergence and decline of a social system, a reflection in that it sums up this movement in a series of concepts. After stressing this point, Engels provides a brilliant sketch of the way in which Marx develops this method. Marx started, says Engels, with the simplest relation to be found, the economic relation first encountered.

We analyse this relation. The fact that it is a *relation* already implies that it has two aspects which are *related to each other*. Each of these aspects is examined separately; this reveals the nature of their mutual behaviour, their reciprocal action. Contradictions will emerge demanding a solution. But since we are not examining an abstract mental process that takes place solely in our mind, but an actual event which really took place at some time or other, or which is still taking place, *these contradictions will have arisen in practice and have probably been solved*. We shall trace the mode of this solution and find that it has been effected by establishing a new relation, whose two contradictory aspects we shall have to set forth and so on. (1971a, pp. 225–6; author's italics)

Very important here is Engels' emphasis upon *practice*. The theoretical concepts which Marx abstracts in the course of his investigations are abstracted from human practice; we are dealing here with 'an actual event' which thought must accurately depict. And because we are dealing with an ever-changing reality our concepts must reflect this continual change; they must flow into each other. Engels now goes on to draw attention to the fact that in the relations between things are expressed definite social relations, that is, definite forms of *practice*. Thus:

> Political economy begins with *commodities*, with the moment when products are exchanged, either by individuals or primitive communities. The product being exchanged is a commodity. But it is a commodity merely by virtue of the *thing*, the product being linked with a *relation* between two persons or communities, the relation between producer and consumer, who are at this stage no longer united in the same person . . . economics is not concerned with things but the relations between persons, and in the final analysis between classes; these relations however are always *bound to things* and *appear as things*. Although a few economists had an inkling of this connection in isolated instances, Marx was the first to reveal its significance for the entire economy thus making the most difficult problems so simple and clear that even bourgeois economists will now be able to grasp them. (p. 226)

And Engels continues his review by stressing the enormous superiority of dialectical thought as against the old metaphysics.

> If we examine the various aspects of the commodity, that is of the fully evolved commodity and not as it at first slowly emerges in the spontaneous barter of two primitive communities, it presents itself to us from two angles that of use-value and exchange-value, and thus we come immediately to the province of economic debate. Anyone wishing to find a striking instance of the fact that the German dialectical method at its present stage of development is at least as superior to the old superficially glib metaphysical method as railways are to the mediaeval means of transport, should look up Adam Smith or any other authoritative economist of repute to see how much distress exchange-value and use-value caused these gentlemen, the difficulty they had in distinguishing the two properly and in expressing the determinate form peculiar to each, and then compare the clear, simple exposition given by Marx. (pp. 126–7)

And he ends this review of the early parts of the *Critique* in the following way:

> After use-value and exchange-value have been expounded, the commodity as a direct unity of the two is described as it enters the *exchange process*. . . . We merely note that these contradictions are not only of interest for theoretical, abstract reasons, but that they also reflect the difficulties originating from the nature of direct interchange, i.e. simple barter, and the impossibilities inevitably confronting the first crude form of exchange. The solution of these impossibilities is achieved by investing a specific commodity – *money* – with the attribute of representing the exchange-value of all other commodities. Money or simple circulation is then analysed in the second chapter, namely (1) *money as measure of value*, and, at the same time, value measured in terms of money i.e. *price*, is more closely defined; (2) money as *means of circulation* and (3) the unity of these two aspects, *real money* which represents bourgeois material wealth as a whole. This concludes the first part, the conversion of money into capital is left for the second part. (p. 227)

Althusser and the early chapters of *Capital*

In order to underscore the significance of the early chapters of *Capital* in the light of Engels' review of the earlier *Critique*, let us take a slight detour and look at the position of Althusser on these early chapters. According to this author, 'we ought to *re-write* Part I of *Capital* so that it becomes a "beginning" which is no longer at all "difficult", but rather simple and easy' (Althusser, 1971, p. 95).

For Althusser, in direct opposition to Lenin, Part I of *Capital* is not the key to understanding the rest, it is a positive *barrier* to that understanding. He therefore gives his readers the benefit of the following advice. 'I therefore give the following advice: put THE WHOLE OF PART ONE ASIDE FOR THE TIME BEING AND BEGIN YOUR READING WITH PART TWO, "The Transformation of Money into Capital" ' (pp. 79–80), adding, 'This advice is more than advice:

it is a recommendation that notwithstanding all the respect I owe my readers, I am prepared to present as an *imperative*' (p. 80). It should be clear from what we said earlier that the real *bête noire* for Althusser is Hegel. He is specific on this point. Many difficulties stand in the way of understanding *Capital* which arise from the 'survivals in Marx's language and even in his thought of the influence of Hegel's thought' (p. 89). As an instance of these supposed 'difficulties' Althusser cites,

> the vocabulary Marx uses in Part I: in the fact that he speaks of *two completely different things* [author's italics] the social usefulness of products on the one hand and the exchange value of the same products on the other, in terms which in fact have a *word in common*, the word 'value': on the one hand use-*value*, and on the other exchange *value*. Marx pillories a man named Wagner (that *vir obscurus*) with his customary vigour in the *Marginal Notes* of 1882, because Wagner seems to believe that since Marx uses the same word, value, in both cases, use-value, and exchange-value are the result of a (Hegelian) division of the concept of 'value'. The fact is that Marx had not taken the precaution of eliminating the word 'value' from the expression 'use-value' and speaking as he should have done simply of the *social usefulness* of the *products*. (p. 91)

What are we to make of this passage? A glance at it reveals that Althusser has made precisely the same mistake as that other '*vir obscurus*' Wagner. For Marx does not derive the terms 'value' and 'use-value', from *any* 'division', Hegelian or otherwise, of the concept of value. He derives both these concepts from an analysis of the *commodity*. And this is crucial. For as we earlier indicated, it means that Marx never starts from any 'concepts' (including therefore the value concept). He begins from the simplest form of bourgeois wealth – the commodity. He shows, as against Althusser, that in the commodity far from being 'completely different things' use-value and value are inseparably united, are *identical*, but identical as opposites. Under conditions of commodity production a product of labour can only assume the value-form if it constitutes a definite use-value. In this respect use-value is *primary* to value in that while use-value can exist independently of commodity production, the reverse is certainly not the case. In unfolding the secret of the commodity form Marx was taking up a problem which had exercised man's mind since antiquity. Aristotle had written that sandals could be used in two ways: in the first place they could be worn, and second, they could be exchanged for another object. If with Aristotle this two-fold nature of the products of labour was still expressed in necessarily primitive form, the economists of the eighteenth century onwards were much more conscious of this division (see the contrast political economy drew between 'values' and 'riches'), even though they failed fully to understand it. And as Engels ('who had touches of theoretical genius marred by a few weaknesses', Althusser tells us; pp. 99–100) makes clear, Marx's ability to provide a clear analysis of the commodity form arose precisely from his indebtedness to German dialectics and principally to Hegel.

We shall return in a moment to Marx's investigation of the commodity. But let us dwell with Althusser a little longer. He wants to leave aside Chapters 1–3 (that is presumably until he has got round to rendering them into simple, non-dialectical language for us). What implications does this 'leaving aside' have? It means, for Althusser, that we can plunge immediately into Part II, 'The Transformation of Money into Capital'. This presents no problem at least for workers, as they will readily understand this section of Marx's work:

> From Part 2 . . . you go straight into the heart of Volume One. . . . This heart is the theory of *surplus-value*, which proletarians will understand without any difficulty, because it is simply the scientific theory of something they experience every day in *class exploitation*. (p. 80)

And this is not an isolated point, an excusable lapse, as it were. For earlier in his 'Preface' to *Capital*, Althusser writes, 'If the workers have 'understood' *Capital* so easily it is because it speaks in scientific terms of the everyday reality with which they are concerned: the exploitation which they suffer because of the capitalist system!' (p. 73) A point emphasized by Althusser, when immediately following we find '*Capital* is a straightforward discussion of their concrete lives' (p. 74).

To take Althusser's specific point: is the essence of *Capital* 'a straightforward discussion of the "concrete lives" of the working class'? It most emphatically is not. Marx's aim was not to show workers that they were exploited, 'something they experience every day'. He aimed for something quite different, something revolutionary in fact. The working class did not need to be told by Marx, or indeed by anybody else, that they were *exploited* – this they had recognized long before the birth of Marxism. It was a recognition which found a reflection, as always, *in practice*, in this case the practice of *trade unionism*. Marx wanted to establish the revolutionary implications of this struggle of the working class. And this revolutionary consciousness does not arise directly from the immediate day-to-day struggle of the working class – it involves grasping the *class struggle as a whole*, on the basis not merely of everyday class exploitation, but on a real understanding of the relationship of all classes to each other and to the state. This is the real message of Lenin's *What is to be Done?* (LCW, vol. 5) against all conceptions of a spontaneous struggle which would automatically generate a scientific consciousness in the working class. The majority of workers 'know' they are exploited; what the working class does *not* spontaneously have is an understanding of the socio-historical roots of this exploitation, nor of all the theoretical and political tasks which are posed in its elimination.

Now this matter has a direct bearing on the status of the early chapters (Chapters 1–3). For it is in these chapters that the logical-historical path whereby capital comes into being is traced. Speaking of the relationship of capital to surplus value, Marx says,

> It is quite simple: if with £100, i.e. the labour of 10 (men), one buys the labour of 20 (men) (that is, commodities in which the labour of 20 (men) is embodied), the value of the product will be £200 and the surplus-value will amount to £100, equal to the unpaid labour of 10 (men). Or supposing 20 men worked half a day each for themselves and half for capital – 20 half-days equal 10 whole ones – the result would be the same as if only 10 men were paid and the others worked for the capitalist gratis. (1972, p. 481)

'It is quite simple.' But Marx immediately adds a point which implicitly refutes Althusser and establishes that it would be quite false to start from the transformation of money into capital without having grasped first of all the nature of commodity exchange.

> The difficulty is simply to discover how this appropriation of labour without any equivalent arises from the law of commodity exchange – out of the fact that commodities exchange for one another in proportion to the amount of labour-time embodied in them – and to start with does not contradict this law. (pp. 481–2)

And it was here that Marx made a development on classical political economy which was to transform completely the science – and this development in this case consisted in tracing the connection between the law of value and the law of surplus value, a connection which utterly eluded Ricardo and company.

Now of course Althusser pays formal acknowledgment to the revolutionary struggle of the working class. But it *is* purely formal acknowledgment. For in his conception the struggles are mechanically, metaphysically separated from the defensive struggle on wages and economic conditions. This is how Althusser poses this relationship:

> The economic (trade union) class struggle remains a defensive one because it is economic (*against* the two great tendencies of capitalism). The political class struggle is offensive because it is political (*for* the seizure of power by the working class and its allies). These two struggles must be carefully distinguished from one another; although they always encroach upon on another; more or less according to the conjuncture. (Althusser, 1971, p. 84)

Here Althusser's 'conjuncture' is introduced as a pure *deus ex machina* to escape from a theoretical impasse. For the problem is *how* is the defensive struggle transformed into the offensive. In the *Manifesto*, Marx shows how the very historical development of capital itself creates the material conditions for the continual growth of the class struggle from defensive concerns (wage regulation, etc.) to offensive concerns (the high point of which is the seizure of power by the working class). *Capital*, from this point of view, is an elaboration and working out in detail of Marx's conceptions, first sketched out in 1848. The point here is this: it is not that the working class is engaged in a defensive struggle which at some unexplained conjunctural moment 'encroaches' upon an offensive struggle. As Althusser presents it here the working class is an inert mass, whose consciousness is raised by entirely outside forces ('theory').[2] This is, however, far from the case. While denying that the working class can *spontaneously* reach a revolutionary consciousness (such a conception is elaborated in the theory of 'spontaneity') Marxism at the same time recognizes that the working class is driven, by the very nature of its struggle *in the direction of* socialist consciousness. And it is this real *movement* of the working class which provides one of the bases for the work of Marxists. Thus in his attack on the economists, Lenin, while denying that socialist consciousness appears as a direct result of the proletarian class struggle, did agree with Kautsky that socialism and the class struggle arise *side-by-side*. In a footnote in *What is to be Done?* Lenin poses the relationship between the working class and a Marxist consciousness which avoids the mistakes of spontaneity but at the same time sees the living connection between Marxism and the working class. 'It is often said,' remarks Lenin, 'that the working class *spontaneously* gravitates towards Socialism.'

This is perfectly true in the sense that socialist theory defines the causes of the misery of the working class more profoundly and more correctly than any other theory, and for that reason the workers are able to assimilate it so easily, *provided*, however, that this theory does not itself yield to spontaneity, *provided* it subordinates spontaneity to itself. Usually this is taken for granted, but it is precisely this which *Rabocheye Dyelo* [*Workers' Cause*, a magazine published by the Economists, 1899–1902] forgets or distorts. The working class spontaneously gravitates towards Socialism, but the more widespread (and continuously revived in the most diverse forms) bourgeois ideology nevertheless spontaneously imposes itself upon the working class still more. (LCW, vol. 5)

The commodity and use-value

Engels' treatment of Marx's method and Althusser's attitude to the early section of *Capital* once more serve to draw attention to the dialectical character of *Capital* as a whole. In considering the nature of Marx's starting point and his dialectical treatment of the commodity, let us recall Lenin's characterization of the most general features of dialectics. Lenin writes: 'The splitting of a single whole and the cognition of its contradictory parts . . . is the *essence* of dialectics' (LCW, vol. 38, p. 359). Now this question of the 'single whole' must be especially kept in mind when considering the point from which *Capital* begins. If Marx's aim was to present the capitalist system in the whole sweep of its development, then the *commodity* had also to be understood in its whole development. The commodity was shown by Marx to be a unity of value and use value. And it was necessary that *both* these 'sides' be kept in view. For a knowledge of *both* these opposites, in their conflict, is necessary if thought is to get near to the real movement of commodity production. Lenin puts this point in the following way 'The condition for the knowledge of all processes of the world in their *"self-movement"*, in their spontaneous development, in their real life, is the knowledge of them as a unity of opposites. Development is the "struggle" of opposites' (LCW, vol. 38, p. 360). As we have seen, for Marx, in the investigation of economic terms *abstraction* was essential. But this process of abstraction is a *contradictory* one. For abstraction to a certain extent kills the living movement of reality. The problem for thought, therefore, is really this: how to depict movement through concepts. The ancient Greek rationalist Zeno regarded movement as 'sensed truth'. But he did not rest on a mere admission of fact. He was among the first in the history of philosophy to show the contradictory aspects of movement – the contradiction between 'discreteness' and 'continuity' of 'rest' and 'motion'. He was among the first of those who attempted to understand the connection between these aspects; but he was unable to comprehend this contradiction in terms of fixed concepts, and therefore, as a rationalist, came to a denial of the reality of movement. But the question is not whether there is such a thing as movement; that is acknowledged as a fact of experience and verified in the history of science – the problem for thought is thus how to grasp movement through concepts which inevitably tend to coarsen and strangle reality. As Lenin shows this is not a 'problem' for thought, so much as an expression of the contradictory nature of all reality, a contradiction which finds its essential expression in dialectics. Thus

> We cannot imagine, express, measure, depict movement, without interrupting continuity, without simplifying, coarsening, dismembering, strangling that which is living. The representation of movement by means of thought always makes coarse, kills – and not only by means of thought, but also by sense-perception, and not only of movement, but *every* concept. And in that lies the *essence* of dialectics. And precisely *this essence* is expressed in the formula: the unity, identity of opposites. (pp. 259–60)

And elsewhere in this work Lenin makes this same point when he says that Hegel showed that 'in abstract concepts (and in the system of them) the principle of motion *cannot* be expressed otherwise than as the principle of the identity of opposites' (p. 345).

The way Marx develops his investigation of the commodity testifies both to the truth of Lenin's propositions and the essential sterility of Althusser's position. For Marx does in fact 'hold fast' to both sides of the commodity. He reveals throughout the *whole* of *Capital* how the contradiction of the commodity form unfolds, intensifies and dominates every aspect of bourgeois society. The contradictions of the commodity are *never* left behind; nor are they merely 'returned to' at various points throughout the three volumes. This basic contradiction (use-value, value) continually reappears in newer and higher forms which grow out of the lower forms as part of an uninterrupted process. It is through the development of these forms that development in the sphere of economy takes place.

Let us examine the question more specifically, from the point of view of the place occupied by use-value in Marx's analysis. One considerable debt we owe to Rosdolsky lies in the fact that he has done much to clear up the confusion surrounding this matter in most popularizations of *Capital*. (See Rosdolsky, 1977, Ch. 3). Summing up his discussion and making what is the decisive point he says, 'Engels was surely right when he perceived in Marx's treatment of use-value, and its role in political economy, a classic example of the use of the "German dialectical method" ' (p. 95).

Among Marx's many criticisms of Ricardo's work was the fact that he had tended to ignore the place of use-value in his economics. For Ricardo, says Marx, it 'remains lying dead, as a simple pre-supposition' (G, p. 320). He was, adds Marx, only 'esoterically concerned' with this category (G, p. 647). Now, as Rosdolsky makes clear, the importance of these comments had certainly escaped many writers on *Capital*. Sweezy's case is typical and important if only because his *Theory of Capitalist Development* has long been recognized as perhaps the standard popularization of Marx's political economy. Sweezy clearly gets the matter of use-value quite wrong. And one source of his error is undoubtedly the confusion of 'use-value' with the concept of 'utility' found in bour-geois economics. Sweezy writes, 'Marx excluded use-value (or as it would now be called "utility") from the field of investigation of political economy on the ground that it does not directly embody a social relation' (1946, p. 26). And pointing out that bourgeois and Marxian value theories are 'diametrically opposed', Sweezy adds, 'Nor should it be made a matter of reproach against Marx that he failed to develop a subjective value theory, since he con-sciously and deliberately dissociated himself from any attempt to do so' (p. 26). Now 'utility' is a subjective, a social category con-cerned with the relationship between an individual's supposed men-tal state and material objects. Marx, of course, entirely rejects this starting point as having anything to do with science. For it pretends to deduce social laws from states of mind. It would have been *impossible* to develop a *value* theory from such a standpoint. The theory of marginal utility was not a rival *value* theory, for value is, as a social relation of a specific kind, precisely what is excluded by the upholders of marginal utility theory. But when we come to consider use-value we are dealing with an entirely different matter. Use-value is the *substance* of all wealth, with an entirely objective existence. Use-values are produced under all social conditions. Thus far from being uninterested in this category, Marx is vitally concerned with it in so far as it is itself a 'determined economic form'. This is what he says on the subject:

To be a use-value is evidently a necessary pre-requisite of the

commodity, but it is immaterial to the use-value whether it is
a commodity. Use-value as such, since it is independent of the
determinate economic forms, is outside the sphere of
investigation of political economy. *It belongs to this sphere
only when it is a determinate form.* (author's italics; I, p. 28)

The key point here is that Marx is not interested in use-value *as
such*. He is interested solely in it in connection with the analysis of
given economic forms. His answer to Wagner clears up the matter
at issue:

> Only an obscurantist who has understood not a word of
> *Capital* can conclude: Because Marx repudiates all Germanic
> professional nonsense about 'use-value' *in general* [author's
> italics] in a note to the first edition of *Capital*, and refers
> readers who wish to know something about actual use-values
> to 'Introduction to Commodity Theory' – for that reason, *use-
> value* plays no role in his work. Naturally, it does not play the
> role of its contrary, 'value', which has nothing in common
> with it apart from the fact that 'value' occurs in the term 'use-
> value'. He could just as well have said that 'exchange-value' is
> ignored in my work because it is only appearance-form of
> value, but it is not 'value', since for me the 'value' of a
> commodity is neither its use-value nor its exchange-value.
> (Marx, 1976, p. 215)

And Marx goes on:

> If one has to talk of analysing the 'Commodity' – the simplest
> economic concretum – then one must keep all relationships
> distant which have nothing to do with the proposed object of
> analysis. What is to be said of the commodity in so far as it is
> a use-value, I have said in a few lines, therefore, but on the
> other hand have emphasized the *characteristic form* in which
> the use-value (the labour product) appears at this point,
> namely [here Marx quotes from the first volume of *Capital*] 'A
> thing can be useful and a product of human labour without
> being a commodity. Whoever satisfies his own need by his
> product creates a use-value, admittedly, but not a commodity.
> In order to produce a commodity, *he not only has to produce
> a use-value, but a use-value for others, social use-value*' . . .

> Thereby use-value (as use-value of the 'commodity' itself)
> possesses a history-specific character . . . Thus it would be
> pure babbling (as emerges from the preceding) in the analysis
> of the commodity – since it manifests itself on the one hand as
> use-value or good and on the other hand as 'value' – to 'tie
> on' upon this occasion all sorts of banal reflections concerning
> use-values or goods which do not fall within the realm of
> commodities. (pp. 215–16)

Immediately following this passage Marx says that Wagner failed
to see that in *Capital* 'use-value plays a very important role different from in previous Economics, but that it precisely only comes
from the analysis of a given economic structuring, not from intel-
lectualizing hither and yon about the concepts or words "use-
value" and "value" ' (p. 216). Karl Korsch got this question right,
even though one would wish to dissent strongly from him on many
others. He writes:

> With Marx . . . use-value is not defined as a use-value in
> general, but as the use-value of a commodity. This use-value
> inherent in the commodities produced in modern capitalist
> society is however, not merely an extra-economic
> presupposition of this 'value'. It is an element of the value,
> and itself is an economic category. The mere fact that a thing
> has utility for any human being, say for its producer, does not
> yet give us the economic definition of use-value. Not until the
> thing has social utility (i.e. utility 'for other persons') does the
> economic definition of use-value apply. (Korsch, 1963, p. 123)

(In his last sentence Korsch is not strictly correct; as Engels points
out in a parenthesis (I, p. 41) in *Capital*, commodities do not
involve only the production of 'social use-values'; this use-value
'must be transferred to another, whom it will serve as a use-value,
by means of an exchange'.)

Thus, far from being excommunicated from the investigation of
capitalism, use-value plays a central role. We can see this in connection with surplus value itself which, as Marx shows, arises from
the use-values of the commodity labour-power. But let us give a
series of examples to indicate the role played by use value.

1 Marx gives one clear example in connection with the deter-

mination of the rate of profit, to the extent that the rate of profit depends on fluctuations in the value of raw materials. For, as Marx puts it,

> it is especially agricultural produce proper, i.e. the raw materials taken from nature, which . . . is subject to fluctuations of value in consequence of changing yields etc. Owing to uncontrollable natural conditions, favourable or unfavourable seasons, etc. the same quantity of these use-values may therefore have different prices. (III, pp. 117–18)

Such variations must always affect the rate of profit 'even if they leave the wage untouched and hence the rate and amount of surplus value too' (III, p. 115).

2 As a second instance of the role of use-value in the investigation of economic forms we can take the case of the Reproduction Schema given in the second volume of *Capital*. For Marx the problem of capital turnover was a two-sided one. In the first place, in order that reproduction may be achieved, the total value embodied in the commodities produced must be *realized*, that is sold at prices equivalent to their value. But at the same time, we are not dealing with a purely *value*-creating and realizing process. For at the same time reproduction always requires, if it is to be crisis-free, that the use-value of the commodities produced should fulfil definite material conditions for the recommencement of production. If, in an extreme case, all commodities produced were raw materials, workers and capitalists alike would starve (assuming no reserves of food were available). Or if all commodities produced were consumer goods there would be no resources to make good wear and tear of machinery and the economy would eventually grind to a halt. So the use-value composition of the outputs of Departments I and II is clearly a crucial factor in an analysis of the conditions of potential equilibrium and breakdown alike.

3 As a final example of the importance of a proper consideration of the use-value side of commodity production let us take the example of money. Even with simple commodity circulation, with the emergence of the money-form of the commodity, the value of a commodity must be represented in the form of use-value, that is in the natural form of the commodity. This means that not only must money itself be a commodity, but also that this use-value

must be connected to quite specific material properties of this money-commodity. As Marx puts this point,

> In proportion as exchange bursts its local bonds, and the value of commodities more and more expands into an embodiment of human labour in the abstract, in the same proportion the character of money attracts itself to commodities that are *by Nature* fitted to perform the social function of a universal equivalent. These commodities are the precious metals. (I, p. 89; author's italics)

And Marx immediately adds 'although gold and silver are not by Nature money, *money is by Nature gold and silver*' (I, p. 89; author's italics).

The formation of money

The first three sections of the opening chapter of *Capital* are concerned with the formation of money. For Marx, the problem was not to show that money was itself a commodity (in the case of gold this was obvious) but to demonstrate the transition from the most simple, elementary relation of the commodity to money. 'The difficulty,' as Marx puts it, 'lies not in comprehending that money is a commodity, but in discovering how, why and by what means a commodity becomes money' (I, p. 92). But before looking at the manner in which Marx sets out to trace this process, it is necessary to stress once more that Marx is not engaged in some mere manipulation of concepts, 'applying' a few Hegelian concepts and phrases. Marx warns against precisely this view when he tells us:

> It will be necessary later, before the question is dropped, to correct the idealist manner of its presentation, which makes it seem as if it were merely a matter of conceptual determination and of the dialectic of these concepts. Above all in the case of the phrase: product (or activity) becomes commodity; commodity exchange value; exchange-value, money. (G, p. 151)

Here Marx is making a point he made over and over again: namely that economic categories reflect real human practice. Engels' insistence on the unity of the 'logical' and the 'historical' can be seen in practice in *Capital* (as well as in the *Grundrisse*) where the logical derivation of the concepts 'value' and 'money' is paralleled with a historical derivation of these same categories. Marx always confronts the results of his abstract analysis with actual historical developments. The exchange of commodities arises from a long process of economic development and presupposes a certain level of the productivity of labour. The decisive point for the development of commodity production arises when communities are able to produce more than they require for their immediate subsistence, that is as soon as this labour can regularly generate a 'surplus product'. Now the exchange of products, says Marx, tends not to take place *within* communities, but *between* them. This primitive barter is still, however, a long way (both logically and historically) from developed exchange. For this, developed exchange, exchange value has to acquire an independent form. This fact is revealed in two ways. The production of use-value remains the purpose of society. Use-values cease to be merely use-values and become means of exchange or commodities, only after a larger amount of them has been produced than is needed for consumption. But even when this occurs, this surplus takes the form of commodities only within the limits set by the nature of these use-values. Thus 'the commodities to be exchanged by their owners must be use-values for both of them, but each commodity must be a use-value for its non-owner' (*Contribution*, p. 50). It is only when a portion of the products of labour are produced with a special view to exchange that,

> the distinction becomes firmly established between the utility of an object, for the purposes of exchange. Its use-value becomes distinguished from its exchange-value. On the other hand, the quantitative proportions in which the articles are exchangeable, becomes dependent on their production itself. Custom stamps them as values with definite magnitudes. (I, p. 88)

So the appearance of the value-form is a reflection of the growth of the productive forces: 'The necessity for a value-form grows with the increasing nature and variety of the commodities exchanged. *The problem and the means of solution arise simul-*

taneously' (p. 88; author's italics). Commercial exchange in which commodity-owners exchange and compare articles, never takes place unless the different kinds of commodities belonging to different owners are exchanged for, and equated at values with, one single further kind of commodity. And this commodity thereby acquires, albeit at first within narrow limits, the form of a universal social equivalent. But it lacks as yet any real stability. It appears and disappears with the momentary, often accidental contacts (between communities) which call it into being. It is attached first to this, then to that commodity. It is only with the development and growth of exchange that it fixes itself to particular types of commodities – that is, it is crystallized out into the money form.

To start with, Marx indicates that a commodity will serve as money which represents in a given community the predominant form of wealth – that is to say the commodity most frequently exchanged and circulated as an object of consumption. At this stage, the commodity 'selected' is determined by the particular usefulness of the commodity as an object of consumption (salt, hides, etc.) or of production (slaves). In the case of a higher development this situation is transformed into its exact opposite, now it is the commodity which has the *least* utility as an object of consumption or production that best serves the needs of *exchange as such*. In the first case, the commodity becomes money merely because of its particular use-value, in the latter case it acquires use-value precisely because of its serviceability as money. This makes the precious metals especially suitable – they are easily divisible and combinable, they are readily transportable owing to the compression of considerable value in a little space.

Having stressed the historical-practical nature of the process which brings the money-form into being, let us now consider how Marx traces this appearance in logic. We know already that the products of labour only constitute values in so far as they embody the same social substance, general human labour. But we know also that it is the labour of individuals, expressing different degrees of intensity, skill, etc, in short definite *concrete* labour 'which assimilates particular natural materials to particular human requirements' (I, p. 42). As such this labour is always objectified 'in a definite particular commodity, with particular characteristics, and particular relations to needs', but as human labour in general it needs to be embodied 'in a commodity which expresses no more than its quota or quantity, which is indifferent to its own natural properties, and which can therefore be metamorphosised onto – i.e. exchanged for – every other commodity which objectifies the same labour-time' (G, p. 168). This means that 'The commodity, as it comes into being, is only objectified individual labour-time of a specific kind, and not *universal* labour-time. The commodity is thus *not* immediately exchange-value but has still to become exchange-value' (*Contribution*, p. 43). It is of course important to keep in mind the fact that this contradiction between individual and universal labour is a reflection of the contradictory nature of the commodity itself, that is of *objectified* labour. Thus, 'Two commodities, e.g. a yard of cotton and a measure of oil, are different by nature, have different properties, are measured by different measures, are incommensurable,' (G, p. 141). While,

Considered as values, all commodities are qualitatively equal and differ only quantitatively, hence can be measured against each other and substituted for one another . . . in certain qualitative relations. Value is their social relation, their economic quality. . . . As value a commodity is an equivalent for all other commodities: as an equivalent, all its natural properties are extinguished: it no longer takes up a special, qualitative relationship towards the other commodities: but is rather the general measure as well as the general representative, the general medium of exchange of all other commodities. As value, it is money. (G, p. 141)

And it is for this reason that value must take on an existence independent of the bodily existence of the commodity. Marx explains that vital point in the following way;

The property of being a value not only has but *must* achieve an existence different from its natural one. Why? Because commodities as values are different from one another only quantitatively; therefore each commodity must be qualitatively different from its own value. Its value must therefore have an existence which is qualitatively distinguishable from it, and in actual exchange this separability must become a real separation, because the natural distinctness of commodities must come into contradiction with their economic equivalence, and because both can exist together only if the commodity achieves a double existence, in which it is a mere symbol, a cipher for a relation of production, a mere symbol for its own value. (G, p. 141; author's italics)

The elementary form of value

We can now examine Marx's analysis of the movement from direct barter; the succession of the stages of exchange – the 'simple', the 'total' and the 'general' value-forms. As Marx notes:

Everyone knows, if he knows nothing else, that commodities have a value-form common to them all, and presenting a marked contrast with their varied bodily forms of their use-value. I mean their money-form. Here, however, a task is set us, the performance of which has never yet even been attempted by *bourgeois* economy, the task of tracing the genesis of this money-form, of developing the expression of value implied in the value-relationship of commodities, from its simplest almost imperceptible outline to the dazzling money-form. By doing this, we shall, at the same time, solve the riddle presented by money. (I, pp. 47–8)

We should note, in passing, that despite the fact that Marx here tells us that in tracing the genesis of the money-form he was attempting something never properly considered by bourgeois economy, very few writers on *Capital* have paid the slightest attention to the sections in *Capital* dealing with the value-form and its growth. The late Ronald Meek in his *Studies in the Labour Theory of Value* dismissed the analysis of the value-form in one short paragraph. 'There is no need', he writes,

for us to follow Marx's rather complex analysis of the 'elementary', 'expanded' and 'money' forms of value in any detail. Essentially, what he is trying to do here is to reveal the contradictions which result from the reciprocal interaction of the two sides of the value equation, and to demonstrate the nature of the solutions of these contradictions which logic – and history – demand and provide. (Meek, 1973, pp. 173–4)

In our opinion this is quite inadequate,[3] Marx's analysis on this question cannot be dismissed on the grounds that it is 'rather complex'. For, as we will endeavour to show, the proper appreciation of the elementary value-form, that is the exchange of two commodities (20 yards of linen = 1 coat), not only provides the key to understanding the nature of money (which classical economy, let alone modern economic theory, failed to understand), but also the key to Marx's notion of fetishism, which Rubin (1972) in particular has so correctly insisted is one of the foundations of Marx's entire analysis of capitalism.

Let us follow Marx's argument. From the beginning he indicates that in the elementary or accidental value-form (x commodity A = y commodity B) is expressed, in 'external' form the 'internal' contradiction within the commodity itself. In the first edition of *Capital* we find the following crucial passage.

> The inner opposition contained in the commodity of use-value and value is thus manifested by an external opposition; that is the relationship of two commodities of which the one counts immediately only as use-value, the other immediately as exchange-value, or in which both of the opposite determinants of use-value and exchange-value are apportioned among the commodities in a polar manner. (Marx, 1976, p. 61)

And a similar passage is found in the third edition where we read:

> The opposition or contrast existing internally in each commodity between use-value and value, is therefore, made evident externally by two commodities, being placed in such relation to each other, that the commodity whose value it is sought to express, figures directly as a mere use-value, while the commodity in which that value is to be expressed, figures directly as mere exchange-value. Hence the *elementary* form of value of a commodity is the elementary form in which the contrast contained in that commodity between use-value and value, becomes apparent. (author's emphasis; I, p. 61)

These passages are crucial and worth considering carefully for the following reason: Marx is here presenting value in truly dialectical manner. For value is an *inner relation* of the commodity to itself, reversed in *outward form* through the relation to another commodity. This other commodity (here the coat) plays the *passive* role of the mirror in which the inwardly contradictory nature of the commodity that expressed its value (the linen) plays the *active* role. Here is expressed the fact that dialectics obliges one always to discover, behind the outward form of a thing's relation to another thing, its own inner nature, its own being. (We should note that the *properties* of a thing – say the linen – are not the result of its relation to other things – the coat – but only *manifest* themselves in such relations.) Of course dialectics does not *reduce* the external contradictions (between two commodities in the elementary form of exchange) to the internal contradiction of the commodity. The question was not one of reduction, but of *deriving* the former from the latter and thus comprehending both in their objective necessity. Exchange-value has to be derived from the contradiction between value and use-value within the cell of bourgeois society.

True to the dialectical conception of the whole work, Marx tells us that this elementary form is the key to understanding the mystery of the entire value-form, just as the contradictory nature of the commodity is the 'germ' of all the more developed contradictions. Thus, 'The whole mystery of the form of value lies hidden in this elementary form. Its analysis, therefore, is our real difficulty.' It is, putting the matter more concretely, the contradictions of this elementary form which provide the essential key to all the higher, more general contradictions: 'We perceive, at first sight, the deficiencies of the elementary form of value; it is a mere *germ* which must undergo a series of metamorphoses before it can ripen into the price-form' (I, p. 62; author's italics). Thus Marx says, 'The antagonism between the relative form of value and the equivalent form, the two poles of the value-form *is developed concurrently with the form itself*' (I, pp. 67–8). Now it is precisely because the equation 20 yards of linen = 1 coat is the 'germ' of all the contradictions of capital that we must investigate it thoroughly. Lenin spoke specifically of this point in *Capital* when he wrote:

> Just as the simplest form of value, the individual act of
> exchange of one given commodity for another, already
> includes in an underdeveloped form *all* the main
> contradictions of capitalism – so the simplest *generalization*,

the first and simplest formation of notions (judgements, syllogisms, etc.) already denotes man's ever deeper cognition of the objective connection of the world. Here is where one should look for the true meaning, significance and role of Hegel's *Logic*. This NB. (LCW, Vol. 38, p. 178)

In other words, as Lenin points out elsewhere in the *Philosophical Notebooks*, even in the simplest copular judgment ('Fido is a dog') is found the germ of dialectics (the relation between the individual and the universal, between chance and necessity, the identity of opposites, etc.) so in the elementary value-expression is found the as yet hardly perciptible germ of the entire movement of capital.

Now in this elementary value form (for simplicity's sake we will throughout use Marx's example, 20 yards of linen = 1 coat) the linen plays the active role, the coat the passive. The qualitative-quantitative contradiction of the commodity linen is 'resolved' in the relationship of this commodity linen to its equivalent-form, the coat. But it is not resolved in the sense that the initial contradiction disappears − it is heightened into an even sharper antagonism. Thus, 'The relative form and the equivalent form are two intimately connected, mutually dependent and inseparable elements of the expression of value; but at the same time are mutually exclusive, antagonistic extremes, i.e. poles of an expression' (I, p. 48). (We can note in passing that this antagonistic nature of the elementary value-form comes across even more strikingly in German by the fact that linen is a feminine word and coat a masculine.) At the outset Marx leaves aside an investigation of the purely quantitative side of this relationship. Here alone is revealed one important aspect of Marx's difference with the political economists whose attention, as we have seen, was directed almost wholly to this quantitative side. Marx says, on this point,

It is the expression of equivalence between different sorts of commodities that alone brings into relief the specific character of the value-creating labour, and this it does by actually reducing the different varieties of labour embodied in the different kinds of commodities to their common quality of human labour in the abstract. (I, p. 49)

Two points should be noted in connection with this and many

similar passages. First, one already made and therefore a question that need not detain us, namely the *objective* character of this reduction of concrete to abstract labour. Second, the fact that the two-fold character of labour embodied in the commodity is only made manifest, only 'brought into relief' in the elementary value-form, in the simple relation between two commodities. Just as the two-fold character of the commodity is only made visible through its relations with another commodity, the same is equally true for the two-fold nature of the labour which produces the commodity.

But, notes Marx, it is not adequate merely to grasp the value-creating nature of labour (that is, abstract labour); it is necessary to see that the reduction of concrete labour to abstract labour is not and cannot be a *direct* one. It is, by its very nature, a *mediated* process, one in which the abstract labour congealed in the commodity in congealed in the form of some object and only in this indirect way can it become 'value'. In a passage which shows the not immodest distance separating Marx from all those who read him as a 'consistent empiricist' we find:

> There is however something else required beyond the expression of the specific character of the labour of which the value of the linen consists. Human labour-power in motion, or human labour, creates value, but is not itself value. It becomes value only in its congealed state, when embodied in the form of some object. In order to express the value of the linen as a congelation of human labour, that value must be expressed as having objective existence, as being something materially different from the linen itself, and yet a something common to the linen and all other commodities. The problem is already solved. (I, p. 51)

Marx is here stressing the fundamental fact that in a society of atomized private producers the labour of the individual is not *directly* social, nor can it ever be. The labour of the individual becomes social only through the negation of its own original character, by appearing in a directly opposed form. Despite the increasingly socialized nature of production under the capitalist system, there is no unified, conscious, mechanism of social planning. The only 'planning' takes place through the blind force of the market. 'The total movement of this order is its disorder.' Hence, Marx, in summing up his discussion of the relative form, says, 'The value of the commodity linen is expressed by the bodily form of the commodity coat; the value of one by the use-value of the other. . . . Thus the linen acquires a value-form different from its physical form' (I, p. 52). Speaking of the linen, Marx says, 'In order to inform us that its sublime reality as value is not the same as its buckram body, it says that value has the appearance of a coat, and consequently that so far as the linen is value, it and the coat are as like as two peas' (I, p. 52). Marx then turns to the *peculiarities* of the equivalent form (the coat). It is through an examination of these 'peculiarities' that he shows how the contradictions in the elementary form of value are in fact overcome – overcome by being taken into a higher unity in the money form. For the peculiarities of the form 20 yards of linen = 1 coat highlight with even more force the indirect, unconscious nature of the process of production under capitalism, a process which therefore demands, and finds, some universal value-form (money) in which this indirectness is turned into its opposite. The three peculiarities are:

1 'Use-value becomes the form of its manifestation, the phenomenal form of its opposite, value.'

2 The fact 'that concrete labour becomes the form under which its opposite direct human labour manifests itself.'

3 The fact 'that the labour of private individuals takes the form of its opposite, labour directly social in its form' (I, pp. 55–8).

Here are brought out by Marx (brought out after the detailed investigation of the elementary form which has so often been neglected in commentaries on *Capital*) all the major contradictions of capital – although naturally only in embryonic form. In particular we should note the fact that the two-fold character of labour which is first revealed in the elementary value-form (remembering the importance of the concrete-abstract labour distinction in Marx's work):

> The body of the commodity that serves as the equivalent, figures as the materialization of human labour in the abstract, and is at the same time the product of some specifically concrete labour. This concrete labour becomes therefore the medium for expressing abstract human labour (I, p. 58)

And further

If on the one hand the coat rates as nothing but the embodiment of abstract human labour, so, on the other hand, the tailoring which is actually embodied in it, counts as nothing but the form under which that abstract labour is realized. In the expression of the value of the linen, the utility of the tailoring consists, not in making clothes but in making an object, which we at once recognize to be value, and therefore to be a congelation of labour, but of labour indistinguishable from that revealed in the value of the linen. In order to act as such a mirror of value, the labour of tailoring must reflect nothing besides its own abstract quality of being human labour generally. (I, p. 58)

The development of the value-form

Precisely because of the unresolved contradictions of the elementary value-form, it must develop into newer higher forms in which these contradictions are never lost, but always sublated. Out of the internal contradictions of the form 20 yards of linen = 1 coat grows the expanded value-form, namely 20 yards of linen = 1 coat, 2 sheep, ½ ton of iron etc. This form comes into actual existence for the first time as soon as a particular product of labour, such as cattle, is no longer exceptionally, but habitually, exchanged for various other commodities (I, p. 66). (This stage corresponds to the 'particular' in Hegel's logic: a series of particular commodities play the role of equivalent alongside each other.)

Having looked at Marx's treatment of the elementary form in some detail, this expanded form need not detain us over-long. However, we need to draw attention to the fact that the relations which were in the elementary form (the individual) relatively imperceptible now manifest themselves with greater force and clarity in this higher form.

It is thus that *for the first time* that value *shows itself* in its true light, as a congelation of undifferentiated human labour. For the labour that creates it, now stands *expressly revealed* as labour that ranks equally with every other sort of human labour, no matter what its form, whether tailoring, ploughing, mining etc. (I, p. 63; author's italics)

Expressed in the expanded form is an expansion of the actual social relations of commodity production. For the linen, by virtue of its form of value, no longer stands in a social relation with merely one kind of commodity, but 'with the whole world of commodities' and becomes a true citizen of the world of commodities (I, p. 63). The *semblance* of the relations of the elementary form now takes on *apparent* form in another sense. (We should note that Marx here deals quite consciously with this movement from 'semblance' to 'appearance', an appearance in which it becomes possible to identify clearly the opposites in the phenomena under investigation.) For what seemed previously mere *chance* is now revealed to be *necessity* in this expanded form.

> In the first form . . . it might for ought that otherwise appears, be pure accident, that the two commodities are exchangeable in definite quantities. In the second form on the contrary, we perceive at once the background that determines and is essentially different from this accidental appearance. The value of the linen remains unaltered in magnitude, whether expressed in coats, coffee, or iron, or in numberless different commodities, the property of as many different owners. The accidental relation between two individual commodities disappears. (I, p. 63)

Further, says Marx, 'It becomes plain that it is not the exchange of commodities which regulates the magnitude of their value; but on the contrary, that it is the magnitude of their value which controls their exchange proportions', a point which, incidentally, makes clear Marx's conception of the relationship of 'production' to 'exchange'. And just as in the case of the elementary form so now in the case of the expanded, Marx goes on to reveal the deficiencies of this total form.

> In the first place, the relative expression of value is incomplete because the series representing it is interminable. The chain of which each equation of value is a link, is liable at any moment to be lengthened by each new kind of commodity that comes into existence and furnishes new material for a fresh expression of value. (I, p. 64)

This form, precisely because it is always by its nature incomplete and 'deficient in unity' (I, p. 64) gives way to a higher form, the General Form of Value, expressed as follows

    1 coat
    10 lbs of tea   = 20 yards of linen
    40 lbs of coffee, etc.

This form, like all economic forms, has a definite material base, that is, a definite foundation in human history. This form 'expresses the value of the whole world commodities in terms of a single commodity set apart for the purpose, namely, the linen, and this represents to us their values by means of their equality with linen' (I, p. 66).

It is in this General Form that all the different, opposed, commodities (and by extension all the particular concrete types of labour embodied in these commodities) are *united* in one commodity. The previous 'deficiency in unity' of the total form is now overcome. As such this General Form of Value preserves within it the elementary form, but in an inverted way:

> All commodities now express their value (1) in an elementary
> form because in a single commodity; (2) with unity, because
> in one and the same commodity. This form of value is
> elementary and the same for all, therefore general. (I, p. 65)

And this unity, summed up in the General concept is no mere mechanical unity, no mere addition of each commodity, individually, apart from the rest, 'finding' the form of its value in one single, excluded commodity. Quite the contrary: the unity is a *dialectical* unity, for in one excluded commodity is represented the *ensemble* of all commodities, their *joint* action. (This should be seen in the light of the earlier discussion of the nature of dialectical concepts as opposed to those constructed on the basis of purely formal thought.) This point is made clear when Marx compares the elementary and expanded forms with the general.

> The two earlier forms either express the value of each
> commodity in terms of a single commodity of a different kind,
> or a series of many such commodities. In such cases, it is, so
> to say, the special business of each single commodity to find

an expression for its value, and this it does without the help of the others. These others, with respect to the former, play the passive parts of equivalents. The general form of value, C, results from *the joint action of the whole world of commodities, and from that alone.* A commodity can acquire a general expression of its value only by all other commodities, simultaneously with it, expressing their values in the same equivalent; and every new commodity must follow suit. It thus becomes evident that, since the existence of commodities as values is purely social, this social existence can be expressed by the totality of their social relations alone, and consequently that the form of their value must be socially recognized form. (I, p. 66; author's italics)

Thus it is not that each commodity 'finds' its value in its passive opposite. Now we have a *transformation* of opposites. For the excluded commodity (here the linen) finds the value of all the other commodities in an objective process, one where 'every new commodity must follow suit'. The passive has now become active and the active passive. The social relations of commodities are now revealed as *objective* relations in and through which 'by joint action' the value of each commodity is expressed in the one excluded commodity. If the General value-form embraces, as it does, the whole world of commodities in their movement, then it must be the abstract epitome, a condensed history of this whole world, or, as Marx says (I, p. 67), the 'social résumé' of that world.

Now we are on the edge of the emergence of the money-form, expressed by:

20 yards of linen
1 coat
40 lbs of coffee   =2 ounces of gold
10 lbs of tea, etc.

Money appears when the exclusion of one commodity, seen in the General Form, becomes finally restricted to one commodity, gold. A commodity which may have served as a single equivalent in isolated exchanges (elementary form) or as a particular equivalent alongside several others (the expanded form) now serves as a universal equivalent. Only when this monopoly position is firmly established does the general form give way to the money-form.

Clearly, not all aspects of this opening chapter of *Capital* have been examined. But in tracing the transition from commodity to money, Marx was laying the essential basis for the rest of his work as well as making an enormous advance over anything achieved in political economy. For he has now traced the *origin* of money and in this way laid the foundation for understanding the mystery which surrounds this fetishized form in which men's social relationships appear embodied in a metal. Precisely because even the best figures in political economy were unable to tackle the problem of the historical nature of the predominant forms of bourgeois economy, for them money did remain a mystery, merely a thing, merely a symbol. We can best look at this problem by examining Marx's theory of fetishism and the place which it occupies in his work.

5 · Some aspects of Marx's notion of commodity fetishism

> When therefore Galiani says: Value is a relation between persons . . . he ought to have added: a relation between persons expressed as a relation between things. (I, p. 74)

In his important book *Essays on Marx's Theory of Value*, I. I. Rubin draws attention to the fact that 'Marx's theory of commodity fetishism has not occupied the place which is proper to it in the Marxist economic system' (1972, p. 5).[1] As he observes, many writers have failed to grasp the relationship of this notion to Marx's critique of political economy – it has, he says, often been regarded as a 'brilliant sociological generalization, a theory and critique of all contemporary culture based on the reification of human relations'. Rubin was surely right to oppose such a view and also that which seeks to separate out Marx's notion of fetishism as some independent entity, having hardly any connection to *Capital* as a whole. Rubin's book was first published over fifty years ago, but in the light of the many distortions of this aspect of Marx's work which have appeared in recent years, what he said then carries even more force today. In fact we shall seek to show that for Marx his notion of fetishism is no mere literary digression, something ancillary to the main text. On the contrary, as Rubin, I think, has adequately shown, it provides one of the key elements in the foundation of Marx's entire theory and is in particular directly bound up with his conception of economic crisis. We know that a separate treatment of fetishism did not appear in the first edition of *Capital*, even though the concept is implicitly present. Only with the second and third editions (the basis for the English translations) did a separate section 'The Fetishism of Commodities and the Secret Thereof' appear at the end of Chapter One. We know that it was the first chapter which gave Marx the greatest difficulty. He wrote and re-wrote the sections dealing with the value-form, seeking to present in the clearest way possible the contradictory nature of the commodity-form and reveal the results of these contradictions. It is no accident that the section on fetishism appears after those dealing with the value-form and no accident that this section was added as part of Marx's struggle to present the value-form in the most adequate manner. But although there is a separate section dealing with fetishism, it is not as though Marx deals with this matter and then drops it. It is a notion which is present throughout the entire three volumes, and one which he develops and concretizes in these volumes as well as in the *Theories of Surplus Value*. (See also Kemp, 1978, where Marx's conception of fetishism is discussed.)

Fetishism and social being

Let us start by recalling that Marx took the political economists severely to task for having accepted the reified, alienated forms of bourgeois economy at face value, for having failed to inquire into the historical and social basis of these forms. In this critique of the work of his predecessors, Marx rejected all notions which sought to 'derive' value (a social relation) from use-value (a material phenomenon). ('The mystical character of commodities does not originate in their use-value', I, p. 71). In similar fashion, Marx opposed all those views which explained the nature of money in terms of the material-technical properties of gold, just as he poured scorn on all those who sought to understand capital from the technical nature of the means of production. What all these 'errors' had in common for Marx was this: they failed to distinguish between the technical role of the instruments of labour on the one hand, and their social form on the other. For Marx the essence of fetishism was this: under commodity production, relations between men take the form of relations between 'things'. The social relations are *indirect* relations, relations mediated through these things, and men simply 'represent' or 'personify' these things in the market place. Now Marx chastised the political economists for taking these forms 'as given' (by Nature) and not as *social* forms arising under definite historical conditions, forms which would therefore disappear under new social conditions. Those who accept the social relations of capital 'uncritically' in effect attribute to things in their immediate manifestation properties which, in point of fact, have nothing in common with this immediate material manifestation as such. The attention of Ricardo was directed almost exclusively to discovering the material base of definite social forms. These forms of social being were taken as read and therefore lying outside the scope of further analysis. It was Marx's aim to discover the origin and development of these social forms assumed by the material-technical production process at a definite stage in the development of the productive forces. Here, incidentally, is a further clue to the distinction between classical political economy and its later degenerate form in vulgar economy. In the latter case, vulgar political economy, certain properties materially inherent in things are assigned to the social form of these things. Hence the power inherent in the means of production to raise labour productivity – that is the power to increase the production of use-values for a given expenditure of labour-time – is ascribed falsely to *capital*, and by extension, to the *owner* of capital. From this notion comes the apologetic theory of the 'productivity' of capital. Classical economy, on the other hand, ascribed economic forms to the specific property of things. It attempted to derive social phenomena directly from material-technical phenomena. Hence capital was 'stored-up labour', rent arose from the soil, etc. Now whatever the inadequacies of the notion that 'capital is stored-up labour', it at least had the merit over vulgar economy that the connection between 'labour' and 'capital' was kept in sight, even if this connection was misunderstood. In the case of vulgar economy, its apologetic nature reaches its high point with the formula: land–rent, capital–interest, labour–wages. For as we have already noted, in this formula the categories of capitalist production do not face each other as alien, hostile forms, but rather as heterogeneous and different forms. The different revenues are derived from different sources, one from land, one from labour and the other from capital. All notions of any inner connections are obliterated. The three categories work together harmoniously in the cause of production as do the plough and the land. In so far as any contradiction is admitted by the vulgar school, it is one merely concerned with distribution – one about the distribution of the value jointly created by the three agents. As we have seen, it was John Stuart Mill, with his division between conditions of production (fixed by nature and therefore immutable) and conditions of distribution (fixed socially and therefore within limits amenable to modification) who elaborated this aspect of vulgar economy into a system which was taken over by Fabianism and various other brands of reformism. Before turning to look at Marx's notion of fetishism in more detail, we should say a little about the origin of this idea and its connection with the development of Marx's work. The notion of fetishism, sketched out in the *Critique* and more fully in *Capital*, is the product of a long line of development, going back to *The Holy Family* (in Marx and Engels, 1975b), with its contrast between 'social' relations and materialized forms. We find Marx, in this early work, saying that property, capital, money, wage labour and similar categories, do not, in themselves, represent phantoms of the imagination, but very practical, very concrete products of the self-alienation of the worker. The material element, dominating all economic relations, is contrasted with an ideal, with a view of the world as it should be. In *The Poverty of Philosophy* Marx says that 'Economic categories are only the theoretical expressions, the abstractions, of the social relations of production'. Marx, in opposition to Proudhon, now grasped that social relations of production stand behind the material categories of the economy. But he did not yet ask why this relationship was a necessary one under commodity production. It was only with the *Critique* and *Capital* that this problem is thoroughly examined and made the basis of the criticism of political economy as a whole. Now it is explained – and this is the essential point in the notion of fetishism – that the:

> absence of direct regulation of the social process of production necessarily leads to the indirect regulation of the production process through the market, through the products of labour, through things. Here the subject is the 'materialization' of productive relations and not only 'mystification' or illusion.
> (Rubin, 1972, p. 59)

It is especially important to stress this last point – that fetishism is not mere illusion, that 'Fetishism is not only a phenomenon of social consciousness, but of social being' as Rubin (p. 59) correctly puts it. For fetishism is often wrongly equated with mystification, merely an ideological category. (We shall return to this point.) It would of course be quite wrong to see a fully worked-out theory of fetishism in Marx's early writings, but it would be equally one-sided to draw a rigid distinction between Marx's early formulation of this question and its rounded out version in *Capital*, a position in general adopted by the Althusserian school. For one element found in the *Economic and Philosophical Manuscripts of 1844* (Paris Manuscripts, in Marx, 1975a) is returned to throughout all Marx's later work – namely that under capitalist relations, the products of the workers' labour confront him as something coercive and this is a *real* coercion, with a definite material base. This we find in this early work:

> The worker puts his life into the object; but now his life no longer belongs to him but to the object. Hence, the greater this activity, the greater is the worker's lack of objects, whatever the products of his labour is, he is not. Therefore the greater this product, the less is he himself. The alienation of the worker in his product does not only mean that his labour becomes an object, an external existence, but that it exists outside him, independently as something alien to him, *and that it becomes a power of its own confronting him; it means that the life which he has conferred on the object confronts him as something hostile and alien*. (Marx, 1975a; author's italics)

We shall see how this theme, far from being dropped, is enriched and developed in *Capital*.

Rubin is absolutely right to say that fetishism is a phenomenon of social being and because of this alone it is present in consciousness. And this 'social being' is commodity production and commodity production alone. Marx is quite explicit on this point.

> The relation of the producers to the sum total of their own labour is presented to them as a social relation of objects which exists outside them. . . . It is a particular social relation between men themselves which in their eyes assumes a phantasmagorical form of a relation between things. . . . This is what I call fetishism; it attaches itself to the products of

labour as soon as they are produced as commodities, *and it is therefore inseparable from the production of commodities.*
(I, p. 72)

Here Marx indicates clearly that the fetishism of economic relations arises only with commodity production. Of course ideology is not a product of capitalism only; false consciousness is a product of *all* societies divided into classes. But it is only under conditions of capitalism that men's economic relations appear to them in the shape of things. So this form of false consciousness, the fetishization of the economic relations, is unique to commodity-capitalist production. This must be stressed against those who wish to see fetishism as for example a product of the division of labour. According to this view, the division of labour means that the individual interest diverges from the general interest, that the deployment of activity is not determined voluntarily, but by circumstances apparently independent of man. Man's own activity thus becomes, by virtue of this division of labour, an alien force which confronts and enslaves him, something not controlled by him. Each member has an exclusive field of activity; the division of labour means that each individual can only take on a partial view of the social whole. What this view 'misses' is that while it is certainly the case that in all pre-capitalist modes the conditions of production dominate men, only under capitalism does this take the form of the dominance of *things* over men. And these things dominate men not by virtue of a growing division of labour, but because of the social role the products of men's labour actually play. Under capitalism the social relations of production are established by means of the transfer of 'things' from individual to individual. This movement of things is a coercive power over men – for it is through the movement of these 'things' (commodities, money, etc.) that production is organized, and not according to any conscious plan on the part of the producers. Thus in the elementary value-form (20 yards of linen = 1 coat) we have a movement of 'things' but simultaneously a definite transfer of economic forms, of definite activities, activities which correspond to definite social relations of production. So it must be stressed that it is only with commodity production (and of course its developed form, capitalism) that definite economic forms attach themselves to things and develop through these things. Thus, says Marx of pre-capitalist society:

> this economic mystification arose principally with respect to money and interest-bearing capital. In the nature of things it is excluded, in the first place, where production for use-value, for immediate personal requirements, predominates; and secondly, where slavery and serfdom form the broad foundation of social production, as in antiquity and during the Middle Ages. Here the dominance of the producers by the conditions of production is concealed by the relation of dominance and servitude, which appear and are evident as the direct motive power of the process of production.
> (III, p. 810)

Referring to the Middle Ages, Marx notes that:

> The practical and natural form of labour, and not, as in a society based on the production of commodities, its general abstract form is the immediate social form of labour . . . the social relations between individuals in the performance of their labour, appear at all events as their own mutual personal relations, and are not disguised under the shape of social relations between the products of labour. (I, p. 77)

And this same point is made about those early societies:

> in which primitive communism prevailed, and even in the ancient communal towns, it was the communal society itself with its conditions which appeared as the basis of production, and its reproduction appeared as its ultimate purpose. Even in the medieval guild system neither capital nor labour appear untrammelled, but their relations are rather defined by their corporate rules, and by the same associated relations, and corresponding conception of professional duty, craftsmanship etc. (I, p. 77)

These passages (and many others could be cited) express the fact that the uniqueness of bourgeois society consists in the peculiar fact that the most basic relations established between human beings in the social production and reproduction of their lives can be known to them only *after the event* and even then solely in the 'opposed' 'inverted' form of the relations between things. Or rather not 'even then' but precisely because the relations are unplanned, knowable *a posteriori* they can become visible only through the *results* of man's activities, through the things he has produced. Under capitalism, man's reflections on the forms of social life and therefore his scientific investigation of these forms take a path which is not merely *different* but is in fact the *direct opposite* to that of the actual emergence and development of these forms. He begins, as he must, with the result of these activities. That is why, for instance, the proportions in which the products of man's labour exchange, appear, and can only appear, to result from the very nature of the products themselves. Thus: 'The quantities vary continuously, independently of the will, foresight and action of the producers. To them, their own social action takes the form of the action of objects, which rule the producers, instead of being ruled by them' (I, p. 75). It is necessary to keep in mind the fact that when we say that men's social relations of production affix themselves to things, are moved by these things, this is no illusion, to be demystified by some pure thought. Matters appear *necessarily* this way. The inverted form taken by man's consciousness is a *necessary* inversion. It is precisely because fetishism is inherent in commodity production that it cannot be 'demystified' in thought alone but only in practice, in the overthrow of those social relations which create the very conditions for this fetishism. This is how Marx expresses this point.

> The life-process of society, which is based on the process of material production, does not strip off its mystical veil until it is treated as production by freely associated men and is consciously regulated by them in accordance with a settled plan. This however, demands for society a certain material ground-work or set of conditions of existence which in their form are the spontaneous product of a long and painful process of development. (I, p. 80)

Only under communism will fetishism disappear, for it is only under commodity production and above all under capitalism – where production is unplanned, where economic and social crises strike the working class as a kind of natural catastrophe, as something having nothing to do with human activity – that the basis for fetishism exists. As Marx says, the formulae whereby labour is represented indirectly, in fetishistic form, in the value of its product and labour-time represented indirectly by the magnitude of its value, bear stamped upon them the fact 'that they belong to a state of society in which the process of production has the mastery over man, instead of being controlled by him' (I, p. 81).

Disappearance of fetishism

Involved here is the notion that if fetishism will only be finally overcome in a society of freely associated producers, then it is equally true that the transparency of the economic relations of pre-capitalist economy was a product of the backwardness of the productive forces. Marx makes this explicit in the following passage:

> The ancient social organisms of production are extraordinarily much more simple and transparent than the bourgeois organism, but they are based either on the immaturity of the individual man who has not yet torn himself from the umbilicus of the natural species-connection with the other men or based upon an immediate master-slave relationship. They are conditioned by a lower level of the productive powers of labour, by correspondingly restricted relationships of men within their material process of the constitution of their life, and consequently to one another and to nature. (Marx, 1976, p. 38)

Therefore the loss of the transparent quality of the social relations marked by the advent of commodity production – a loss which becomes increasingly pronounced with the development of capitalism – must not be evaluated in purely *negative* terms. For the fact that men's social relations in production become increasingly indirect, the fact that the internal vein connecting man to man becomes more and more embodied in the connection between things, testifies to a *development* of the productive forces. The point here is that while the conditions of production rule producers in ancient, Asiatic, feudal and capitalist economy alike, in the case of pre-capitalist modes, these conditions were more immediately *natural* – climatic changes, soil fertility etc. Under capitalism man gains increasing control over these immediately *natural* conditions (although of course it can never be complete) and this is reflected in the fact that men become increasingly dependent on social conditions to secure their means of life. Under capitalism, the more man gains control over nature the more he becomes dependent on capital. And this dependency takes the form of a growing domination of 'things' over man and his activities. Thus changes in the price of a metal (gold) can, under certain conditions, not only seem to create economic crises – unemployment, currency depreciation, stock collapses, etc. – but actually do result in these phenomena.

As anybody familiar with *Capital* knows, Marx continually draws an analogy between the commodity-form of production and the religious conceptions developed by man. And this is important for us here, because it underlines the fact that the reified character of the products of man's labour just like religion has a definite objective basis in the social relations of production. Religion can never be fully understood if it is regarded merely as an ideological device, carrying a definite function – for instance, to reconcile the masses to the conditions of their exploitation and poverty. Undoubtedly this is one side of religion ('the opium of the people') but for Marx only one side. For the fact must not be lost sight of that religion has definite material roots – it expresses man's inadequate knowledge and control over nature, a lack of development of the productive forces and the fact that in class society he confronts nature indirectly through a set of (antagonistic) social relations. Only the removal of these social relations and conditions can lay the basis for the final disappearance of religious conceptions. Thus 'The *religious reflections* of the real world can only disappear as soon as the practical workaday life represents for men transparently resolvable relationships to one another and to nature' (Marx, 1976, p. 38). Neither religion nor fetishism arise from a wrong way of viewing the world to be righted by the disembodied intellectual who has grasped the 'real' relationship between man and the products of his labour. Just as 'after the discovery by science of the component gases of the air the atmosphere itself remains unaltered' (I, p. 74), in the same way,

The determination of the magnitude of value by labour-time is therefore a secret, hidden under the apparent fluctuations in the relative values of commodities. Its discovery, while removing all appearance of mere accidentality from the determination of the values of products, yet in no way alters the mode in which that determination takes place. (I, p. 75)

Because of many quite erroneous views on the nature and source of fetishism let us consider this last point further by looking at one criticism directed by Marx against Thomas Hodgskin, a member of the 'proletarian opposition' to political economy (Marx, 1972, p. 267), and a writer for whom Marx had much admiration. At one place Hodgskin attacked the notion, prevalent amongst the economists, that the level of employment together with the standard of living of the working class depended on the amount of circulating capital available. Marx quotes from Hodgskin's 'correct' reply. Hodgskin says, 'The number of labourers must at all times depend on the quantity of *circulating capital*; or, as I should say the *quantity of co-existing labour*, which labourers are allowed to consume' (p. 295). And Marx comments:

What is attributable (in the economists' conception) to *circulating capital* to a stock of commodities, is the effect of 'co-existing labour'. In other words, Hodgskin says that the effects of a certain social form of labour are ascribed to objects, to the products of labour; the relationship itself is imagined to exist in *material* form. We have already seen that this is a characteristic of labour based on commodity production, or exchange-value and this *quid pro quo* is revealed in the commodity, in money . . . to a still higher degree in capital, in their personification, their independence in respect of labour. They would cease to have these effects if they were to cease to confront labour in their *alienated form*. The *capitalist*, as capitalist, is simply the personification of capital, that creation of labour endowed with its own will and personality which stands in opposition to labour. (pp. 295–6)

So, for Marx, Hodgskin recognized that political economy made a fetish of the social conditions of capital. But for Hodgskin, Marx proceeds to point out, this fetish was a subjective illusion, an illusion advanced, thought Hodgskin, to cover up the class interest of the owners of capital.

> Hodgskin regards this as a pure subjective illusion which conceals the deceit and the interests of the ruling classes. *He does not see that the way of looking at things arises out of the actual relation itself*; the latter is not an expression of the former, but vice versa. In the same way English socialists say 'we need capital, but not the capitalists'. But if one eliminates the capitalists, the means of production cease to be capital.
> (p. 296; author's italics)

This is a vital point made by Marx against Hodgskin. For it involves questions not so much in economics, as in the Marxist theory of knowledge. If social being determines social consciousness, then this consciousness cannot be reduced to a series of mere 'illusions' or 'mystifications', the product of a distorted way of looking at things. To see the matter this way would amount to sheer idealism. Marx's consciousness is a product of his social being, of his social practice. Thus the manner in which man conceives his social relations, the *form* taken by his consciousness, cannot be divorced from these relations. 'The way of looking at things arises out of the actual relation'. Man's social relations are reflected in his mind and translated into thought-forms. But these social relations are always reflected in thought in an *inverted* form. And this inversion arises from the fact that man's social relations under capitalism are formed without first passing through consciousness. This last point actually provides the criterion whereby Marxism distinguishes between social relations and ideological relations. Speaking of the ideas of that group of Enlightenment thinkers which found classical expression in Rousseau's *Social Contract*, Lenin says:

> So long as they confined themselves to ideological social relations (i.e. such as, before taking shape, pass through man's consciousness) they could not observe recurrence and regularity in the social phenomena of the various countries. . . . The analysis of material social relations (i.e. of those that take shape without passing through man's consciousness: when exchanging products men enter into production relations

without even realising that there is a social relation of production here) at once made it possible to observe recurrence and regularity. (LCW, Vol. 1)

Fetishism as illusion

Thus it is not at all true that the value-relations appearing in the exchange of the products of labour as commodities are not 'really' relations between things, but merely imaginary relations having a mystical quality. This view is directly refuted by Marx in many places, for instance when he says,

> The labour of the individual asserts itself as part of the labour of society, only by means of the relations which the net of exchange establishes directly between the products, and indirectly through them, between the producers. To the latter, therefore, the relations connecting the labour of one individual with that of the rest appear not as direct social relations between individuals at work, *but as what they really are* material relations between persons and social relations between things. (I; author's italics)

This point, that the attachment of the social relations of production to things is no mere illusion, not something to be explained from some self-contained 'ideological sphere', is brought out strikingly by Marx in the *Critique.*

> A social relation of production appears as something existing apart from individual human beings, and the distinctive relations which they enter in the course of production in society appear as the specific properties of a thing – it is this perverted appearance, *this prosaically real, and by no means imaginary* mystification that is characteristic of all social forms of labour positing exchange-value. This perverted appearance manifests itself merely in a more striking manner in money than it does in commodities. (Marx, 1971a, p. 49; author's italics)

It should be clear from the above that (a) Marx understood fetishism as an objective phenomenon, a product of definite social conditions and (b) the basis for overcoming fetishism is provided by the development of the productive forces. From this standpoint it is clearly impossible to treat Marx's notion of fetishism as merely mystification. It is here that once again we must take issue with Althusser. For this is precisely how he treats the notion of fetishism. In his view ideology (false consciousness) is not a product of definite social conditions but something playing what is essentially a functional role in all societies. He tells us, 'Ideology is not an aberration or a contingent excrescence of History: it is a structure essential to the historical life of societies' (Althusser, 1969, p. 232). And it follows necessarily from this that 'historical materialism cannot conceive that even a communist society could ever do without ideology be it ethics, art or "world outlook" '. (Althusser, 1969, p. 232). Ideology, for Marx a product of definite social conditions (and in particular the division between mental and manual labour which arises with class society), is made by Althusser into a product of *all* societies. Fetishism (which Marx sees arising specifically in connection with commodity-capitalist economic forms) can for Althusser have no specific material basis in definite production relations.

One task involved in refuting Althusser's view – which involves amongst other things the attempt to draw a rigid distinction between 'ideology' and 'science' – is to demonstrate how Marx traces the fetishistic forms associated with capitalist economy from their simplest forms to the more complex, which are discussed in *Capital*, Volume III. Here again it is necessary to bring out the connection, the unity, between 'logic' and 'history', of being and social consciousness. If the commodity is the cell-form of *all* the social relations of capital, the embryo out of which all those higher forms historically emerge, then the commodity constitutes also the cell-form for all those 'necessary illusions' which dominate present society. We shall, in dealing with this problem, have to stress one point: Marx does much more than recognize that political economy deals uncritically with reified categories. Nor was he content merely to reveal that the inverted way in which the social relations appear in capitalist society arises from the essence of the social relations of production which form the basis of this society. He wanted to show that the more the capitalist mode of production develops, the more the social relations increasingly confront men as an external dominating power.

> By means of its conversion into an automaton, the instrument of labour confronts the labourer, during the labour-process in the shape of capital, of dead labour, that dominates and pumps dry, living labour-power. The separation of the intellectual powers of production from the manual labour, and the conversion of those powers into the might of capital over labour, is, as we have already shown, finally completed by modern industry erected on the foundation of machinery. The special skill of each individual insignificant factory operative vanishes as an infinitesimal quantity before the science, the gigantic physical forces, and the mass of labour that are embodied in the factory mechanism and, together with that mechanism, constitute the power of the 'master'. (I, p. 423)

And this power is a real, not 'illusory' power. And because it is a real power, it brings *real powers*, the working class, into conflict with it. Marx stresses this point in the course of his discussion 'Machinery and Modern Industry':

> Hence the character of independence and estrangement which the capitalist mode of production gives to the instruments of labour and to the product, as against the workman, is developed by means of machinery into a thorough antagonism. *Therefore it is with the advent of machinery, that the workman for the first time brutally revolts against the instruments of labour.* (I, p. 432; author's italics)

In other words, the very development of the fetishism of the products of man's labour under capitalism − seen in naked form with the emergence of modern industry − brings with it, at the same time, the social force with the potential to bring about an end to this fetishism. History does not set only 'problems', it always, in setting these problems, also brings into being the necessary forces through which these problems can be overcome.

> Mankind thus inevitably sets itself only such tasks as it is able to solve, since closer examination will always show that the problem itself arises only when the material conditions for its

solution are already present or at least in the course of
formation. (Marx, 1971a, p. 21)

So for Marx the growth of fetishism, far from being an indication
of the growing ability of capital to suppress the revolutionary
struggle of the working class, is on the contrary an expression of
the ever-growing contradictions of capitalist society which bring
the working class face-to-face with these contradictions.

> The growing accumulation of capital implies its growing
> concentration. Thus grows the power of capital, the alienation
> of the conditions of social production personified in the
> capitalist, from the real producers. Capital comes more and
> more to the fore as a social power, whose agent is the
> capitalist. This social power no longer stands in any possible
> relation to that which the labour of a single individual can
> create. It becomes an alienated, independent social power
> which stands opposed to society as an object, and as an object
> that is the capitalist's source of power. The contradiction
> between the general social power into which capital develops,
> on the one hand, and the private power of the individual
> capitalists over these social conditions on the other, becomes
> even more irreconcilable and yet *contains the solution of the*
> *problem* because it implies at the same time the
> transformation of the conditions of production into the
> general, common, social, conditions. This transformation
> stems from the development of the productive forces under
> capitalist production, and from the ways and means by which
> this development takes place. (III, p. 259; author's italics)

As we have said, Marx's task was to reveal the origin of this
reification in its most simple form, commodity production. Let us
begin with the simplest expression of this perversion which reaches
its high point in capital – that is with the elementary value form
itself, 20 yards of linen = 1 coat. This is the first expression of the
'externalization' or 'alienation' of the opposition between value
and use-value which exists in every commodity. From this point
all the higher forms of fetishism can be considered as a growth in
the contradiction between the production of use-values and the
social forms through which that production develops. When com-

modities come into the world as use-values this is merely their 'plain, homely, bodily form'.

> They are, however, commodities only because they are something two-fold, both objects of utility and at the same time depositories of value. They manifest themselves therefore as commodities, or have the form of commodities only in so far as they have two forms, a physical or natural form and a value-form. (I, p. 47)

It is this fetishism, inherent in commodities, which is more clearly and strikingly expressed in gold. In making this point, Marx refers to the value-form of the commodity as 'ideal'.

> The price or money-form of commodities is, like their form of value generally, a form quite distinct from their palpable bodily form, it is therefore, a purely ideal or mental form. Although invisible, the value of iron, linen and corn has actual existence in these very articles. (I, p. 95)

Now what does it mean to say that the value-form is 'purely ideal'? Does this mean that, like value, money is purely a mental state, a figment of individual imagination? Clearly this is *not* what Marx means.

The ideality of value

For Marx, value is an expression of a definite social relation. And we know that for Marx social relations were *objective* – therefore value cannot be something present merely in consciousness. Similarly, Marx explicitly rejected the idea that money was a mere symbol, that is, he rejected the notion that money was something purely imaginary, thus 'although gold and silver are not by Nature money, money is by Nature gold and silver'. What does Marx mean therefore, when he tells us that money is a purely ideal form? In his essay 'The Concept of the Ideal', the Soviet philosopher Ilyenkov, in examining this question of Marx's use of the term 'ideal', has done much to throw light on the notion of fetishism (see Ilyenkov, 1977a, pp. 71–99). As he notes, the term 'ideal' is used today largely as a synonym for 'conceivable', phenomena that are represented, imagined and thought. (If we were to follow this definition, as he correctly points out, there would be no point in talking about any 'ideality' existing outside human consciousness.) When Marx uses the term ideal in connection with the value-form, he certainly does not mean something present only in consciousness. On the contrary – and this is Ilyenkov's main point in connection with the value-form – Marx means that the value-form is 'ideal' because it is totally distinct from the palpable, corporeal form of the commodity in which it is *presented*. In other words, the value-form is 'ideal' but certainly exists outside human consciousness. As Ilyenkov states, in what is a clear reference to the degeneration of philosophical work under the impact of Stalinism,

> This use of the term may perplex the reader who is
> accustomed to the terminology of popular essays on
> materialism and the relationship of the material to the 'ideal'.
> The ideal that exists outside people's heads and consciousness,
> as something completely objective, a reality of a special kind
> that is independent of their consciousness and will, invisible,
> inpalpable and sensuously imperceptible, may seem to them
> something that is only 'imagined', something 'supersensuous'.
> (1977a, p. 72)

As Ilyenkov argues, the term 'ideal' in this debased version of materialism, has more in common with Kantianism and the pre-Hegel tradition in philosophy than it has with Hegel (and, by extension, with Marx). For Hegel,

> This relationship of representation is a relationship in which
> one sensuously perceived thing performs the role or function
> of representation of quite another thing, and, to be even more
> precise, the universal nature of that other thing, that is,
> something 'other' which in sensuous bodily terms is quite
> unlike it, and it was this relationship that in the Hegelian
> terminological tradition acquired the title of 'ideality'. (1977a,
> p. 84)

It is clear that if we follow this line, Marx's designation of the value-form as 'ideal' takes on a quite different meaning than it would for a 'simplistic' materialism, and a meaning which throws much light on Marx's notion of fetishism. By 'ideal' Marx in no way means that the value-form exists only in the brain of the commodity owner, but in the fact that the corporeal form of a thing (the coat) is only a form of expression of a quite different 'thing' (linen as a value) with which it has nothing in common. The nature of this linen is *represented*, expressed, embodied, in the form of a coat and the coat is the 'ideal' or 'represented' form of the value of the linen. And far from being something expressed only in consciousness, this representation expresses a relationship entirely objective, which actually determines the behaviour of man without his being aware of it. The social relations under which the linen is produced find their embodiment, their representation, not directly, not immediately, but in the mediated form of the coat. These social conditions are alienated in the form of the coat. The transformation of nature by man which is involved in the production of linen, a definite form of human objective activity, is represented in an 'object', the coat. And this is what Marx means by ideality – the form of human social activity represented in a thing. Ilyenkov puts the point this way:

> 'Ideality' is a kind of stamp impressed on the substance of nature by social human life activity, a form of the functioning of the physical thing in the process of this activity. So all the things involved in the social process acquire a new 'form of existence' that is not included in their physical nature and differs from it completely – their ideal form. (1977a, p. 86)

The commodity form is 'ideal' precisely because it does not include a *single* atom of the substance of the body in which it is represented, because it is the form of quite *another* body. And this other body exists only ideally; the chemical analysis of gold will find within it not a single atom of boot polish. Nevertheless gold 'represents' a hundred tins of boot polish (say), and this representation is performed not in the consciousness of the seller of the polish – it takes place through a market according to forces which in no sense depend on any consciousness of the money-form. Everybody spends money without necessarily being aware of what he is spending. (As Ilyenkov correctly notes, 'In *Capital* Marx quite consciously uses the term "ideal" in this formal meaning that it was given by Hegel, and not in the sense in which it was used by the whole pre-Hegelian tradition.' This example alone serves to show that Marx did far more than 'coquette' with Hegel's terminology.)

It is in this sense that the simplest value-form (20 yards of linen = 1 coat) contains the essence of the fetishism inherent in all bourgeois economic forms. The 'peculiarities' of this form (abstract labour in the linen taking a form directly opposed to it, the concrete labour in the coat, etc.) thus contain the key to grasping the riddle and source of the fetishism of all bourgeois economic forms.

The reification of production relations associated with simple commodity production develops further with money. The 'riddle of the money fetish now becomes dazzling to our eyes', says Marx. In one of his earliest economic writings he had written about the fetish quality of money as follows:

> Why must private property develop into the *money-system*? Because man as a social being must proceed to exchange and because exchange – private property being pre-supposed – must evolve *value*. The mediating process between men engaged in exchange is not a social or human relationship, it is the *abstract relation* of private property to private property and the expression of this abstract relationship is value – whose real existence as value constitutes *money*. Since men engaged in exchange do not relate to each other as men, *things* lose the significance of human personal property. (Marx, 1975a, pp. 212–13)

This was written in 1844 as notes on James Mill's *Elements of Political Economy*. It serves to indicate once more that Marx's notion of fetishism found in *Capital* was a true development of *all* his previous economic writings right back to the 1840s. (It puts Althusser's much vaunted 'epistemological break' into true perspective.) Marx continues:

> The personal mode of existence of money as money – and not only as the inner, implicit, hidden social relationship or *class relationship* between commodities – this mode of existence corresponds more to the essence of money, the more abstract it is, the less it has a *natural* relationship to other commodities, the more it appears as the product and yet the non-product of man.

All the products in a situation of commodity production have first to be exchanged for a third material thing, in order that these commodities can receive their adequate social validation. This material medium has become independent of the world of commodities – this provides the basis for the emergence of money. And it is through this medium of money and through it alone that man's social bond is established. Man carries his social power in his pocket. In this sense, as the power of money grows, it constitutes the 'objective bond of society' the 'real community' as Marx at one point characterizes it. Thus, far from money overcoming the reification inherent in the simplest exchange of two commodities, this fetishism is heightened and intensified. Thus Marx tells us,

> The same contradiction between the particular nature of the commodity as product and its general nature as exchange-value, which created the necessity of positing it doubly, as this particular commodity on the one side and money on the other . . . contains from the beginning the possibility that these two separated forms in which the commodity exists are not convertible into one another. (G, pp. 147–8)

That is, the contradiction between use-value and value is not definitely, finally, resolved in money, it is externalized, made more open, more antagonistic. Not merely does the value of one commodity have to realize its value in another commodity, now, in the money form, *all* commodities have to express their value in *one* single commodity. This reification of social relations is more extreme, but, by this very fact, so is the possibility of crisis. Hence:

> As soon as money has become an external thing alongside the commodity, the exchangeability of the commodity for money becomes bound up with external conditions which may or may not be present, it is abandoned to the mercy of external conditions. (G, p. 147)

And this is not all. In the exchange of commodities further contradictions arise. For the act of exchange is split into two mutually independent acts, namely exchange of commodities for money and exchange of money for commodities – in short purchase and sale (C–M–C). The acts take place at different times and places and their immediate identity is destroyed. If purchase and sale balance, this balance can only be the result of accident, never of conscious will.

> Circulation bursts through all restrictions as to time, place, and individuals, imposed by direct barter, and this it effects by splitting up, into the antithesis of a sale and a purchase, the direct identity that in barter does exist between the alienation of one's own and the acquisition of some other man's product. To say that these two independent and antithetical acts have an intrinsic unity, are essentially one, is the same as to say that this intrinsic oneness expresses itself in an external antithesis. If the interval in time between the two complementary phases of the complete metamorphosis of a commodity becomes too great, if the split between purchase and sale becomes too pronounced, the intimate connection between them, their oneness, asserts itself by producing a crisis. (I, pp. 113–14)

Fetishism and economic crisis

Marx immediately follows this with a passage which underlines the point we are here at pains to stress – that the growing reification of economic relations – the process whereby they are increasingly attached to things and their connection with human labour, man's practice, appears to be less and less immediately obvious, involves the very same process which creates within capitalism the source of its breakdown. That is, the theory of fetishism and theory of capitalist crisis are in *Capital* completely united, *inseparable*.

> The antithesis, use-value and value: the contradictions that private labour is bound to manifest itself as direct social labour, that a particular concrete kind of labour has to pass for abstract human labour; the contradiction between the personification of objects and the representation of persons by things; all these antitheses and contradictions, which are *immanent* [author's emphasis] in commodities, assert themselves and *develop their modes of action in the antithetical phases of the metamorphosis of a commodity*. (G, p. 414)

Purchase and sale are equally essential but 'there must come a moment when the independent form is broken and when their inner unity is established externally through a violent explosion . . . there lies the *germ* of crisis' (G, p. 198). Here is only a *germ*, a 'possibility' of a crisis and further development is required before this possibility is transformed into a reality. Hence 'The conversion of this mere possibility into a reality is the result of a long series of relations, that, from our present standpoint of simple circulation, have as yet no existence' (I, p. 114).

This path, from possibility to reality, is treated by Marx when he traces the growing independence of this money-form, separated from the products it 'represents'. Exchange separates itself out as an independent aspect, cut off from the actual production of commodities. Now commodities are bought not only for consumption but for resale. The obtaining of exchange-value becomes the object of these latter transactions. 'The rise of exchange (commerce) as an independent function torn away from the exchanges corresponds to the rise of exchange-value as an independent entity in money, torn away from products' (G, p. 149). And here the possibility of crisis is now considerably enhanced:

> This doubling of exchange – exchange for the sake of consumption and therefore exchange for exchange – gives rise to a new disproportion. . . . The possibility of commercial crisis is already contained in this separation. But since production works directly for commerce and only indirectly for consumption, it must not only create but also and equally be seized by this incongruity between commerce and exchange for consumption. (G, p. 149)

And finally, the emergence of money as the general equivalent in which all concrete labour is objectified cannot escape the contradiction that while money is a commodity unlike any other particular commodity, it nevertheless does remain a particular commodity. Gold still has to be brought out of the ground, refined, transported, etc. It still has to be produced as a commodity. The opposition of the money-commodity to the world of commodities can never be absolute. As Marx says of money: 'It is not only the exchange-value, but at the same time a particular exchange-value.

Hence a new source of contradictions which make themselves felt in practice' (G, p. 151).

Now of course the analysis of the fetish character of money does not *exhaust* the fetishism of bourgeois economy. This fetishism grows and develops along with the emergence and development of capital. As we have seen, it is a growth in which (a) the social relations between men, based upon their labour, become increasingly obscured, hidden behind the things which this labour produces. The inner connection between these outward forms is increasingly lost and can only be grasped through strict scientific analysis but (b) this development is accompanied, and must be accompanied, by an equal growth in the coercive power of these alienated forms (money, capital, etc.) which increasingly stand as oppressive forces, opposed to the needs of the working class. So the increasing 'reification' of these forms goes hand-in-hand with the conditions for their overthrow. The growing social power of capital brings it increasingly into conflict with the needs of society as a whole. The growth of this fetishism inherent in commodity production reaches its consummate expression in interest-bearing capital (M–M′). This, says Marx, is the 'mystification of capital in its most extreme form' (Marx, 1972, p. 494). And elsewhere,

> of all these forms, the most complete fetish is *interest-bearing capital*. This is the original starting point of capital-money and the formula M-C-M′ is reduced to its true extremes M-M′, money which creates more money. It is the general formula of capital reduced to a meaningless résumé. (1972, p. 453)

Interest-bearing capital is capital which 'no longer bears any birth mark of its origin'; it represents 'the perversion and objectification of productive relations to the highest degree'; it is 'only form without content' (1972, p. 384).

In a very interesting passage Marx deals with the various forms of capital in order to demonstrate that this interest-bearing capital is the automatic fetish, where money appears to breed money, where capital appears able to expand without reference to any natural-objective factors such as the length of the working day, size of the proletariat, etc. To illustrate his point, Marx takes the elements of the Trinity Formula in full:

The *land* or *nature* as the source of *rent* i.e. landed property is fetishistic enough. But as a result of a convenient confusion of use-value with exchange-value the common imagination is still able to have recourse to the productive power of nature itself, which, by some kind of hocus-pocus, is personified in the landlord. (1972, p. 454)

Marx turns next to the formula 'Labour is the source of wages', and demonstrates that here there is a confusion between labour as a material activity and labour in a definite social form. However, despite this,

the common conception is so far in accord with the facts that even though labour is confused with wage-labour and, consequently, wages, the product of wage-labour with the product of labour, it is nevertheless obvious to anybody who has commonsense that labour itself produces its own wages. (1972, p. 454)

Similarly, when capital is considered as part of the *productive process*, it still continues to be regarded as an instrument for acquiring the labour of others, and 'here the relationship of the capitalist to the worker is always presupposed and assumed'. (1972, p. 454). And even though in the case of merchant capital, capital appearing in the process of circulation where ideas that profit arises from swindling, 'buying cheap and selling dear', etc. – even here profit is explained as a result of exchange, that is, arising from a social relation and not from a thing (1972 p. 454). Quite different is interest-bearing capital:

It is capital in its finished form – as such representing the unity of the productive process and the circulation process [here is the subject of Volume III] and therefore yields a definite profit in a definite period of time. In the form of interest-bearing capital only this function remains, without the mediation of either productive process or circulation process. . . . Interest-bearing capital is the consummate *automatic fetish*, the *self-expanding* value, the money making money, and in this form no longer bears any trace of its origin. The social relation is consummated as a relation of things (money, commodities) to themselves. (1972, p. 454)

Marx deals with these forms in Volume III but the actual growth of the fetishism is traced throughout the entire work. Considering 'the road travelled by capital before it appears in interest-bearing capital' (1972, p. 481), Marx examines the connection between the circulation process and the creation of surplus value. Whereas, in the immediate production process, the relationship is still very obvious or cannot be misunderstood, 'The circulation process obliterates and obscures the connection. Since here the mass of surplus-value is also determined by the *circulation time of capital*, an element foreign to labour-time seems to have entered' (1972, p. 482). And when we come to profit (as distinct from surplus value) the inner connection between labour-time and the economic forms is even more obscured and reified in things.

> This profit is first received for a definite period of circulation of capital, and this period is distinct from the labour-time; it is secondly, surplus-value calculated and drawn not on the part of capital from which it originates directly, but quite indiscriminately on the total capital. In this way its source is completely concealed. Thirdly, although the mass of profit is still quantitatively identical in the first form of profit with the mass of surplus-value produced by the individual capital, the rate of profit is, from the very beginning, different from the rate of surplus-value; since the rate of surplus-value is s/v and the rate of profit is s/c+v. Fourthly, if the rate of profit is presumed given, it is possible for the rate of profit to rise or fall and even to move in the opposite direction to the rate of surplus-value. (1972, p. 482)

The price of production and fetishism

And the matter becomes even more obscured when we consider the *average* rate of profit and with it the conversion of values into cost prices. Here,

> the profit of individual capital becomes *different* from the surplus-value produced by the individual capital in its particular sphere of production, and *different*, moreover, not only in the way it is expressed – i.e. rate of profit as distinct

from rate of surplus-value – but it becomes substantially different, that is, in this context, quantitatively *different*. (1972, pp. 482–3)

In this form of profit:

> Capital more and more acquires a material form, is transformed more and more from a relationship into a thing, but a thing which embodies, which has absorbed, the social relationship, a thing which has acquired a fictitious life and independent existence in relationship to itself, a natural-supernatural entity; and in this form of *capital* and *profit* it appears superficially as a ready-made precondition. It is the form of its reality, or rather its real form of existence. And it is the form in which it exists in the consciousness and is reflected in the imagination of its representatives, the capitalists. (1972, p. 483)

The point here is this: the formation of 'prices of production' constitutes a more perverted and estranged form than 'value' for now, outwardly, the price of production depends not upon labour, but upon capital. This development of fetishism is a reflection not only of increasing mystification but of the contradictory development of the social relations of production. That the formation of an average rate of profit – and the contradiction this entails between value and price – is itself engendered by the development of the productive forces was many times stressed by Marx. Thus:

> What competition, first in a single sphere achieves, is a single market value and market price derived from the various individual values of commodities. And it is competition of capitals in different spheres which first brings out the price of production equalising the rate of profit in the different spheres. *The latter process requires a higher development of capitalist production than the previous one.* (III, p. 177; author's italics)

It is because of the growing disparity in the organic composition of capitals between and within industries, that values are transformed into production prices. The regulator of capital accumulation, the establishment of an average rate of profit, *demands* a deviation, a 'contradiction' between price and value; this is a contradiction made not in thought but in material reality. In this form, 'price of production', is reflected the growing social power of capital. For now the capitalists *as a class* take part in the exploitation of the working class *as a class*. Expressed in this 'thing' the price of production, is the growing antagonism between the two major classes, an antagonism raised to the level of society *as a whole*:

> In each sphere [it transpires that] the individual capitalist, as well as the capitalists as a whole, take part in the exploitation of the total working class by the totality of capital and in the degrees of that exploitation not only out of general class sympathy, but also for direct economic reasons. For, assuming all other conditions . . . to be given, the average rate of profit depends on the intensity of exploitation of the sum total of labour by the sum total of capital. (III, p. 193)

In this form (production prices) Marx notes 'capital becomes conscious of itself as a *social power* in which every capitalist participates proportionally in his share of the total social capital'. (III, p. 191). The capitalists now become communists, as Marx wryly observes. But at the same time the material conditions are laid for the *unity* of the working class in its sturggle against the entire capitalist class.

Enough has been said about these forms of surplus value to reveal the truth of Marx's proposition that economics is not concerned with things, but with relations between people, and in the last resort between classes, but that these relations 'are always bound to things and appear as things' (Engels). In place of the fetishized categories which bourgeois social science uncritically adopted, Marx presented a quite different conception of the process of social production, that is, one which started not with a view of things 'in themselves' but a process in which men, in unity with nature and with other men, continually renew both themselves and the world of wealth which they create. As Rubin has rightly said, this revolutionary conception of the scope and nature of political economy involved drawing a consistent distinction between productive forces and productive relations, between the material process of production on the one hand and its social form on the other. It is under capitalism (as it develops out of commodity production) that these social relations acquire a material form and because of this the 'things' to which the social relations are attached play a definite social role: as the 'bearer' of the given social relations. The basic notions of political economy express the essence of the various social-economic *forms* which in turn express the developing production relations between the classes in capitalist society. As Rubin has said, 'some of these relations between and among people presuppose the existence of other types of production relations among the members of a given society and the latter do not necessarily presuppose the existence of the former' (1972, Ch. 4). He gives, as an example, the relationship between finance and industrial capital (*ibid.* p. 32). This relationship involves industrial capital's receiving loans from finance capital; but presupposed here, or more accurately, *sublated* here are the relations between industrial capital and wage labour. On the other hand this latter relationship — between industrial capital and wage labour — does not *necessarily* involve relations between industrial and finance capital. From this it is clear that the economic categories 'capital' and 'surplus value' precede the categories 'interest-bearing' capital and 'interest'. To take this point further, the relations between industrial capital and the working class take the form of the sale and purchase of labour-power. Sublated here are the relations of simple commodity producers without which the buying and selling of labour-power would, of course, be impossible.

The functions of money

We have noted in several places that in Marx's opinion classical economic theory had singularly failed to grasp the nature of money.[2] And the confusion which surrounded this problem amongst the leading bourgeois economists in the first decades of the nineteenth century found its reflection amongst the theoreticians of the working class. This is clear in Marx's polemics against Proudhon and his analysis of the writings of the English socialists on the nature of money. The mistakes committed by these writers amounted, in essence, to a failure to understand the fetishism inherent in money; or where there was some inkling of this fetishism (Hodgskin has already been mentioned), its source was not appreciated. We can therefore conveniently draw together some of the points made about Marx's notion of alienation by considering the functions performed by money in capitalist economy as well as the mistakes made by Marx's opponents on this question. For Marx, money fulfils the following functions:

1 Measure of value
2 Medium of commodity circulation
3 Means of accumulation (hoarding)
4 Means of payment
5 World money

Right from the start we should be careful to realize that Marx is not 'defining' money in any abstract sense. 'It is not a question here of definitions which things must be made to fit. We are dealing here with definite functions which must be expressed in definite *categories*' (II, p. 230). This point, which has considerable importance for Marx's method as a whole, applies entirely to his notion of money. Marx, in his treatment of the functions of money, is actually pointing to the role which money, appearing as a thing, plays in the organization of the social relations of capitalist production. As with all his categories, the functions of money express production relations and the various functions represent the changes taking place in the production relations which the development of capitalism brings. This is stressed by Marx when he says,

> The particular functions of money which it performs, either as the mere equivalent of commodities, or as a means of circulation or means of payment, as hoard, or as universal money, *point, according to the extent or relative preponderance of the one function or another, to very different stages in the process of social production.* (I, p. 170; author's italics)

Here once more is expressed the great gap separating Marx from vulgar political economy. Conventional economic thought contents itself with enumerating various types of money systems, some of which exist in reality, others merely in the imagination. Marx used to remark ironically how proud the economists were with the discovery that money was a commodity. But vulgar economy has forgotten even this discovery of its predecessors. For economic theory, especially since the collapse of the Gold Standard in the 1930s, the commodity is only one of a number of possible money-forms. On this view we seem to be offered a choice, as if we were able to select the most suitable money-type after considering all the advantages and disadvantages of the various possible alternatives. Needless to say, all such 'theories' are quite devoid of any historical sense. Neither money, nor any of the various functions it fills, are the result of 'discoveries'; the various money systems did not arise because people consciously weighed their comparative advantages. They have all emerged out of definite social relations, or, more specifically, out of the contradictions of commodity production and circulation. For Marx, money reflects definite social relations, a point emphasized by Rubin when, in his discussion of the nature of fetishism, he deals with the various functions of money in the following way:

1 If the transfer of goods from sellers to buyers and the inverse transfer are carried out simultaneously, then money assumes the function, acts as, a 'medium of circulation'.

2 If the transfer of goods *precedes* the transfer of money, and the relation between sellers and buyers is transformed into a relation between debtor and creditor, then money has now assumed the form of a 'means of payment'.

3 If the seller keeps the money which he receives from his sale, postponing the moment when he enters a new relationship as a purchaser, then money has acquired the function-form of a 'hoard'.

4 Once the emergence of capitalism takes place and a relationship between a commodity owner (capitalist) and a commodity owner (the worker selling his labour power) is established through the transfer of money, then money has become transformed into *capital*. The money which directly connects the capitalist with the worker plays the role, or takes the form of 'variable capital'. But to establish the necessary relationship with the worker, the capitalist must of necessity possess means of production, or money with which to buy the means of production. In this form money plays the role of 'constant capital'.

Here are expressed the various 'sides' or 'aspects' of money, as they have actually come into being. Marx's task (as with all the reified forms of bourgeois economy) was to grasp the historical character of the various functional forms of money, or its 'conceptually determined forms of existence', as the *Grundrisse* puts it. So the various functions of money cannot be reduced to a series of formal definitions, akin to those encountered in conventional textbooks of economics. The functions dealt with in *Capital* were the ones which money has actually played (and continues to play) in the evolution of bourgeois economy. The properties of money were abstracted from history. Thus the first specific form of money lies in its function as a measure of value – the first because it emerges directly from commodity circulation 'The principal difficulty in the analysis of money is surmounted as soon as it is understood that the commodity is the origin of money' (I, p. 64). And all the functions, as evolved in Marx's analysis, must be seen in the same way – as expressions, in the alienated form of this metal, of definite social relations. As commodity production develops so money assumes its various roles, revealing its essential quality in its highest form as world money, universal money.

> It is only in the markets of the world money acquires to the full extent the character of the commodity whose bodily form is also the immediate social incarnation of human labour in the abstract. Its real mode of existence in this sphere adequately corresponds to its ideal concept. (I, p. 142)

All the mistakes of political economy in connection with money take the following basic form: one aspect of money, one of its several functions, is isolated from the rest and elevated to the rank of being the *defining* function of money, one from which all the rest can be derived. Rosdolsky quotes H. Black, a critic who none the less appears to have some insight into Marx's work,

> The strict division of these functions from the substance of money (social value) and likewise the separation of the functions from one another, is a striking feature of Marx's theory of money. Other theoreticians define money as a means of commerce, a unit of account, a means of exchange or a means of payment, i.e. they elevate one particular function to the position of being the determining function on money and then somehow derive all the remaining functions from the main one. In contrast to this Marx strictly separates the

essence of money from the services which it is able to perform, owing to its particular character. (Rosdolsky, 1977, p. 135)

But if political economy derived the functions of money from one basic function this derivation was necessarily devoid of any historical content. And for Marx this mistake – which led to a confusion of money's various functions – is one concerned not with economic theory as such, but again involves philosophical questions. For political economy, as we have seen, the social relations of capital were fixed by Nature. It was the very nature of 'things' which determined the social relations of capital. The political economists did not grasp that these 'things' were the bearers of historically changing and developing social relations and therefore the changing *social* function of these 'things' (money, means of production, etc.) had to be examined. For Marx the various functions of money, as they had evolved, represented the development of the social relations of modern society. This is why *all* the various functions of money, in their transition and interconnection, had to be investigated. To abstract merely one function of money (as instrument of circulation, means of accumulation) was, in effect, to deny the historical character of bourgeois social relations. For this had the result of isolating this 'thing' (gold) from that totality of social relations which this metal, in its diverse functions, represented. To grasp the role of money in modern society (that is to grasp it concretely) it was necessary to *combine* its many abstract properties into a series of concepts. This is why the essence of money only emerges at its highest level when it fulfils the role of *world* money and hence 'Its real mode of existence in this sphere adequately corresponds to its ideal concept.'

Mistakes of the type we have mentioned were clearly evident in the metalist theory of money, a theory which is associated with the early development of capitalism. The early representatives of this school, such as Thomas Mun (1571–1641), held that gold and silver were the only true forms of wealth, trade capital the only legitimate form of capital, and they confined the functions of money to the single one as a means of accumulation (money as a hoard). They attempted to explain this single function of gold by reference to its very nature. In replying to these ideas, Marx shows that objects of one kind or another only assume the various functional forms of money as the social relations demand. This the adherents of metalism failed to grasp. Contemporary metalists aim to show, but without success, that the instability of capitalist economy and its contradiction can be eliminated and capitalism rescued by means of the 'miraculous' power of gold.

Marx's treatment of 'money as hoard' also brings out another important point connected with the question of fetishism. When we said that Marx 'combined' the abstract properties of money, this should not be taken to mean that he eclectically pulled together the various functions of money as they had existed historically. This 'combination' is always undertaken from the standpoint of developed capitalist relations. (The analogy of the relationship of ape to man holds fully here.) The hoard is, in one respect, the clearest form of money's anatomy. But although the formation of hoards is a process common to all commodity production, it constitutes an end in itself only where this commodity production remains underdeveloped — that is, where it has not reached the level of capitalist commodity production. This is so because the less intensively and extensively has commodity production developed, the more does money appear as actual wealth, wealth as such, wealth in general. The accumulation of wealth in the form of the precious metals precedes the accumulation of wealth in the form of other commodities. This is due to the natural properties of the noble metals — their durability, etc. Under developed capitalist conditions hoarding continues and money, in one of its functions, plays the role of hoard, as one of the means of accumulation. But this role is now qualitatively different. The same object (metal) now assumes a quite new role, expressing quite new, more developed, social relations. Needless to say, therefore, these social relations can in no way be deduced from the natural qualities of this metal. Now the function of money as hoard must be understood from the point of view of the circuit of capital in general (M–C–M'). Hoarding is now a resting place in this process. Whereas in pre-capitalist economy the accumulation of hoards signified wealth, now their over-accumulation signifies stagnation, a withdrawal from the circuit of capital, an interruption in the process of their metamorphosis. Thus:

Countries in which the bourgeois form of production is developed to a certain extent, limit the hoards concentrated in the strong room of the banks to the minimum required for the proper performance of their peculiar functions. Whenever these hoards are strikingly above their average level, it is, with some exceptions, an indication of stagnation in the circulation of commodities, of an interruption in the even flow of their metamorphosis. (I, p. 145)

Ricardo's notion of money

This same mistake — taking one particular function of money out of its real historical context and deriving the rest from it — was made by Ricardo and his school, although from a different angle than in the case of metalism. The error committed by Ricardo consisted of the fact that he raised to the level of dogma that money was merely a medium of circulation. According to Ricardo's conception, money is only an instrument for the circulation of commodities. It was not, for him, a necessary form of the existence of the commodity in which the contradictory nature of the labour embodied in the commodity (abstract and concrete labour) must manifest itself in exchange-value, as general social labour. Money was, for the Ricardians, a means for effecting the union of purchase and sale, of the buyers and sellers of *products*. The exchange of commodities was transformed unwittingly into the mere *barter* of products, of simple use-values. This represented a return not only to pre-capitalist production relations, but even to conditions prior to simple commodity production. Circulation, like all economic relations, has two aspects, closely related. In so far as this circulation transfers commodities from those for which they constitute non-use-values to those for whom they are use-values, this process consists simply of the appropriation of objects for human needs. However, to the extent that this process takes place through private exchange, mediated by money, and the relations between these commodities (and indirectly the buyers and sellers of the commodities themselves) to one another are objectified in the different forms of money, then it gives rise to definite social relations. Marx is careful to distinguish these two aspects, making the latter the subject matter of political economy. But Ricardo reduces this latter relationship to the former. And implied here was the denial of any possibility of capitalist crisis. This was so precisely because the first, basic, condition of capitalist production, is that the product of labour must assume the commodity-form, and therefore this product must express itself in the alienated form of money.

> Since the transformation of the commodity into mere use-value (product) obliterates the essence of exchange-value, it is just as easy to deny, or rather it is necessary to deny, that *money* is an essential aspect of the commodity and that in the process of metamorphosis it is *independent* of the original form of the commodity. (Marx, 1971b, pp. 501–2)

This same point is made against vulgar economy with even more force.

> With regard to this subject, we may notice two methods characteristic of apologetic economy. The first is the identification of the circulation of commodities with the direct barter of the products, by simple abstraction from their points of difference; the second is, the attempt to explain away the contradictions of capitalist production, by reducing the relations between the persons engaged in that mode of production, to the simple relations arising out of the circulation of commodities. The production and circulation of commodities are, however, phenomena that occur to a greater or lesser extent in modes of production the most diverse. If we are acquainted with nothing but the abstract categories of circulation, which are common to all these modes of production, we cannot possibly know anything of the specific points of difference of these modes, nor pronounce any judgement upon them. In no science is such a big fuss made with commonplace truisms. For instance, J. B. Say sets himself up as a judge of crises, because, forsooth, he knows that a commodity is a product. (I, footnote, p. 114)

It was the ahistorical, formal view of money which Ricardo developed into the quantity theory of money. This theory, which affirms that the value of money (be it gold or paper) is determined exclusively by the quantity of it in circulation, took shape in the eighteenth century. Its principal exponent at that time was Hume, who held that money lacked any innate value, that its value arose solely as a result of its functioning as currency. With Ricardo's view of the essence of money one can see yet another example of the inconsistency of his economic theory. From the standpoint of the law of value he held that gold and silver did indeed have an innate value, determined (as in the case of all commodities generally) by the quantity of labour involved in their production. At the same time he held that gold coins had more or less value according to the number in circulation and that, as the quantity of gold increased, its value would fall. Here was a clear deviation from Ricardo's value theory. Reducing the essence of money to a simple function (instrument of circulation) the upholders of the quantity theory of money confused the laws of full-value gold money and token money (paper money) and wrongly assumed that any quantity of full-value gold money could be in circulation at any one moment. From this it followed that commodities entered circulation without a price and money without a value, and that prices of commodities altered according to the quantity of money on the market. In criticizing this theory, Marx shows that only the quantity of full-value money actually needed enters circulation and this quantity is fixed spontaneously, according to the law of value. Money (gold) has its own value, formed in production before the process of circulation. It fulfils its function as the measure of value of commodities *before* the direct act of purchase and sale. Marx says,

> The first chief function of money is to supply commodities with the material for the expression of their values, or to represent their values as magnitudes of the same denomination, qualitatively equal, and quantitatively comparable. It thus serves as a *universal measure of value.* And only by virtue of this function does gold, the equivalent commodity *par excellence* become money. (I, p. 94)

Commodities therefore enter circulation with a price and money with a specific value and it is thus impossible for the quantity of gold money to be more or less than that needed. Hence the depreciation of monetary gold in the seventeenth century (to which those adhering to the quantity theory usually referred) was the result not of a surplus of gold in circulation, but of an increase in the productivity of labour in gold mining and a consequent fall in the *value* of gold.

This inability to see in money the universal measure of value led not only to a series of mistakes about the determination of the general price level. It was directly connected with Ricardo's false search for an invariable measure of value. This is a problem we have already looked at, but can return to briefly in the light of the discussion of fetishism. To insist, as we have done, that fetishism is a phenomenon of the very *being* of capital amounts to exactly the same as insisting that the 'measurement' of all commodities in one alienated (money) commodity is an objective, necessary process and not the 'invention' of man. All those who think there can be some invariable measure of value in fact completely misunderstand the nature of capital. It is because man's production relations are indirect, relations mediated through things, that there can never be any invariable measure of value, be it 'labour', 'money' or the currently fashionable Sraffian 'standard commodity'. Values are measured spontaneously, becoming embodied in one commodity (money) because the production relations are not, and cannot be, planned in advance. To deny this is to deny one of the basic qualities of capitalism as a mode of production. The task of true science here is therefore not to invent fictitious 'measures' but to demonstrate how this spontaneous process of measurement actually takes place. The neo-Ricardian school does not even begin to understand this point. All those who wish to discover some standard of value in effect want to transform capitalism into a system capable of conscious planning. In short they want to retain capital while removing its contradictions. Stressing the need for money as a 'thing' in which the values of all commodities must be alienated, Marx says,

> To the owner of a commodity, every other commodity is, in regard to his own, a particular equivalent, and consequently his own commodity is the universal equivalent for all others. But since this applies to every owner, there is, in fact, no commodity acting as universal equivalent, and the relative value of commodities possesses no general form under which they can be equated as values and have the magnitude of their

values compared. So far, therefore, they do not confront each other as commodities, but only as products or use-values. (I, p. 86)

How is this contradiction resolved? Not through the 'invention' by men of some invariable measure of value of the sort after which Ricardo searched. The problem is solved in practice, spontaneously:

> In their difficulties our commodity owners think like Faust: 'Im Anfang war die That'. ['In the beginning was the deed'] They therefore acted and transacted before they thought. Instinctively they conform to the laws imposed by the nature of commodities. They cannot bring their commodities into relation as values, and therefore as commodities, except by comparing them with some other commodity as the universal equivalent. (I, p. 86)

And Marx stresses that this process whereby all commodities find their representation is one alienated commodity is a social act:

> a particular commodity cannot become the universal equivalent except by a social act. The social action therefore of all other commodities, sets apart the particular commodity in which they all represent their values. Thereby the bodily form of this commodity becomes the form of the socially recognized universal equivalent. (I, p. 86)

There is here no question of gold being an invariable measure of value. Quite the contrary: precisely because gold is a commodity its value must fluctuate. Its fluctuation in no way impairs its function as a standard of prices. Nor does it interfere with its functions as a measure of value for 'The change affects all commodities simultaneously, and, therefore *caeteris paribus*, leaves their relative values *inter se*, unaltered, although those values are expressed in a higher or lower gold price. (I, p. 98).

This futile search for a standard of value for the 'economist's stone', should perhaps enable us to put into some perspective the work of those who believe that Marx's work suffers from precisely the absence of such a standard. It is no accident that there is no trace of the notion of fetishism in the work of what might be called the 'Sraffa School' which has returned to Ricardo for some answers to the current crisis in economic theory. For it is precisely this school which has grappled with what we have tried to show is a quite mistaken problem – namely the search for some abstract standard of value – be it a 'standard' or 'composite' commodity. Nor is it any accident that this school has 'discovered' (one hundred years after Marx!) that capital is a social relation. No doubt this is a welcome advance over the orthodox conception that capital is a stock of goods used in the production of other goods. But in the light of what we have tried to show it must be said that it is quite inadequate merely to stress that capital is no mere thing but a social relation. This was not Marx's position: he insisted always that capital was a social relation, but one affixed to 'things'. Marx's qualification to Galiani involved no small quibble. For in this caveat to Galiani is expressed the essential point of Marx's notion of fetishism, a notion which is fundamental to his entire analysis of capitalist economy.

Notes

1 Introduction

1 We cannot here go into all the details of this degeneration. But it was Stalin's now notorious *Dialectical and Historical Materialism*, first published in 1938, which controlled all philosophical activity in the USSR for almost twenty years. Printed in over 200 million copies, this pamphlet stultified all creative work in the field of philosophy and did much to discredit Marxism. What is important to note about Stalin's pamphlet is that it attempted rigidly to separate out the Marxist 'method' from philosophical materialism. Thus Stalin writes about dialectical materialism as follows: 'It is called dialectical materialism because its approach to the phenomena of nature, its method of studying and apprehending them, is *dialectical*, while its interpretation of the phenomena of nature, its conception of these phenomena, its theory, is *materialistic*' (Stalin, 1950, p. 5). Stalin went on, in the next paragraph, to speak of historical materialism as an 'application' of the principles of dialectical materialism to the study of society and its history. Stalin's position is a direct repudiation of Lenin's position in the *Philosophical Notebooks*, where he insists throughout on the unity of dialectics, logic and epistemology and where he continually stresses that concepts are not applied to nature and society but on the contrary must be *abstracted* from reality. Under Stalin all serious work on the elaboration of the categories of materialist dialectics ceased and Hegel's philosophy was largely ignored or in extreme cases condemned as an aristocratic reaction to the French Revolution and to French materialism. Once more this was a direct negation of Lenin's stance. In his essay 'On the Significance of Militant Materialism' (LCW, Vol. 33) written in connection with the launching of the journal *Under the Banner of Marxism* in 1922, Lenin had proposed that those associated with the journal should constitute themselves into a kind of 'Society of Militant Friends of the Hegelian Dialectics'.

197

2 Marx's critique of classical economics

1 An earlier, shortened, version of the material in this chapter appeared as 'What is Revolutionary in Marx's *Capital?*' in *Labour Review*, vol. 1, no. 5, pp. 279–95

2 For Keynes's discussion of his definition of classical economics, see his *General Theory* (1936), footnote, p. 1.

3 There we find the following: 'Once for all I may here state, that by classical Political Economy, I understand that economy which, since the time of W. Petty, has investigated the real relations of production in bourgeois society, in contradistinction to vulgar economy, which deals with appearances only, ruminates without ceasing on materials long since provided by scientific economy, and there seeks plausible explanations of the most obtrusive phenomena, for bourgeois daily use, but for the rest, confines itself to systematising in a pedantic way, and proclaiming for everlasting truths, the trite ideas held by the self-complacent bourgeoisie with regard to their own world, to them the best of all possible worlds.'

4 It was this side of Smith's value theory which was taken up by Malthus and the apologetic wing of political economy and was developed into the utility theory of price.

5 In his *In Defence of Marxism* Trotsky takes up a philosophical struggle against this non-Marxist method of analysing the class nature of the USSR. His leading opponent in this dispute was James Burnham, later famous as author of *The Managerial Revolution*. Burnham's book was based largely upon Bruno Rizzi's work of 1933 *La Bureaucratisation du monde*. In connection with Rizzi, Trotsky says, 'Bruno R. places both the Soviet and fascist regimes under the category of "bureaucratic collectivism", because the USSR, Italy and Germany are all ruled by bureaucracies: here there are the principles of planning; in one case private property is liquidated, in another limited, etc. Thus on the basis of the *relative* similarity of *certain* external characteristics of different origin, of *different* specific weight, of *different* class significance, a fundamental identity of social regimes is constructed, completely in the spirit of bourgeois professors who construct categories of "controlled economy", "centralised state", without taking into consideration whatsoever the class nature of one or the other. Bruno R. and his followers, or semi-followers like Burnham, at best remain in the sphere of social classification on the level of Linaeus, in whose justification it should be remembered however that he lived before-Hegel, Darwin and Marx' (Trotsky, 1966, p. 68). This same method, characterized elsewhere by Trotsky as the purely normative method in sociology, still passes for much Marxist analysis of the USSR.

6 In connection with the argument which follows see Ilyenkov's

Dialectical Logic: Essays on its History and Theory, particularly chapter 10. The whole of this work should be read in that it represents a conscious effort to re-examine the relationship between Hegel and Marx in a manner quite different from that found in Soviet philosophy during the period of Stalinist orthodoxy. Although taking up a series of issues in the history of philosophy, Dr Ilyenkov's work has direct bearing on an appreciation of the method of *Capital*. One of the virtues of the book is that it goes back to Lenin's *Philosophical Notebooks* for its starting point and throughout stresses that logic, being dialectical, is not confined to the science of 'thinking' but embraces also the science of the development of all things, both material and 'spiritual'. Not only is Ilyenkov repudiating neo-positivism, in whose hands logic became a purely technical discipline, a description of systems of manipulations with the terms of language, but also Stalinism with its notion of dialectics as a 'method' separate from the movement of the world. Ilyenkov's work has a direct relationship to the themes we are discussing in that he consistently draws attention to the opposition between dialectics and a purely formal logic. He demonstrates that the old (pre-Hegelian) logic could not investigate the forms of thought scientifically because it took them to be universally valid, and therefore separate from man's practice and devoid of content. Against this, 'Dialectics . . . was the form (or method or schema) of thought that included both the process of elucidating contradictions and of concretely resolving them in the corpus of a higher and more profound stage of rational understanding of the same object, on the way toward further investigation of the essence of the matter' (p. 190).

7 This point is true of Ricardo's entire procedure. Thus the question 'how from the mere determination of the "value" of the commodities their surplus-value, the profit and even a general rate of profit are derived remains obscure to Ricardo' (Marx, 1969, p. 190). And this same confusion, arising from the lack of any notion of mediation between essence and phenomenon, was true in the case of Ricardo's conception of the relationship of surplus value to profit. Thus 'Where he correctly sets forth the laws of surplus value, he distorts them by immediately expressing them as laws of profit. On the other hand, he seeks to present the laws of profit directly, without the intermediate links, as laws of surplus-value' (Marx, 1971b, p. 374).

8 Marx always stressed that in the categories of political economy were expressed real social contradictions. And the *opposition* to political economy – in the shape of both utopian socialism and the vulgar school – reflected these very same social contradictions. Thus 'the development of political economy and the opposition to which it gives rise keeps pace with the real development of social

contradictions and class conflicts inherent in capitalist production
. . . *Ricardo* and the further advance in political economy caused by
him provides new nourishment for the vulgar economist (who does
not produce anything himself): the more economic theory is
perfected, that is the deeper it penetrates its subject matter and the
more it develops as a contradictory system, the more it is
confronted by its own, increasingly independent, vulgar element,
enriched with material which it dresses up in its own way until
finally it finds its most apt expression in academically syncretic and
unprincipled eclectic compilations. To the degree that economic
analysis becomes more profound it not only describes
contradictions but it is confronted by its own contradictions
simultaneously with the development of the actual contradictions in
the economic life of society. Accordingly, vulgar political economy
deliberately becomes increasingly *apologetic* and makes strenuous
attempts to talk out of existence the ideas which contain the
contradictions' (Marx, 1972, p. 501).

9 As this idea is important for their work as a whole, it is important
to show that Cutler *et al.*'s contention that the law of value holds
for every form of society has no basis in Marx's writings. In *Anti-
Dühring* (to which Marx contributed a chapter and which he read
in the manuscript) Engels deals with this very point. In the chapter
'Distribution' he says (1947, part III, ch. IV), 'Commodity
production . . . is by no means the only social form of production.
In the ancient Indian communities and in the family communities of
the southern Slavs, products are not transformed into commodities.
The members of the community are *directly* associated for
production; the work is distributed on the basis of tradition and
requirements and likewise the products in so far as they are
destined for consumption. Direct social production and direct
distribution exclude all exchange of commodities, therefore also the
transformation of the products into commodities . . . and
consequently also their transformation into values' (author's italics).
Engels is here underlining a point implicitly denied by Cutler *et al.*,
namely that the category value reflects a situation where the
relations between men assume the fetishized form of relations
between the products of their labour. In a letter to Kautsky written
in September 1884 Engels is even more explicit in repudiating the
sort of position held by Cutler. '[You say that] value is associated
with commodity production, but with the abolition of commodity
production value too will be "changed" that is *value as such* will
remain, and only its form will be changed. In actual fact however
economic value is a category peculiar to commodity production and
disappears with it . . . just as it did not exist before it. The relation
of labour to its product did not manifest itself in the form of value
before commodity production, and will not do so after it' (Marx

and Engels, *Sochineniya*, ed. V. Adoratsky, Moscow, 1935, vol. XXVII, p. 406, quoted in Meek, 1973, p. 257).

10 Speaking of the formation of an average rate of profit, Marx makes a point he held to be true of all laws of bourgeois economy 'Under capitalist production the general law acts as the prevailing tendency only in a very complicated and approximate manner, as a never ascertainable average of ceaseless fluctuations' (III, p. 161).

11 This particular work of Dobb opens with a chapter entitled 'Requirements of a Theory of Value'. From the very outset the author reveals that his method is quite opposed to that of Marx. For the problem does not lie in finding some abstract criteria against which the 'adequacy' of various value theories can be judged. Such a method of approach is essentially Kantian in that it seeks a set of abstract norms, derived from outside the development of the phenomena under investigation. Once these criteria are selected – and the selection must be arbitrary and subjective – the spit is then turned and they are in turn 'applied' to the phenomena concerned. This method lands Dobb and others in considerable difficulties. At one point he admits 'Quite a number of theories of value can be derived with no means of choice between them except their formal elegance.' This being so, we are inevitably driven towards instrumentalism for 'The ultimate criterion [for the 'adequacy' of a theory] must be the requirements of practice: the type of question which one requires to answer, the purpose of the inquiry in hand' (1940, p. 8). For a fuller discussion of Dobb's position see Pilling (1972).

12 An example of a work which places a similar notion of economic surplus at the centre of its analysis of contemporary capitalism is Baran and Sweezy's *Monopoly Capital*. This book is important in that it points to some of the serious implications involved in a rejection of the Marxian notion of surplus value. Defining economic surplus these authors say (p. 9), 'The economic surplus, in the simplest possible definition, is the difference between what a society produces and the costs of producing it.' Having abandoned the concept of surplus value in favour of what is essentially an asocial category, they then proceed to dispense with the law of value. For, according to them, the size of this surplus can be explained in terms of the pricing policies of the oligopolists who dominate capitalism in its monopoly phase. Indulging in open and tacit price agreements, such oligopolists can ensure an ever rising economic surplus. The way is then cleared for a conception of the problems of capitalism which is almost entirely focused on the means available for disposing of this mounting surplus. In short, the work is given a Keynesian orientation, taking it in the direction of an 'underconsumptionist' notion of economic crisis. The actual social conditions under which surplus value is extracted from wage

labour, and the contradictions specific to this process are left entirely out of account.

13 Cf. Lafargue (1975). 'Political economists have laid it down as an axiom that Capital, the form of property at present predominant, is eternal; they have tasked their brains to show that capital is coeval with the world, and that as it has no beginning, so it can have no end. In proof of which astounding assertion all the manuals of political economy repeat with much complacency the story of the savage who, having in his possession a couple of bows, lends one of them to a brother savage, for a share of the produce of his chase. So great were the zeal and ardour which economists brought to bear on their search for capitalist property in prehistoric times, that they succeeded, in the course of their investigations, in discovering the existence of property outside the human species, to wit amongst the invertebrates: for the ant, in her foresight, is a hoarder of provisions. It is a pity that they should not have gone a step farther, and affirmed that, if the ant lays up stores, she does so with a view to sell the same and realise a profit by the circulation of her capital.'

3 The concepts of *Capital*

1 Cutler *et al.* reject all the basic concepts of *Capital* and do so quite explicitly. 'Much of the sterility of modern Marxist economic theory is an effect of the point of departure to which it attempts to be all too loyal, *Capital* (that this loyalty is often a travesty is another matter). Many of the central concepts and problems in *Capital*, far from constituting a point of departure, are actually *obstacles* to the new kinds of theoretical work socialists need to undertake if they are to come to terms with modern capitalism.' They then proceed to reject the category 'value'; the conception of the capitalist mode of production and its laws of motion as well as the notion – basic to Marx's understanding of fetishism – of the 'personification' of economic functions by individuals in the capitalist mode of production (p. 3). Many critics have been anxious to defend the Marxian law of value against this attack. But such a line of reply is inadequate inasmuch as this work is not so much an effort to 'reconstruct' *Capital* as a direct attack upon the whole of Marxism. This is evident in the conclusions to the work where the authors make clear their rejection of the materialist conception of history, and accept (rightly) that such a rejection must lead to the abandonment of revolutionary politics. Thus, 'Denying the effectivity and existence of any *necessary* tendencies in the capitalist mode of production is therefore a radical challenge to the foundation of certain political positions widely influential on the Left. . . . The central problems to be thought out are the

construction of a strategic power bloc in the absence of its necessity, and the seizure and exercise of power under conditions other than those of armed insurrection' (pp. 240–1). Now, if the tendencies of capitalist economy do not pose *as a necessity* the question of the overthrow of existing society, the entire material and scientific basis for socialism completely disappears. How a 'strategic power bloc' (whatever this might be) can be constructed in the absence of any material basis for such a construction is not made clear. In fact such a conception reduces socialism to words, to mere propagandism outside any social struggles and certainly outside the struggle of the working class. It is easy to understand the superficial appeal of such theory in some academic circles.

2 Lenin certainly never took such a position. Indeed he was at all times anxious to refute those who accused Marxism of 'sectarianism' as a doctrine having no connection with the highest conquests of human thought. 'The genius of Marx consists precisely in his having furnished answers to questions already raised by the foremost minds of mankind. His doctrine emerged as the direct and immediate *continuation* of the teachings of the greatest representatives of philosophy, political economy and socialism' (LCW, vol. 21). Prior to Marxism, it was Hegel who more than any thinker insisted that history could not be chopped up into discrete bits. History must be seen in the whole sweep of its development, as a contradictory unity. Hegel writes on the history of philosophy as follows: 'In the history of philosophy the different stages of the logical Idea assume the shape of successive systems, each based on a particular definition of the Absolute. As the logical Idea is seen to unfold itself in a process from the abstract to the concrete, so in the history of philosophy the earliest systems are the most abstract, and thus at the same time poorest. The relation too of the earlier systems of philosophy is much like the corresponding stages of the logical Idea: in other words, the earlier are preserved in the later; but subordinated and submerged. This is the true meaning of a much misunderstood phenomenon in the history of philosophy – the refutation of one system by another, of an earlier by a later. Most commonly the refutation is taken in a purely negative sense to mean that the system refuted has ceased to count for anything, has been put aside and done for. Were it so, the history of philosophy would be of all studies most saddening, displaying, as it does, the refutation of every system which time has brought forth. Now although it may be admitted that every philosophy has been refuted, it must in an equal degree be maintained that no philosophy has been refuted, nay or can be refuted. And this in two ways. For first, every philosophy that deserves the name always embodies the Idea; and secondly, every system represents one particular factor or stage in the evolution of

the Idea. The refutation of a philosophy, therefore, only means that its barriers are crossed, and its special principle reduced to a factor in the completer principle that follows' (Hegel, 1975, pp. 125–6). Such passages in Hegel are worth considering in the light of the attempt to separate Marx absolutely from all preceding efforts by bourgeois thinkers in all fields of science, including political economy; Hegel's approach also indicates how sterile, and ultimately childish, are those efforts to divide Marx's own development into rigidly separated periods after the manner of Althusser and his followers.

3 In the *Communist Manifesto*, Marx and Engels deal with the formation of consciousness in the working class from the point of view of the transition from immediate, sensuous knowledge to the emergence of definite concepts. In the early phase of the growth of the working class, there does not yet exist in this class a scientific understanding of the actual nature of its conflict with capital. The worker is directly in conflict with the individual capitalist. Many of the facts of capitalist exploitation which the worker experiences and witnesses he tends to ascribe to the personal qualities of his own employer. The employer, in this stage of the development of class consciousness, emerges as something distinct from the capitalist class as whole, just as the worker does not, at this point, yet see himself as part of the working class as a whole. The many different aspects of capitalist reality do not yet emerge in the understanding of the worker as manifestations of a universal class antagonism running through the whole of modern society, but as a series of isolated, chance phenomena without any internal necessity or interconnection. To develop this still limited and partial understanding to a richer and fuller synthesis of these apparently disconnected facts, the concrete experience of the worker must be permeated by a much richer and wider knowledge which reflects a world-historic practice by the whole of mankind. Knowledge of the actual complexities of the capitalist system, which sublates within it all the foregoing history of mankind, requires generalization so wide as to be beyond the grasp of separate groups of workers – considering their position in capitalist society – and far beyond their immediate circle of vision. It was Marxism which provided – on the basis of the class struggle – this generalized view of the class struggle as a whole, a view which was able to penetrate to the essence and real, historical significance of the struggle of the working class. It is exactly this wholeness, this survey of the facts in their mutual dependence, the simultaneous grasping of the many contradictory aspects of reality which Lenin stresses as the characteristic of genuine scientific thought. It is a scientific thought which is distinguished from a mere direct perception of reality. As Engel's puts it in *Anti-Dühring*, 'Actually all really exhaustive

knowledge is thus characterised: in our thoughts we take a single
thing out of its singleness and turn it into a particularity, and this
latter into a generality – that is we find infinity in finity, the eternal
in the transitory.'

4 The more petty philosophers dispute whether essence OR that
which is immediately given should be taken as basis (Kant, Hume,
all the Machists). Instead of *or* Hegel puts *and*, explaining the
concrete content of this 'and' (LCW, vol. 38, p. 134).

5 It is worth noting that although Lukàcs has a quite different
position from Althusser, he also at one point makes the following
statement in his *History and Class Consciousness*: 'Even if one were
to suppose, without accepting, that modern research has
demonstrated the factual inaccuracy of all Marx's scientific
propositions, an orthodox Marxist could accept all these new
discoveries and reject all Marx's propositions without being in any
way compelled to renounce his Marxist orthodoxy. Orthodox
Marxism does not mean an uncritical acceptance of the results of
Marx's research . . . it refers exclusively to Marx's method.' Here
Lukàcs tends to transform the Marxist method into a fetish. We
have already argued that Marx's 'results' cannot be taken as things
in themselves. But at the same time they certainly cannot be
ignored. If all Marx's results had proved historically to be wrong,
then Marxism must certainly fall to the ground. The point is that
the results of Marx's scientific work must be seen in their *unity*
with the method which enabled him to arrive at these results.

6 It was this mechanical standpoint which led to a neglect of form in
the investigation of matter, a neglect which was translated into
classical political economy with results which I shall later explore.
In ancient philosophy, for example with Aristotle, form was
understood as an active principle, creative and constructive,
whereas matter was believed to be passive. When the mechanical
world outlook became predominant, form came to be interpreted as
merely the outer integument, a configuration of the material object
having no connection with its inner essence, with its structure.

4 The significance of the opening chapters

1 A flavour of this polemical character can be seen in Marx's
comments on Edmund Burke: 'This sycophant who, in the pay of
the English oligarchy, played the romantic laudator temporis acti
against the French Revolution, just as, in the pay of the North
American Colonies at the beginning of the American troubles, he
played the Liberal against the English oligarchy, was an out and
out vulgar bourgeois. "The laws of commerce are the laws of
Nature and therefore the laws of God." No wonder that, true to

the laws of God and of Nature, he always sold himself in the best market' (I, p. 760).

2 Attacking the 'humanist-historicist' interpretation of Marxism Althusser (*Reading Capital*, pp. 140–1) argues that 'Marxist theory is produced by a specific theoretical practice, *outside* the proletariat, and that Marxist theory must be '*imported*' into the proletariat.' He claims that this quite one-sided view was actually upheld by Lenin.

3 This omission on the part of Meek and most others is surprising given Marx's many explicit statements on the problem of the form of value. Urging Marx not to change a draft he had made of the early sections of *Capital*, Engels writes (16 June 1867), 'The second sheet especially bears rather strong marks of your carbuncles, but that cannot be altered now and I do not think you should do anything more about it in an addendum, for, after all, the philistine is not accustomed to this sort of abstract thought and certainly will not cudgel his brains for the sake of the form of value. At most *the points here established dialectically* might be set forth historically at somewhat greater length, the test to be made from history, so to speak, although what is most necessary in this respect has already been said. But you have so much material that you can certainly still make quite a good digression upon it, which will demonstrate to the philistine from history the necessity for the development of money and the process which takes place in connection with it.' (Marx and Engels, 1956, p. 226; author's italics). And Marx's reply to this point is equally instructive in bringing out the importance of the value-form and its dialectical character. Marx says (p. 228), 'As to the development of the *form of value* I have and have *not* followed your advice, in order to behave dialectically in this respect as well. That is to say I have 1) written an *appendix* in which I describe *the same thing* as simply and pedagogically as possible, and 2) followed your advice and divided each step in the development into paragraphs, etc. *with separate headings*. In the *preface* I then tell the *"non-dialectical"* reader that he should skip pages x–y and read the appendix instead. Here not merely philistines are concerned but youth eager for knowledge etc.'

5 Some aspects of Marx's notion of commodity fetishism

1 Rubin's book is amongst the very few which since 1917 have done real justice to the method of *Capital*. It is important to note that, like Rosdolsky, Rubin was associated with theoretical and political trends hostile to Stalinism. He was born in 1886 and from 1905 was an active participant in the Russian revolutionary movement, after 1926 being employed at the Marx-Engels Institute. Between

1924 and 1930 he completed several works in the field of political economy, covering various aspects of the history of economic thought. In 1930 he was arrested, accused of belonging to an organization which never existed, forced to confess to deeds never committed and eventually murdered. He was amongst a generation of brilliant Soviet economists wiped out by Stalin. It is to be hoped that some of his other work will be translated into English.

2 Adam Smith was in this respect no exception. Starting with the division of labour and the process of commodity exchange, Smith then raises the question of money, without which regular exchange is impossible. In the brief fourth chapter Smith discusses the nature of money and the history of its emergence from all other commodities as a special commodity. Although Smith returns to the problems of money and credit throughout *The Wealth of Nations* these economic categories play only a minor role in his writing. He sees in money only a technical device making possible the course of economic progress – 'the great wheel of circulation'.

Credit is similarly regarded as a technical device through which capital is activated.

Bibliography

1 Works by Marx

(1934), *Letters to Kugelmann*, New York, International Publishers.
(1955), *The Poverty of Philosophy*, London, Lawrence & Wishart.
(1962), *Critique of the Gotha Programme*, in Marx and Engels, *Selected Works*, vol. 2, London, Lawrence & Wishart.
(1969), *Theories of Surplus Value*, part I, London, Lawrence & Wishart.
(1971a), *Critique of Political Economy*, London, Lawrence & Wishart.
(1971b), *Theories of Surplus Value*, part II, London, Lawrence & Wishart.
(1972), *Theories of Surplus Value*, part III, London, Lawrence & Wishart.
(1976), *Value: Studies by Marx*, London, New Park.

2 Works by Engels

(1947), *Anti-Dühring: Herr Dühring's Revolution in Science*, London, Lawrence & Wishart.
(1960), *Dialectics of Nature*, London, Lawrence & Wishart.

3 Works by Marx and Engels

(1956), *Selected Correspondence*, London, Lawrence & Wishart.
(1970), *The German Ideology*, ed. C. J. Arthur, London, Lawrence & Wishart.
(1975a), *Collected Works of Marx and Engels*, vol. 3, London, Lawrence & Wishart.
(1975b), *Collected Works of Marx and Engels*, vol. 4, London, Lawrence & Wishart.

4 Works by other authors

Althusser, L. (1969), *For Marx*, London, New Left Books.

Althusser, L. (1971), *Lenin and Philosophy and Other Essays*, London, Allen Lane.

Althusser, L. and Balibar, E. (1970), *Reading Capital*, London, Allen Lane.

Baran, P. A. and Sweezy, P. M. (1966), *Monopoly Capital: An Essay on the American Economic and Social Order*, New York, Monthly Review Press.

Brunhoff, S. de (1973), 'Marx as an a-Ricardian: exchange value and money at the beginning of *Capital*', *Economy and Society*, vol. 2, pp. 421–30.

Cutler, A., Hindess, B., Hirst, P. and Hussain, A. (1977), *Marx's Capital and Capitalism Today*, London, Routledge & Kegan Paul.

Dobb, M. H. (1940), *Political Economy and Capitalism*, London, Routledge & Kegan Paul.

Eatwell, J. (1974), 'Controversies in the Theory of Surplus Value: Old and New', *Science and Society*, vol. 38(3), pp. 281–303.

Fine, B. and Harris, L. (1976), 'Controversial Issues in Marxist Economic Theory', in R. Miliband and J. Saville, eds. *Socialist Register*, London, Merlin Press.

Hegel, G. W. F. (1968) *Lectures on the History of Philosophy*, vols 1 and 2, trans. E. S. Haldane and F. H. Simson, London, Routledge & Kegan Paul.

Hegel, G. W. F. (1969), *Science of Logic*, trans. A. V. Miller, London, Allen & Unwin.

Hegel, G. W. F. (1971), *The Phenomenology of Mind*, trans. J. B. Baillie, London, Allen & Unwin.

Hegel, G. W. F. (1975), *Logic* (the 'Encyclopaedic Logic'), trans. W. Wallace, Oxford University Press.

Hilferding, R. (1973), *Böhm-Bawerk's Criticism of Marx*, Clifton, N. J., Kelley.

Hindess, B. and Hirst, P. (1975), *Pre-Capitalist Modes of Production*, London, Routledge & Kegan Paul.

Hodgson, G. (1973), 'Epistemology and the Transformation Problem', *Bulletin of the Conference of Socialist Economists*.

Hunt, E. K. and Schwartz, J. G., ed. (1972), *A Critique of Economic Theory: Selected Readings*, Harmondsworth, Penguin.

Ilyenkov, E. V. (1977a), 'The Concept of the Ideal', in *Philosophy in the USSR: Problems of Dialectical Materialism*, Moscow, Progress Publishers.

Ilyenkov, E. V. (1977b), *Dialectical Logic: Essays on its History and Theory*, Moscow, Progress Publishers.

Kemp, T. (1978), 'Commodity Fetishism in Marx's *Capital*', *Labour Review*, vol. 1, no. 10, pp. 601–13.

Keynes, J. M. (1936), *The General Theory of Employment, Interest and Money*, London, Macmillan.

Korsch, K. (1963), *Karl Marx*, London, Russell & Russell.

Lafargue, P. (1975), *The Evolution of Property*, London, New Park.

Lukàcs, G. (1967), *History and Class Consciousness*, London, Merlin Press.

Meek, R. L. (1967), 'The Decline of Ricardian Economics in England', in R. L. Meek, *Economics and Ideology*, London, Chapman & Hall.

Meek, R. L. (1973), *Studies in the Labour Theory of Value*, London, Lawrence & Wishart.

Pilling, G. (1972), 'The Law of Value in Ricardo and Marx', *Economy and Society*, vol. 1, no. 3, pp. 281–307.

Pilling, G. (1977), 'What is Revolutionary in Marx's *Capital*?', *Labour Review*, vol. 1, no. 5, pp. 279–95.

Popper, K. (1966), *The Open Society and its Enemies*, vol. 2, London, Routledge & Kegan Paul.

Popper, K. (1972), 'What is Dialectic?', in K. Popper, *Conjectures and Refutations. The Growth of Scientific Knowledge*, London, Routledge & Kegan Paul.

Ricardo, D. (1951), *Principles of Political Economy and Taxation*, ed. P. Sraffa, London, Cambridge University Press.

Ricardo, D. (1952), *Letters 1816–18*, vol. VII of *The Works and Correspondence of David Ricardo*, ed. P. Sraffa, London, Cambridge University Press.

Robinson, J. (1966), *An Essay on Marxian Economics*, London, Macmillan.

Roll, E. (1973), *History of Economic Thought*, London, Faber & Faber.

Rosdolsky, R. (1977), *The Making of Marx's Capital*, London, Pluto Press.

Rubin, I. I. (1972), *Essays on Marx's Theory of Value*, Detroit, Black and Red.

Smith, A. (1976), *The Wealth of Nations*, 2 vols, ed. R. H. Campbell and A. S. Skinner, Oxford, Clarendon Press.

Stalin, J. V. (1951), *Dialectical and Historical Materialism*, Moscow, Foreign Languages Publishing House.

Sweezy, P. M. (1946), *The Theory of Capitalist Development*, London, Dobson.

Trotsky, L. D. (1966), *In Defence of Marxism*, London, New Park.

Trotsky, L. D. (1967), *The Revolution Betrayed*, London, New Park.

Trotsky, L. D. (1978), 'Nationalism and Economic Life', *Labour Review*, vol. 1, no. 10, pp. 617–25.

Yaffe, D. (1973), 'The Marxian Theory of Crisis, Capital and the State', *Economy and Society*, vol. 2, no. 2, pp. 186–232.

Yaffe, D. (1975), 'Value and Price in Marx's *Capital*', *Revolutionary Communist*, vol. 1, January.

Name index

211

Subject index

abstract identity, 82–7
abstraction: Aristotle on, 104–5;
  capital in general as, 102–3;
  reality of, 101; value concept
  and, 110
abstract labour, 45–51; classical
  political economy and, 48–50
analysis: role in classical
  economics, 25

boom, post-war, 2–3
Bretton Woods, 4, 126

capital: concept of 113–15; and
  productive forces, 87–90; social,
  102–3
capital-in-general, 92–4, 96–101,
  102
circulation, 121
classical political economy: and
  class struggle, 62–6; definition
  of, 9; ahistorical method of, 10–
  14; vulgar economy and, 9
class struggle, 62–5, 122, 134–5
commodity, 136–42, 144; cell
  form of capital, 124–6;
  contradictory nature, 22; and
  empiricism, 79–82; Lenin's
  analysis, 23; starting point for
  Capital, 120
commodity fetishism, *see* fetishism
concepts: in *Capital*, 67–115
  passim; of capital, 113–15;
  empiricism and, 83–4; of
  feudalism, 90; in Hegel, 83;

sequence of, 114; value concept,
  105–6
concrete and abstract, 112
Conference of Socialist
  Economists, 2
contradiction: James Mill and, 33,
  123; Popper and, 31, 33, 34; in
  Ricardo's economics, 32

dialectical materialism, 81
dialectics, 6, 122, 129, 147

economic crises, 178–82
elementary value form, 146–52;
  see also form of value
empiricism: conception of law in,
  26; concepts in, 83–4; and
  formal logic, 31–2; and problem
  of value and profit, 30–5
esoteric and exoteric (in Wealth of
  Nations), 16
exploitation, 132–3

fetishism, 66, 156, 157–96
  passim; disappearance of, 165–
  8; and economic crisis, 178–82;
  illusion of, 168ff; and price of
  production, 182–5; and social
  being, 158–65
feudalism, 90
formalism, 28–9
formal logic: and dialectics, 38–41
form of value, 43–4, 48, 146–52,
  200, 206; development of, 152–
  6

213